BRYANT ON BOWLS

BRYANT ON BOWLS

David Bryant

PELHAM BOOKS

Stephen Greene Press

PELHAM BOOKS/Stephen Greene Press

Published by the Penguin Group
27 Wrights Lane, London W8 5TZ, England
Viking Penguin, a division of Penguin Books USA Inc,
375 Hudson Street, New York, New York, 10014, USA
The Stephen Greene Press, Inc., 15 Muzzey Street, Lexington, Massachusetts
02173, USA
Penguin Books Australia Ltd, Ringwood, Victoria, Australia
Penguin Books Canada Ltd, 2801 John Street, Markham, Ontario, Canada,
L3R 1B4
Penguin Books (NZ) Ltd, 182-190 Wairau Road, Auckland 10, New Zealand

Penguin Books Ltd, Registered Offices: Harmondsworth, Middlesex, England

First Published 1985 (hardback), 1989 (paperback)

Reprinted 1990

Printed and bound in Great Britain by Butler and Tanner, Frome.

A CIP catalogue record for this book is available from the British Library

ISBN 0 7207 1905 4

CONTENTS

INTRODUCTION   page 7

ACKNOWLEDGEMENTS   page 8

CHAPTER ONE   page 9
Father's influence – learning from the green's bank – Exmouth the yearly apex – our garden lawn and control – father; finesse better than force – how a mathematical mind helps – the start of my crouch delivery – the motivation to strive seriously

CHAPTER TWO   page 18
Delving deeper into the game – how unthinking practice can develop faults – sufficient application and determination masters fundamentals – differences between line and length – why you must never fear defeat – total belief in your shot is vital – the importance of 'body language' – the basic shot in bowls – coping with disappointment

CHAPTER THREE   page 26
Broadening horizons – the causes of poor performance – learning the rules imperative – the three grips – differences between slow and fast greens – the dangers of 'skidding' your deliveries – forget the green, play the opponent – buying your bowls – three ways of maintaining your line

CHAPTER FOUR   page 34
Love of the game the way to excellence – why strong and supple legs are vital – finding your length – mental rehearsal and visualisation – where 'hookers' go wrong – the importance of your right foot – correct use of your eyes – six reminders before delivering – teachers may be the pools of knowledge but you are the one who has to learn

CHAPTER FIVE   page 43
The knack of winning – overtaking the legendary Percy Baker – preparing for the 1962 Commonwealth Games – differences between Australian and British greens; adapting – the duties of a lead – adjusting to greens of differing speeds – principle of correct elevation when delivering – six 'musts' for draw shot devotees

CHAPTER SIX   page 56
The coming of World Championships – growth of indoor bowls – launching of National Indoor Championships – start of a new partnership – preparing for Kyeemagh – take care of your back – ways and means of husbanding nervous energy – unusual scoring system works against England – the stressful road to Kyeemagh gold – the value of left handedness; and why – the match that earned me gold – love of bowls gains me an important victory – the value of relaxation in match play

CHAPTER SEVEN   page 70
Danger of tiredness; how it works – value of a sound, simple delivery – facing of the deliverer's hand palm – analysis of compactness – avoiding jerking – merits of tilting my bowl – curing wobble – why practice demands as much concentration as match play – causes of trouble – gravity versus muscle power – the finer points of delivery – causes of bumping – I win gold at Edinburgh ... and know I have more to learn

CHAPTER EIGHT   page 85
Temptations to emigrate – the Banyo Masters – my most consistent years – problems besetting the 1972 World Championships – my mistaken choice – a left hander, Maldwyn Evans, wins the singles – severe lessons alert me about the future – using time positively when off the mat – accepting what cannot be changed – building up your 'know how' bank – crisis shots an occupational hazard

CHAPTER NINE   page 100
EBA Championships move to Worthing – the best green in England – two defeats that were good for bowls – RAF wartime discoveries about performance – psychological skills for successful skipping – the need to keep calm; to be a master tactician – transmission of confidence – the need for total awareness – deploying a left hander – dangers of complacency – the nine commandments for skips

CHAPTER TEN   page 109

Scottish supporters rouse their team – hazard training – living in the 'now' (current second) pays dividends – on green conference turns the tables – open bowls on the horizon – value of yoga – dangers of over-trying – value of basic solidity – why bad shots must be eliminated – the third World Championships series – 106,492 fans flock to Zoo Park, Johannesburg – 'staying with your opponent' – unruffled concentration and unruffled tranquillity essential – the inverted 'U' and optimum performance – value of planning pre-match strategy

CHAPTER ELEVEN   page 132

The sadness of Dad's illness – vivid memories of his friendship – training for the Commonwealth Games – how to shed 18lb of weight – why bowlers suffer when tired – launch of Kodak Masters – the 'South African Clinic' (semi-fixed) delivery shows some advantages – my rivalry with Precious McKenzie – why forewarned is forearmed – the immense test of 14 matches – when and why to use your favourite shot – winning with honour

CHAPTER TWELVE   page 147

EIBA find outlet in the rules – short cut to Open bowls – value of self-discipline – inaugural Embassy World Indoor Bowls Championship – inner calm triumphs – growth of bowls as a spectator sport – 'being there' to the rescue – the shot that won the Kodak Masters – my opponent's 'never up, never in' helps my win – danger stimulates my motivation – dangers in breaking rules – challenge more effective than cash as a motivator – dangers in breaking rules – challenge more effective than cash as a motivator – most amazing final of my life

CHAPTER THIRTEEN   page 161

Impending arrival of Open bowls – new forms of bowls – sets scoring the best; and why – need of one rink greens – what tempts sponsors most – selection for the 1980 World Championships – special skills needed by World Championship class skips – new use of number twos – preparation leads to tranquillity and wins – how I acquired inbuilt know-how – inner calmness is a learned skill – cherish the thrills of competition – why I made Allcock take-over – why the decision paid off – Frankston sharpens my mental toughness, it pays me back with gold

CHAPTER FOURTEEN   page 176

Nine countries in Embassy World Championship – dealing with defeat – severe test in retaining my title – end of my amateur career – five days later I win £2000 – the value of daring – cheque a lesser incentive than an enthralled crowd – how women may bridge the bowls gap with men – consistency outbalances irregular brilliant shots

CHAPTER FIFTEEN   page 184

The Queen bestows my greatest honour – British varying bowling codes draw closer – Embassy World Championship goes 'Open' – John Player Classic at Darlington becomes valuable warm-up – how psychological 'warfare' overtakes Norma Shaw – beating Mal Hughes peaks my game – knock out system better than groups – how to dismiss panic – how it helped me retain Embassy title – how to feel at peace when beaten – why John Watson refused £4000 – spectator bowl events necessitate new promotional methods – birth of the CIS UK Open Indoor Singles Championship – scientific analysis reveals how and why I won the British Isles singles title – problems of the over 50s – how I tore two hamstrings – the joys of coaching

CHAPTER SIXTEEN   page 205

My techniques for winning break all records – TV hours increasing – preparing for the Aberdeen World Championships – why and how I changed my drive technique – my experience overcomes Belliss in Gateway Masters final – dismay about the Aberdeen format – why it was unsatisfactory – how just two shots in fifteen days of matches reduced me to bronze and silver medals – why bowls is a strange game – improving skills opens new horizons – why I shall never stop looking for them

EPILOGUE   page 216

Measuring your powers of concentration – practising 'being there'

INTRODUCTION

The majority of world champions attribute their supremacy to 30 per cent technical skills and 70 per cent intangibles which are related to the mind, self-discipline, attitudes, dedication, learning ability and a host of other factors embraced by the personality.

People frequently remark upon my concentration, calmness, inventiveness etc., and it is true that throughout my career I have constantly sought for knowledge in parallel with the development of my technical skills, styles and methods.

There are already a number of bowls books which set out sufficient methods of playing the game to satisfy almost every beginner or average club player. None has delved into the mind to attempt the teaching of the game's intangibles.

So with this book I have taken the plunge. Not so much by instructing you to 'do this' or 'do that', but by describing my last twenty-five years as a competitor and by outlining how the visible parts of my game have been affected by my attitudes and disciplines and vice versa.

My progress has not come easily and it has necessitated dedication, thoroughness and the use of special methods which now keep me calm and objective in every kind of competitive crisis. Most of the skills I now possess were learned. In describing how and when they came about I am dealing with personal facts though many engaged my mind for long periods before they became everyday facets of my general make-up.

Given that you love the game of bowls and are persistent in nature, you should be able to improve your standing in your club, county or country by developing similar intangibles suited to your overall personality.

My ideas may sometimes create disbelief but I hope you will give them careful study before you cast them aside. They worked for me as well as for such sporting 'greats' as Bjorn Borg, Steve Davis, Billie-Jean King and hosts of others.

Give my ideas a try. At best they will improve your game enormously and at worst may give you many new thoughts that should enrich your pleasure in playing the challenging game we love so much.

ACKNOWLEDGEMENTS

I would like to thank Clarence Jones for all his devoted assistance in the preparation of this book, particularly for his painstaking research, his valuable experience as a Member of the British Society of Sports Psychology and the resultant tests which appear at the end of this book. His pictures, too, have been very valuable.

The photographs are reproduced by permission of: Peter Baker page 16 (bottom); *Belfast Telegraph* page 49; BIPPA page 53; Albert Evans page 72 (top); Feature Press Photo Agency page 185; Fox Photos page 13 (bottom); Ken Fraser pages 13 (top) and 72 (bottom); John Harvey pages 16 (top) and 59 (bottom); Clarence Jones pages 38, 59 (bottom), 81, 96, 97, 106, 111, 119, 121, 129, 158, 189 and 203.

Every effort has been made by the author to trace the copyright owner but in some cases this has not been possible and it is hoped that any omissions will be excused.

The line drawings are by Pan Tek.

AUTHOR'S NOTE

At the end of each chapter I have included a 'Loser's guide to Winning' which I hope you will find helpful.

CHAPTER ONE

It might well have been a conspiracy the way my father, mother, grandparents and great uncle Sam involved me in their abounding passion, bowls ... or lawn bowls as it is officially known around the twenty or so countries comprising the International Bowling Board.

My involvement began in my very early childhood as bowls was a regular topic of conversation, not only in the home but through-out the family, as three of my grandparents were regular partici-pants. My first memories of the Clevedon Club were of my father and grandfather Bryant, who was a founder member, playing in Saturday afternoon matches; and I suppose this was the initial influence which sparked off my interest in the game. My grand-father, although a fine player who represented his county on numerous occasions, never achieved the prowess of my father Reg who, at that time, was a regular Middleton Cup skip for Somerset and who later was to represent his country as an Indoor Inter-national. It was not surprising therefore that as my fascination for the game increased I supported my father at every opportunity. I remember that I particularly enjoyed watching him compete in both club and county competitions eagerly awaiting the specta-cular drive which scattered the bowls in all directions and which to me, at that time, was the most exciting shot in the game. Those memories stay as vividly in my mind as my father's unwavering advocacy of length and direction as a player's most valuable assets – even though at first I didn't know exactly what he meant.

During the late 1930s my visits to the Clevedon Bowling Club became more frequent as my route home from Junior School very conveniently took me past the club and I regularly perched myself on a seat by the greenside, eyes glued to the play. Seemingly, the sun always shone and I lived every shot I saw. Tranquillity seemed to dominate those absorbing afternoons and if today I am noted for my concentration and inner calmness then those afternoons played a major role in their development.

Watching may be a splendid hobby but I am one of the 'What if I do that?' brigade and in a very short time this led to my fidgeting to bowl, with my mother (although at that time she did not actually play) taking up position as my first tutor and father's analytic eyes acting as a monitor.

The Exmouth Open Tournament provided the climax to each year, with the first week of the Bryant family holiday spent busily on the beach. Then came the tournament, with mother and me abandoning the beach each lunchtime to take our places by the greenside in readiness to watch and applaud each bowl delivered by my father. They say opportunity only knocks once and, for me, that once arrived when I found four old lawn bowls half

Sixteen-year-old David Bryant delivering, left arm flying.

hidden behind the Exmouth Club's pavilion. Pestering my ever-patient father, I persuaded him to approach the groundsman and, in exchange for five shillings, the bowls became my most treasured possession. They were soon augmented by twelve croquet balls, discards collected from a relative's house in the course of a social visit to Taunton.

Croquet balls are unbiased and made to run true, those used for bowls are biased so that they run in a curve when traversing a green. Neither factor mattered because my practice area, the

With Great Uncle Sam, left arm anchored in variations of style.

front garden at home, curves in two directions; and to increase one's problems a large flower bed stands sentinel in the middle of that lawn. Hazardous, of course, yet what a testing and thought-provoking venue this proved for the important international and national matches staged there most days ... with me standing in for each of the eight great champions named for those matches.

In my front garden my 'what if' approach to life and bowls came into its own, with no brakes or inhibitions limiting the limitless experiments I sampled in delivering, gripping, swinging, foot moving, etc. that came to mind. The space was small, the lawn hazardous and understanding control and adjusting to infinite variations of heads demanded total concentration and an abundance of different shots and methods. If concentration and control are among my major assets, then they probably derive from those many summers of experimenting.

Apart from assembling a wide range of different shots, I also learned the mechanics and 'feel' of many alternative deliveries. To this day, I still experiment with new methods and deliveries, sometimes with unexpected results.

Maybe I filled all eight positions in those front garden classics but only in trust for the men I watched daily on my way home from school. I made my debut on the Clevedon Club green at the age of ten in 1942. My competitive instincts were realised that afternoon when my great uncle Sam arrived at the club minus one member of his team. Spotting me seated in my favourite chair I heard him say, 'David will do' and within moments I was enjoying my first sample of testing my skills against real adversaries under match conditions. I loved it then as I do now.

However, at that time I was already playing regularly at the Promenade Club with my mother and grandparents. My mother having decided to take up the game as she had found herself with a lot of time on her hands due to father's enlistment in the services.

During these formative years in the game I would play most days of the week either at the Promenade Club with the family and other members or with my school friends in our front garden which, although comparatively small, had been the venue for many exciting triples and fours games.

Despite his consistency and accuracy with a fast bowl, and it was this which impressed me most in my childhood days, my father was a great believer of finesse rather than force. It blended perfectly with his impeccable green manners and his Olympic

Reg Bryant delivering.

The start of another tranquil afternoon partnering my father.

attitude to competition and sportmanship. Almost inevitably, he preached the values of the draw shot, length bowling and a tactic all too often overlooked, the importance of being content with second wood when the head starts to look ominous. His own mastery of those shots compelled me to practise them by the hour but many years went by before I came to value them as he did; how valuable they proved over all my years of international and national competition.

However, in those early days my experiments embraced the more glamorous cannons, yards on shots, jack trailers and, above all, the powerful drive. How I loved the speed of a bowl hurtling down the green and the excitement when it crashed into the target and snatched valuable shots from the opposition. Memories of the good ones linger far longer than the many misses that left me desolate. Meanwhile, I doubt if any eleven year old could ever have bettered my accuracy with the drive.

Bowls may have occupied most of my sporting time but I also thoroughly enjoyed cricket and I was opening bat for my school house team. Unlike my bowls, I had very few shots and though I may have plodded my way until about the eighth wicket down, runs never came freely or easily; strangely, now I look back, my insatiable appetite for experimenting never spread to cricket.

That contrasted with my approach to billiards and snooker. Mathematics was a subject in which I specialised as a teacher, and these leanings I believe, nurtured my fascination with playing one ball on to another to discover what happened. Friends say that this early questing shows plainly in my bowls. In order to experiment one must think. Imagination is needed and is invaluable because without imagination there can be no progress on what has already been done. This approach sometimes did not please Dad greatly whose great strength lay in his mastery of length. This talent earned him England Indoor International representation in 1958/59 as well as the English fours title in 1957/68/69 and the British Isles Fours Championship in 1969. Can there be anything more moving than winning such a title together as father and son? If he had enjoyed better opportunities when he was younger, who knows how far beyond that he might have gone?

Father was a Somerset skip for many years but when we played together he encouraged me to skip. Usually he moved to lead and I could not have been blessed with a better one. All the way through, from my games on the front lawn right up to the last tournament in which I participated, I have never lost my belief in experimenting. In the earliest days I had no thoughts about becoming even the County Champion, let alone National or even World Champion. My absorbtion in playing, experimenting and analysing overrode all other ambitions. Practising all the accepted deliveries – and a few that never reached the text books – filled my mind and quite a few notebooks as my findings steadily increased.

Today my delivery differs considerably from the first one I used because, like the majority of players, I automatically chose the upright stance. Early on I found control on the very fast greens difficult which prompted me to experiment with various delivery techniques resulting in the crouch style which I have used over the past thirty years. Normally, as I rise from my crouch I adjust the height of my stance to suit the pace of the green but under certain conditions when the greens are very heavy I sometimes abandon my 'knees bent, up, step and deliver' technique replacing it with the traditional 'upright athletic delivery'. That is the delivery I have always used when driving. 'Driving' is used almost everywhere instead of the term 'firing shot' in the British Isles, and I find 'drive' a less clumsy definition.

Pictures of my delivery in early matches show that at one stage my left arm floated while later I immobilised it by putting my hand on to my front leg when delivering. Developing a technically sound delivery demands constant, highly concentrated practise in grooving it deeply into one's neural system. Like a car repeatedly following the same track going up a driveway, continuity slowly fashions a track which automatically helps continuous repetition. That neural track can be increased by imaginary deliveries made when sitting in a car in a traffic jam or even lounging in one's favourite armchair. This form of mental practise is well validated and widely used, particularly in the USA and among Japanese gymnasts. And Dad's watchful eyes ensured I steered clear of bad habits.

His offer to enrol me as a member of the Clevedon Bowling Club came in October 1947. Strangely, when I look back, I did not immediately jump at the chance but eventually I accepted his generous offer. About that time my eyesight deteriorated considerably, though I did not realise it immediately. Consequently, I could not understand why my batting in cricket was weakening. I also enjoyed tennis, but not when the ball began to look small

Memories of the thrill of my lifetime. The British Isles and England fours champions of 1968, *left to right* Bill Elliott, Reg Bryant, David Rhys Jones and David Bryant.

The first taste of triumph. Roger Harris and me, the 1952 Somerset pairs champions.

and blurred. With bowls continually increasing my inquisitiveness, I decided to give it top priority but supplemented it with table-tennis, snooker and billiards in the winter.

Nowadays educationalists theorise that a balance of practice, stress and enthusiasm helps youngsters to advance and succeed. My quota at the club could scarcely have been bettered. Winning the Clevedon Club Handicap Singles in my first year, I reached the semi-finals of Somerset County Singles Championship the next year. With Roger Harris I reached the finals of the Clevedon Open Pairs where we lost to great uncle Sam and his partner. However, I beat him in the singles. It was a great fillip and I realised that I had some flair for the game. That was the moment I decided to strive seriously to improve.

● Never be afraid of experimentation.
● Try both an upright and crouch delivery and decide which suits you best.
● As a beginner or novice, concentrate on control when practising. Line, then length.
● Take great pains to ensure that each and every delivery you make is well grounded.
● Look at the line and never the target.

CHAPTER TWO

Far from abandoning my experimental attitude, I delved more and more into the game, its techniques and tactics. Then as now, I believed that if one possesses an adequate quota of inherent ability and never deviates from the main objective, success, experiments can do no harm.

Technical development comes from intelligent experimenting, understanding of what is effective, discarding what is not and many hours, days, weeks, months and years of practice. In the last chapter I dwelt briefly on how repetition of a movement slowly develops a groove that makes it easier to repeat that movement with machine-like consistency. It must be emphasised that unthinking practice can, therefore, build in faults if one fails to concentrate minutely on each section of a practice session. I would go so far as to say that detailed, applied concentration is even more important when practising than in a match. In a match one is disciplined by the desire to beat an opponent. There is no such external pressure when practising. Instead, it is dependent upon one's self-motivated urge to achieve.

That particular personality trait is largely inherent, although it can be learned through intense self-discipline and adherence to the factors and habits which pave the way to achievement. I will dwell on a few of those factors later in this book.

Meanwhile, I am convinced that any man or woman with sufficient application and determination can master the fundamentals of a championship class delivery. That learning will produce your capability of always bowling on line. Maintaining line is largely a learned skill.

Control of length is more dependent on touch or 'feel' and I am unsure just how deeply that control is governed by inheritance, as distinct from learning. Certainly, consistency of line is greatly helpful to length, especially as one's experience widens. Whatever the ratio of inheritance to learned skill may be, there can be no questioning the absolute necessity of developing the skills that can be learned – like a sweet delivery – to the utmost of one's potential.

In pursuit of the perfection I believed necessary, if I was to become an effective competitive bowler, I experimented continually ... even to the extent of bowling with my left hand. In so doing I discovered a great deal about balance, body control and other factors which are taken for granted when using one's natural hand.

Now I would say that, inevitably, learning to bowl left handed became a valuable match asset on the occasional situation, notably in those days when the Bristol Indoor Club played on an indoor swimming pool which was converted to a green each winter. Bristol contested many a Denny Cup National Indoor Club Championship match on that green and on one of the rinks it was virtually impossible to avoid one of its 'runs' with my normal delivery. On such occasions I avoided the run by bowling with my left hand, so starting the bowls path down the rink from a point about eighteen inches more to the left. Apart from producing many good shots, I fancy my unexpected, sudden changes of hand exercised a psychological jolt on many an opponent.

Be quite clear, not all experiments succeed. Even so, I believe there is no such thing as total failure; at the very worst a disaster teaches one not to repeat that experiment. Or maybe a slight adjustment here and there will produce something valuable in quite another way. Additionally, by experimenting one learns to use one's best shots when they are needed instead of half-hearted methods that are doomed to failure before they even begin.

Here I am mindful of why Bjorn Borg believed he was the world's number one tennis champion. 'You must never fear defeat' he said, 'if you fear defeat you will never dare to win.' I would change only the last four words, substituting after 'will' '... not use your best shots'.

My first serious taste of this came after Roger Harris and I battled through the 1953 Somerset Pairs Championship and so qualified for the English Bowling Association Championships which, in those days, were staged at the famous Paddington Club. Winning our first and second rounds, we met the crack Northumberland couple Purves and Norman. With four ends remaining we appeared on the verge of a major upset with our three shots lead. The Paddington Club is closely enclosed on all sides by large blocks of flats and, maybe, this tended to keep the greens slightly heavier than those at the Clevedon Club. We were about to bowl to an end which we found somewhat difficult. So I said to Roger 'I think we'll try the backhand; we can't come to much harm'. He dutifully drew his four bowls on the backhand, I followed suit

Happy (bowls) families. Roger Harris and David Bryant (standing) with Reg Bryant and Len Harris proudly displaying the spoils of the 1956 Somerset County Fours Championship.

... and our opponents happily scored a six. Roger and I struggled with all the knowledge and skill we knew to regain our lead but to no avail. Nevertheless, I shall never forget the faces of the people watching from the greenside, their expressions showing utter disbelief that a couple of young bowlers, both twenty-one years old, could be threatening an international trialist and his partner.

With our fathers, Roger and I qualified for the National Fours Championship in 1956, reaching the third round but losing heavily to a Cambridge and County four. We began well but maybe we were too conscious that a number of people were tipping us to win the title. True *or* false, we fell away badly, but the lesson concerning a strong start that crumbles into nothingness lodged in my mind. When we qualified again in 1957 I felt quite an experienced bowler.

That time we contested our first two rounds on the supplementary green at the Brondesbury Club and so the larger crowds were not there to see us. This made for a flatness in atmosphere, for no supplementary club can exude the atmosphere created by the main centre, then known as the 'Mecca of Bowls'.

We began against Cumberland and with two ends remaining I was far from happy. We were leading by one shot when I went to the mat for my last bowl of the 20th end. They were lying seven shots up and the thought of starting the last end six shots down was unpleasantly dismal. Experiment vanished, instead my mind clamped down on all the advice and time devoted by Dad concerning the importance of the draw shot and how best to play it. In situations when one is faced with a crisis and it's difficult to remove, half-heartedness must be completely banished. The mind must decide on the shot to be used and then create a vivid picture of how to produce it successfully. There can be no room for doubt. One must calmly create a total belief that the shot will succeed. Full of mental belief in the shot that was going to save the day, I delivered my bowl; even today I can see my bowl curving through their scorers to seize a single that sent us into the last end two shots ahead.

Success with the shot endured through the rest of the event, the four of us going on to win the title. That provided us with our first National Championship title and lifted my self-belief immeasurably.

Roger and I also qualified for the pairs that year, losing to a famous Sussex pair Gordon Sparks and Arthur Knowling. Arthur holds an enviable record in that event in winning the title twice running partnered by his father. He always demonstrated an important factor in successful bowling, namely tremendous pleasure in playing. Our quarter-final stretched on and on for 105 minutes more than the longest of the other three matches in that event. That and the seemingly magnetic way he held the course of his bowls on a hand swinging five feet as though it was a straight hand are memories that still live in my mind.

His enjoyment derived also from his belief that bowlers are under some obligation to consider the spectators, and that lay behind the sometimes hilarious way he used to chase his bowls up the green after delivering. The apex of that part of his career undoubtedly came at the Crystal Palace indoor club during an important international match. As always, he chased every bowl, the late stages of each run when the bowl was nearing the end of its journey enticing Arthur down on to his hands and knees with his nose close over the bowl. On this day he dropped lower and lower until the moment when his nose dropped so low that it actually touched the bowl itself, stopping its journey. Of course, that meant its removal by the umpire and the immediate reaction was that he had cost his four a valuable bowl. On reflection, and knowing how Arthur had said later 'you must give the crowd some entertainment', I could well believe that he knew the bowl would not have reached the counting cluster near the jack and so gave everyone an extra big laugh.

Do not think that I endorse going to such extremes. No, the reason for playing a match must be for testing one's own skills against those of others. Striving with every scrap of experience, knowledge and technical expertise should be obligatory. Efforts below that demean your opponent and blemish the Olympic ideal. However, I am also sure that obtaining maximum pleasure from the game, with chasing the bowl a part of it, is an antidote to the stress and tension which ruins so many potentially good competitive bowlers. Relaxation and enjoyment of the challenge as much as the play itself increases rather than diminishes performance.

Nowadays one hears more and more the words 'body language' which, loosely, means improving one's own mental strength and self-confidence by good posture. This entails an erect stance and purposeful walk with the chest well up. Apart from the fillip such 'presence' gives oneself, it can and often does apply pressure to the opponent, especially if he in any way lacks self-confidence. 'Walk tall' the song goes. Please do.

It had always been my ambition to qualify for all four National Championship events in one year and 1957 took me to within two matches of such an achievement. They were the semi-finals of the county singles and triples but, maybe, that singles disappointment eventually proved of greater value than if I had won it.

The four years 1956 to 1959 inclusive were, I believe, where I proved myself as a skip, significantly because I was bold and aggressive. That loss in the county singles by 21–18 took place on an exceptionally (for England) fast green and it served as an incentive for a deeper study of techniques and tactics on such greens.

The ultimate effect reduced the aggression and power which had, from my earliest days, always provided pleasure and excitement, replacing it with much more dependable steadiness and adaptability. Those childhood days on the front lawn had generated a full range of shots, all of which I used with gay abandon. Advancing years, experience and a will to win taught me, often by the hard lesson of defeats, that aggression and the sheer joy of succeeding with spectacular shots often go against percentages. The value of caution and when to use it came into my thinking orbit and improved my judgement. On the whole, this was good but there is always the danger of caution degenerating into over-caution and from there to negative thinking and playing. To repeat, in order to win one must have the courage and conviction to use one's best shots when a situation demands them.

Consequently, I believe that my skipping lost some of its earlier fire though my singles play undoubtedly improved. Perhaps of all things, patience is the greatest asset in singles. Patience and concentration, the willingness to go on drawing shot after shot on the right line through meticulous use of a perfectly practised and grooved delivery technique – a learnable skill – and with the intense awareness and feel that ensures control of length.

No matter that an aggressive opponent may drive out many of those micrometrically accurate draw shots; patience and concentration should never waver. Out goes your good shot; you draw in another ... and then another.

Obviously, there will be a few occasions when a drive is essential but your occasional drive will not, normally, apply as much pressure on your opponent as draw shot after draw shot nestling up to the jack.

This in no way implies that the other shots can be neglected. To reach international levels you must be skilled with every known shot ... and maybe a few that aren't so well-known. On certain days your succession of drives may totally wreck your opponent's confidence but that does not negate the fact that consistently drawing to the jack is 'cash in the bank', especially now that the game has become Open.

In my opinion, singles and fours require two entirely different mental approaches. There is no guarantee that a first class skip will excel in singles or vice versa. However, on the whole, specialisation on singles, with its different tactics, can affect a player's all round game. Simply, the skips in a fours match do not deliver a bowl until those before them have clustered their twelve around the jack; well, theoretically clustered them. That can look like a veritable forest with no way of entry.

There was much to be learned in those early developing days, including the realisation that bowls is a good game for children. After a few years at a teacher training college, I became a schoolmaster and, later, a qualified teacher of mentally-handicapped children. Those years were tremendously rewarding in the warmth and friendship bestowed on me by so many children with all kinds of likes, dislikes, capabilities and deficiencies. There are many valuable lessons for children to learn in sport. Bowls is devoid of body contact so that the small and weak can play on equal terms with the rough and husky without any fear of physical damage. Discipline of the mind is essential; in football, tennis and many other games one can shed tension simply by running about energetically. There is no such way out in bowls; it is self-discipline or defeat.

In golf one can hit a magnificent drive close up to the hole and the opponent can do nothing about it. In bowls one can manoeuvre a match winning position with three splendidly controlled bowls edging their ways around the jack, only for the opponent to run the jack through to a cluster of his bowls and perhaps snatch victory for himself. One may feel inwardly infuriated but that is the essence of the game and the options are clear. Either accept what has happened philosophically and patiently, recognising and admiring your opponent's skill, or grumble, grouse and otherwise behave without decorum, patience and the inner determination that next time you will forestall him and win.

Roger and I had a taste of this in 1959 when we qualified for the National Pairs and battled our way into the final where we met Fred Harris and Jim Brayley, a truly formidable combination. Without in any way detracting from their fine skills and tactics, it was one of those days when nothing seemed to go quite right for us. In no way can I write that they were lucky but, from our viewpoint, four good take outs of the jack went fractionally wrong, on the major occasion the jack sliding off to give them five shots that left us 9–15 behind.

We clung on, fought back to 16–all and then lay game when Brayley went to the mat for the last time. Producing unquestionably the shot of the day, he drew a bowl that glided through the forest to rest delicately on mine fractionally closer to the jack. Later, he confessed 'I prayed all the time the bowl travelled down the green.' What can one do in such a situation? The title was almost stolen from us and we were unimaginally disappointed but Brayley's shot was so magnificent that we could only express our admiration. Only self-discipline and the correct, Olympic attitude to sports generally and bowls specifically can cope with such frustration. On the other hand, only such a test can teach one how to deal with disappointment, maintain patience and learn from the upset how to turn it into a valuable lesson.

In bowls, as in other sports, a disciplined, expansive attitude can be nurtured through disappointments and frustrations. Whether or not one grows through such experience is totally up to the individual. I believe one has the freedom to learn and conquer. It is a personal task which can be taught and learned and it is the individual alone who can do the learning.

● Try different sizes, weight and bias before buying your first set of bowls. If uncertain, ask a coach or experienced player to help you choose.

● Once you have decided on your shot, banish half-heartedness. Imagine the path of your bowl, deliver it firmly and take good care of your follow through.

● Applaud when your opponent makes a good shot ... then tell yourself quietly, 'and now I'll show you a better one'.

CHAPTER THREE

The horizons enclosing South West England soon began to increase after our Clevedon success in winning the National Fours Championship. S.W. England and the famous club at Paddington, London, extended to Glasgow when I gained my first England colours in 1958. Dreams about the 1962 Commonwealth Games scheduled for Perth, Western Australia, began to colour the hopes of most of the top grade competitive male players in the four home countries. Strangely, although women's bowls rivals the men in numbers and enthusiasm, their entry to the Commonwealth Games was delayed by nearly twenty years.

Because bowls was then a strictly 'amateurs only' game, those who were ultimately chosen had to negotiate all kinds of compromises with those in command of their jobs or those who might be taking charge of small businesses under players' ownership. Thus, it was imperative that the governing bodies of the four home country National Associations gave those chosen ample time to make all necessary preparations. In our case, we were 'given the nod' about a year in advance and formal selection around nine months in advance.

In this case, I am discoursing on international level bowls. Rose Kennedy, matriarch of the legendary American political family, once wrote a sentence that accords exactly with my beliefs; it expounded that 'accidents are the result of poor preparation'. The first detail of sound preparation must lie in the implements you use, namely your bowls. If you are a beginner, learn your requirements to the limit before spending your money. If you already play but are keen, nay determined, to improve, first learn completely about you and your bowls before rushing in to a new purchase.

First, then, take time to read and digest the International Bowling Board rules on bowls. It can be found in rule nine of the Laws of the Game.

It begins by stipulating that bowls shall be made of wood, rubber or composition and shall be black or brown. If your aim is international representation or competition, each of your bowls must carry on both sides an individual and distinguishing mark.

If your ambition is limited to local or county play the rule reveals there is no need for those marks on each side.

More relevant, perhaps, are the rulings on size. Bowls made of wood (lignum vitae) shall have a maximum diameter of 133.35mm and a minimum diameter of 117mm. In imperial terms the limits are $5\frac{1}{4}$in to $4\frac{5}{8}$in. There are no longer relationships of size with weight. There is a maximum limit of 1.59kg (3lbs 8oz) and that is all.

For all international and Commonwealth Games matches a bowl made of rubber or composition shall have a maximum diameter of 130.175mm ($5\frac{1}{8}$in) with the same 117mm minimum size.

All bowls have to be officially tested against the 'standard bowl' (a replica of the 'Master Bowl' held by the IBB) supplied to the official testers. Your bowls are shaped and the running face worked into them so that on an official tester's minutely accurate table they will not curve less in testing than the official IBB 'master'. They may curve as much as ingenuity can manufacture – but run in a straight line, emphatically 'no'.

So in choosing a suitable bowl you must define, or have defined for you, the size, weight, bias, shape of the area concerned with the running face and the material. Nowadays about 90 per cent of bowlers favour composition so you have one more variable, which form of composition will be best for your individual needs; and around 80 per cent of players use five-inch diameter.

First then, examine yourself as a bowler. How do you grip your bowl when delivering it from the mat? There are three basic grips, namely the cradle, the claw and the finger. Using the cradle, your bowl rests in the palm of your hand. Generally this is probably best suited to slower greens so if you live in a coldish, wet place like Scotland you are more likely to play most of your bowls on a slow, heavy green, compared with, say, New Zealand, where even a sudden puff of wind can send a standing bowl careering off on their hard, glassy greens.

The claw grip comes next. The bowl is held mainly by the fingers and thumb. Contact with the palm is limited to the puffy area at the base of the fingers. In the UK it is the most used grip and is suitable for all conditions. However, the fingertips are the most sensitive part of the human body and on ultra-fast greens such as those which abound in dry, hot, windy areas, that sensitivity of touch is extremely important. Hence the finger grip. With this the bowl is held well forward and is substantially controlled by the fingertips.

Already, then, variables have to be carefully analysed and judged in relative importance. There is more to come, namely the way you approach your bowls; your attitude to the game. Are you forceful by nature rather than a practitioner in finesse? If you are the latter you will probably be best served by a grip that gives you maximum fingertip feel. Again, however, the greens on which you play regularly must be taken into account.

The correct assessment of greens is an important part of preparation and, I suggest, of the type of bowls you eventually settle on. It is customary to talk about the speed of greens in terms of seconds. Maybe you have heard bowlers saying something like 'the green was very slow. It was running only about nine or ten seconds'. Conversely, you may have been told 'it is a fast green. At least 14 seconds'. Maybe you have puzzled on how a 14 seconds green can be faster than one of nine seconds: it doesn't sound logical. But consider for a moment: if the green is heavy and inadequately mown, then the bowl you deliver will run fast for a short while, only to be brought to a halt quite quickly by the braking effect of the heavy green. The ball is slowed down to a stop without any chance of trickling on and bending. On the other hand, if the green is close-cropped, sun-baked and hard, then the bowl will leave your hand at a slower speed and, as it nears the end of its journey down the green, it will meet with little resistance from the surface; the bowl will trickle on and on. Because it is lopsided – the bowls word is 'biased' – it will travel in a curve. In New Zealand during the Commonwealth Games and on a 23 or so seconds green, I once saw a bowl get taken up by the wind so that it slowed down to a stop only after it had covered a 180 degree semi-circle completely round the jack. That is why the greens that allow the bowl to trickle on in a curve are labelled 'fast'.

Tests to match theory with the actual performance of a bowl were carried out at the Mansfield IBC, London late in 1980 by Clarence Jones with Norman King, a former World Championship gold medallist, as the bowler. This was unique in world bowling as no one else possessed the sophisticated electronic equipment and bowls experience. King was chosen because of his sweetness of delivery and constancy of performance.

Preliminary tests established that the rink in question had a start to stop time of 12.612 seconds over a distance of 30.18 yards. The radar gun (an instrument used in the police radar speed measuring system) showed that a bowl projected at 18.43 feet per second took 24.57 yards to come to rest; 29.33 yards needed a projection of 19.21 feet per second.

With those fixed baselines, it was then possible to determine the degree of turn in those last few moments of trickle of King's Henselites. A line was drawn six feet in front of the jack and the timing started when the bowl crossed the line; it was stopped in time with the bowl coming to rest. The distance from the six foot line to the bowl was then measured.

By delivering a great number of bowls and logging times and distance, it became possible to produce a chart showing the curve of the bowl. Tabulated, the varying distances from the front line related to time showed:

Time taken from line to rest	Distance beyond front line
1.2 secs	3 feet
1.43 secs	5 feet
1.46 secs	6 feet
1.48 secs	7 feet

From this skeleton table, plus the other distances not given here, it was possible to show in a simple graph exactly how King's bowls behaved. The curve illustrated (see page 30) is that produced by a mathematical instrument. The dots are those produced and averaged from the abundant deliveries. The two correspond with remarkable similarity.

The pattern of the varying curves was then checked by visual-plus-time observations and they corresponded, bearing in mind that the graph is not necessarily lined up with the course of a full delivery. Nevertheless, the lateral distance of a bowl's travel during its last 1.48 seconds is seven feet. Remembering that the jack was 31 feet from the point of delivery, a trickle time of 1.3 seconds should produce a travel around 54 inches and that is precisely the 'land' taken by King with bowls delivered with that degree of trickle time.

Such detailed observation revealed another important facet of delivery; the variation of skid in any bowler's deliveries, bowl by bowl. King is as sweet as anyone in getting his bowls away but even his delivered bowls skidded for varying distances before running in synchronism with the green. That skidding resulted in similar 'lands' having differing swings at the end of their journeys.

THE WORLD BOWLS MEASUREMENTS

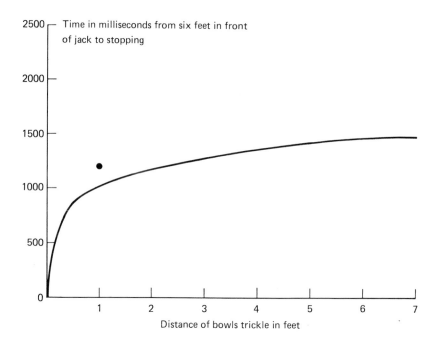

Except for the first second (1000 milliseconds) there is a close
relationship between theory and actual measurements

A further variable inherent in bowling greens, natural or man-
made, is their tendency to set up runs. Just as the drive of a house
will gradually suffer grooves set up by the constant travelling over
the same path by cars, so a green can create runs through bowl
after bowl taking the same route to the head. Such runs can prove
extremely difficult. Delivering a bowl along the run will usually
lead to it staying in the run instead of following the special course
you hoped to find. Delivering inside a run frequently results in the
bowl swinging across the jack and finishing well off the desired
line to the jack. Going outside the run almost always ends in your
bowl staying outside the run, so finishing wide of the jack.

It is also true that grass leans towards the sun. Thus, a tendency
for a rink to swing towards, say, the left in the morning may
change dramatically in the afternoon when the sun has crossed
the sky and pulled the blades across the rink with it.

These hazards are usually less of a problem in practice than
they may seem in theory. On the whole it is usually preferable to

concentrate on your bowl and the course you intend it to traverse. Trying to analyse a rink and then 'beating' it is dangerous; the beating of a rink may easily become more important than beating your opponent. Of course, one must be aware of hazards but a good bowler dominates the green and his bowls. He never lets a rink develop total mastery over him.

The 1983 British Isles Championships singles final provided a good example of this while helping Chris Ward to a 21-9 win over Paul McVeigh, Ireland. Twice England singles champion, Ward is blessed with considerable talent and on that day he used it well.

The rink on which they played had been set up on the middle of two rinks used in the morning semi-finals and this change resulted in varying speeds on three of the four hands.

McVeigh, it seemed, tried to play the green, for he bowled up and down one side of the rink sixty times and only twenty-three times up and down the other side. Ward trusted his ability more than the green and so delivered thirty-five bowls on one side and forty-seven on the other. It was noticeable that more of McVeigh's bowls swung across the jack than did Ward's.

So much for greens. Now comes the choice of bowls best suited to your requirements. You will, almost automatically, think mostly about your style and grip. Personally, I like a bowl which takes a sweep and would always settle for one which is over- rather than under-biased. Maybe if I was leading on a heavy green I might consider a narrower biased bowl but as a skip I have to manoeuvre my bowls round all kinds of obstacles and through multitudes of unusual gaps. That is the time when a bowl that can be varied at the end of different paths is a necessity. That was a major reason for me spending so many years experimenting and testing before I was able to tell myself 'now you've got it right'. So now I use one set of bowls for singles play which are below average bias, but certainly above minimum, as a bowl with too narrow an arc will find every run in the green, more often than not with disastrous results. My second, more heavily biased set are used for team play.

On fast greens a fraction of too much or too little strength can leave one's bowl several feet away from the jack. A sensitive touch is needed and touch is felt best by the fingertips and fingers generally. Because the green is fast, little power of delivery is necessary. In such a situation a bowl many would say is too large for you might well give you that extra finger and hand sensitivity you need.

However, fast greens impose less braking on a bowl than do heavy greens. Maybe, then, you should choose one of the composites that dig more into the green or the latest brands of composites that are endowed with braking power rather than the old, spherical lignums.

On slow greens quite big differences in the power of your deliveries produce tiny variations of length because of the relatively short time taken by a bowl to stop once it loses its early momentum; the distances can be as small as two or three inches. Such differences may cost you a single or a two instead of, perhaps, three or four shots because of those extra twelve inches.

Any bowler intent on becoming a specialist lead should consider seriously the use of a bias that runs straighter than average. With such a bowl an accurate lead can position delivery after delivery straight in front of the jack so making life very difficult for any opponent. This is particularly true in early season, county championship matches when the heavy green in running around nine or ten seconds.

Even indoors, greens are not always as fast as they might be. Most serious competitive bowlers prefer greens around 14 seconds in pace. That gives them scope for exploiting their skills. On a nine seconds green the bowl comes to a stop before it has had the chance to curve its way round a few front shots and through a gap on to the jack.

However, in a 21 ends fours match, complete with two trial ends, there will be a minimum of 368 deliveries. If all come to rest in ten seconds instead of fifteen that match will take thirty minutes less to finish. Any abundantly used indoor club playing four sessions a day can raise it to five sessions by slowing down the green by five seconds. That can add another forty or so green fees per day, to say nothing of extra drink sales. So a slow instead of fast green is financially valuable. Not many clubs have greens as slow as that, but it has happened.

Any beginner who goes straight into his local sports shop and buys a set of bowls is almost begging for trouble. Not because any proprietor or assistant is likely to mislead him deliberately but selection of a set of bowls merits obtaining help from an actual bowler of experience. An eighth of an inch either side of your optimum size – and as a beginner you will not know what that optimum is – is liable to reduce your effectiveness. This weakness will be compounded if you also buy the wrong weight.

Beginners, therefore, should always beg, borrow or steal many different sets for trial. Nowadays most clubs have, or are in contact with, one of the ever growing numbers of bowls coaches who have passed the official examination. When considering that a set of bowls nowadays can cost £100 or more, it is surely worth while having a lesson or two in learning which bowls will suit you best.

- Accidents are the result of poor preparation. Ensure that every detail is right each time you walk on the green.
- If you are to play a match, get to the green early, absorb the surroundings and try to foresee how the green will play.
- Be sure you know the rules back to front. Remember, they often change.
- Remember, the cradle grip is best on heavy greens but fast greens need good touch. That comes best from your fingers.
- If you bump or skid your bowl when delivering, your accuracy will suffer. So always take care to 'ground' each delivery.

CHAPTER FOUR

I am told that all-time tennis great Bobby Riggs decided he would become the world number one before he was big enough to play and that, consequently, he began with table-tennis for preparation. I also understand that Tracy Austin, the tennis player, once said over breakfast 'I want to become the world's best player'; she was eight years old at the time.

No such far off goals came into mind in my early years; indeed, I don't think that I have ever approached any championship with the hard and fast goal of winning in my mind. Obviously, I always prepare for a major event with all the experience and discipline in my possession, and in competing I play with immense will to win. Yet stronger than that is the sheer love of the game and my continuing to play it to the extreme limits of my ability; the challenge is perfection and, as a product of perfection, victories will follow automatically.

This quest embraced many facets of bowls and sports generally, a quest that intensified in the five years that separated the 1957 EBA Fours Championship from the Commonwealth Games at Perth, Western Australia, in 1962. Technique played an important role in the quest.

Consider, a sixteen inch gun is never allowed to move around a battleship; it is always secured strongly to the deck in order that its foundation is unshakeable. This analogy relates to my arrival at the delivery technique which I have been using for thirty years or so.

The sequence is, first a double knee squat from which I assess the direction and strength of the delivery to come. More about direction later but, meanwhile, my aim has always been for compaction. Every part of the movement must be aligned on the attempted path to the shoulder of the overall route of the bowl. There should be no room for flapping arms, feet sticking out in all directions, shoulders shoving or arm hooking in the release zone of the bowl.

Complete stability of my legs is of paramount importance, and to obtain that stability it is imperative that those legs are strong and supple. Special exercises to help strength and suppleness formed a vital part of my pre-Perth preparation ... and they remain so twenty years on from then; with increased determination as I moved towards my fiftieth birthday and onwards. Increasingly, knees and legs stiffen and grow weaker. One becomes vulnerable to injuries, as I discovered when suffering ham string injuries a few years ago. So the squat which heralds the start of my delivery may not last for the rest of my bowling life, especially because the exercising grows ever more demanding. Its key part is not so much the going down but, more, the control of the rise and its control of the length of my forward step in synchronism with the swing of my arm. A twenty-five yard draw on a 15 seconds green necessitates a short step and abbreviated back swing. A yard on shot with the target thirty-five yards from the mat on a heavy green demands a longer step and stronger, synchronising swing. Producing such variations precisely takes a heavy toll on the legs.

While squatting I juggle my bowl fractionally up and down in my hand to establish the sensitivity of feel needed for the correct length.

The number of jiggles varies. I learned from the January 1983 issue of *World Bowls* magazine that during a critical moment in my match against Jim Hobday in the inaugural Triple Crown Classic at Folkestone in November 1982, I actually jiggled my bowl up and down nineteen times; thank goodness for justification in the shape of a 'dead toucher' that robbed Jim of several shots.

Those jiggles are part-manifestation of another important facet of bowls, namely making ultimate use of the time spent between each actual release of one's bowl. There is nothing, other than Divine intervention, that can help one correct the path and length of a bowl once it has left the hand. Every facet of body, legs, arms, hand and mental determination and patience must bear down on that moment of delivery. Years of intelligent, disciplined practice help in achieving the state of isolation which allow one to focus totally on each delivery. Visualisation – mental rehearsal – supports dedicated practice immediately before and during any match.

One's follow through fits importantly into this operation. Factually, if there can be no control once the bowl has left the hand, what matter if the swing stops immediately after release, hooks or one scratches one's ear? Consider a Boeing 747 or other massive carrier of hundreds of air passengers. Its perfect take off follows a long, needle straight run-up followed by a further totally straight lift once the aircraft is in the air. So with the delivery of a bowl.

Theoretically the hook or whatever does not stop until the bowl has been released. In fact, it is extremely difficult to shift from movement to stop instantaneously. The speed of the swing should never be decelerating at the moment of release. Therefore, almost inevitably, hooks and other idiosyncracies come into the action before release of the bowl. Spend a few evenings watching bowlers and you will quickly observe how hookers first tend to deliver bowls that go across the jack and then, in trying to correct, their direction becomes ever more erratic.

I took a long time to develop a follow through that is 'on line' for an overall distance of around two to three feet, varying with the pace of the green. In helping this I do not run through my deliveries. Instead, I let my right leg swing freely upwards, always in line with the direction the bowl sets off down the green.

In refining this form of delivery I have discovered that the direction the right foot is pointing is an important factor in direction of the bowl. Accuracy of direction is at its best when the foot is pointing down the required line as this eliminates or minimises, perhaps, the arm and leg moving in different directions, so inhibiting balance to a greater or lesser degree. One sees on the green, even during the Gateway Building Society EBA Championships, many bowlers who point their back foot inwards and then let their back knee tuck in behind the front leg after release of the bowl. Indeed, one such bowler reached a recent final of the Singles Championship.

All the points I am making are marginal and maybe a highly talented 'natural' can override them. But, given that all other things are equal, the bowler with the superior delivery technique starts with an advantage that brings victory far more often than defeat. So always strive for a better technique.

To achieve consistency in accuracy of line it is of paramount importance that the bowler's eyes are riveted to a point of aim or target. During the delivery action his eyes must never be allowed to stray, thus maintaining total concentration until the bowl has been released and the follow through completed and ensuring that the whole body flows rhythmically down the aiming line.

The actual point of line varies from player to player; in fact, many bowlers claim that they do not look at anything in particular but, of course, this cannot be the case. Having discussed the subject with bowlers of varying abilities over the years, I believe they fall into three categories. Players who take a mark on the bank, players who take a mark on the green and players who bowl to an imaginary shoulder.

Basically, they are all doing the same thing. When a bowl is delivered with perfect green and weight it inscribes an arc before nestling on the jack. At approximately three fifths of the distance from the mat to the jack the bowl reaches its widest point. This is called the shoulder of the arc. As a bowl responds to its bias the moment it is delivered, the degree of which will vary with the pace of the green, the bowl cannot travel in a straight line to the shoulder of the arc. Thus, the initial delivery line must be angled outside it, the degree depending on the pace of the green or, to put it another way, whether it is a narrow, medium or wide drawing hand.

From this it can be deduced that all players using identical bowls must be delivering approximately along the same line, whichever category they fall into. Therefore, if a straight line is drawn on the grounding position of the bowl to the mark or target on the bank, this must be the aiming line down which all players deliver.

The actual point of aim will vary from individual to individual; bowlers in the first category will look at the bank whereas those in the second category may look at a mark anywhere on the green which can vary from match to match. The player who plays to the imaginary shoulder will bowl to a target on this line approximately three fifths of the way to the jack which will be approximately equally distant to the true shoulder. On a slow green with little arc the true and imaginary shoulder will be relatively close together but on greens of 15 seconds or more the two lines can be several feet apart.

A further refinement in my delivery shows in the way I turn my arm and hand inwards during my back swing. I have found this a natural movement when my arm swings backwards and it helps to keep the whole arm on a straight path backwards and forwards.

Understand that I have been outlining my own delivery and the way I experimented, tested and analysed over the years preceding, for me, the then most important international event since 1958, and 1962 Commonwealth Games.

On the whole I encourage experimenting but it comes after one has experienced enough bowls to develop some idea of what the game is all about. Nowadays there is a vast, national network of

Grounding at the moment of delivery is vital for accuracy and consistency. It is helped by a flexible back and knees, as I was able to produce despite any pressures of this EBA singles final at Mortlake.

qualified coaches who can start people off in the game and then help them towards competitive standards. In my case, I observe the following points when teaching.

1. The motive force of a delivery is generated both by weight transfer and arm movement. In general terms the arm is only a partly contributory vehicle. Therefore, the delivery must be conditioned to ensure a smooth and accurate line for the bowl, with good distribution of forces on the muscles that will be used.

2. The bowler must feel comfortable and at ease on the mat. His feet should be sufficiently apart to ensure a good balance, with knees relaxed and body weight slightly forward. The bowl should be held without tension in the wrist or arm.

3. The arm holding the bowl may be slightly to the front but not excessively so. The feet should be positioned on the mat so they

are pointing along the intended line of delivery.

4. Perfect grounding of each and every bowl is essential for consistent accuracy. Other imperatives are rhythmic body movement along the line of delivery starting from the moment of addressing the green from the mat and ending with completion of the follow through. During the delivery the shoulder, elbow, forearm, wrist and bowl should all stay in line and move along the aiming line with a smooth, flowing action.

5. The elbow must not be allowed to stray from the side of the body as it will cause a 'hooked delivery'. The wrist must not be allowed to twist while the bowl is being grounded.

6. During delivery body weight has to be transferred from the right foot to the left foot ... smoothly. To help that smooth action I recommend placing the left hand on the left thigh to act as a prop; this minimises those slight wobbles or body sways that result in a player missing his intended line.

7. In the true athletic delivery (which I normally teach) the actual delivery is a synchronised combination of a forward step with the left foot and pendulum-like swing of the right arm.

8. The bowl is held in front of the body addressing the aiming line. As it is swung back and in passing the body, the left foot is raised and moved forward meticulously along the line of intended delivery. The foot, however, does not make contact with the green until the arm has begun its forward swing. It is essential that the knees are bent and relaxed, so helping a successful transfer of body weight to the left foot.

9. A smooth follow through is essential and this can only be achieved if the body weight is well forward and over the front foot. This necessitates the back foot rising on to the toes or even being elevated above the mat according to the power of the swing.

10. The delivery hand should be pointing along the aiming line during the major part of the follow through in order to minimise any tendencies to hook, jab or flick the bowl. Any of those three faults can play havoc with both line and length.

11. The bowler's eyes should be looking at the target which is marking the intended line of delivery. They must remain on that target in order to eliminate all tendencies to lift the head, or to look to where the bowl is going, until total completion of the follow through. It is natural for the body to flow forwards along the line so it is imperative that the back foot does not move forward past the front until the bowl is well on its way down the

green. It is all too easy for a forward movement of the back foot to tilt the body to the left and so ruin the intended line of delivery. It is a good habit to take several steps along the path of the bowl while regaining an upright position *after completion of the follow through*.

Probably you will read these details while sitting in your favourite armchair. You may remember them all clearly ... until you actually stand on a mat in readiness to bowl.

For protection, run through these quick reminders before delivering.

a Relaxed and comfortable stance.

b Right foot pointing along the aiming line, left foot alongside helping sound balance.

c Shoulder, elbow, wrist and bowl smoothly down the aiming line.

d Knees relaxed, especially at the moment of delivery.

e Ground the bowl perfectly.

f Rivet eyes on given point throughout the action.

So far I have dwelt on two methods of delivery, my own and the athletic, sometimes known as the upright. The two have something in common in that the forward swing of the arm is synchronised with a forward movement of the left foot.

There are two other methods which are used by a significant number of players. One is called the fixed stance, the other the semi-fixed.

The fixed is so called because the front foot is placed down the delivery line and there it stays throughout the whole of the action. It is, perhaps, the best stance for men suffering from a physical incapacity or by veterans who have lost much of their youthful flexibility and leg mobility. In first standing erect and then swinging, stepping forward and bending low they are liable to spoil overall control through malfunction of one, maybe all, physical deficiencies. In starting with the left foot firmly planted and the left hand placed on the upper leg for stability, they eliminate many of the dangers of instability.

However, that stability is achieved through the abandoning of free flowing, body movement and this can be a severe handicap when bowling on the ten second, heavy greens all too often found in Great Britain. Conversely, the fixed stance delivery can be advantageous when the green is very fast and the problem is cutting down power rather than increasing it. The best practitioner of the fixed stance I have ever met was the late Tom Fleming who won a gold medal at the 1962 Commonwealth Games and was runner-up in the EBA Singles Championship in 1959 and 1960, that second time to me. However, Tom had longish arms and was 6'2" tall so his physique endowed him with the leverage to compensate for loss of much of his body weight.

The semi-fixed stance is a cross between the athletic and mixed stances and is often mistaken for the athletic. When taking his stance on the mat the player adopts a similar position to the athletic delivery but his front foot is moved partly down the delivery line, the degree of which is determined by the pace of the green; shorter for a heavy green, longer for a fast green. During delivery the front foot moves forward to complete the step. The main merit of this particular stance is the selection and part commitment to the delivery line of the front foot in the initial stage. This must surely minimise error in missing the correct line and increase the percentage of well-greened bowls. As in the fixed stance, the body is stabilised by the free hand grasping the thigh or knee of the front leg.

Reviewing what I have written so far, I believe there is much you can learn from these written words. There is also an important point to make. It is that many teachers are veritable fountains of knowledge but they cannot make anyone learn. The learning situation is entirely under the control of the pupil. He must possess two main factors; one is total belief in the tutor and what the tutor is saying, and the other is unwavering enthusiasm and determination to master and put into operation all that he is learning. What is it that we are sometimes told – you can take a horse to water but you cannot make him drink.

All this is strongly linked to the 1957–62 period. It was in about 1962 that my inquisitiveness led me ever deeper into the off green aspects of improving my bowls; into a region of sport which embraces a number of aspects and techniques which are frequently called the 'intangibles'.

Clearly, they can be realised and even learned to some degree on the green itself. Probably not greatly in run-of-the-mill practice but the pressures and anxieties of international competition are hard masters where the variations of experience teach valuable lessons. One can also learn massive amounts simply from considering and analysing techniques and skills when at rest in one's home, on holiday stuck in a traffic jam, and so on. As a school teacher I had always been aware of the intangibles of life and those 1962 Commonwealth Games caused me to consider them more and more.

- If you are over fifty do not be too proud to change from an upright to crouch delivery. Consider yourself and not the spectators as well as the conditions when deciding.
- Take your time when lining up your feet, especially the back one. Gain complete balance and comfort before delivering. Strong and supple legs are a great help.
- Try 'weighing' (jiggling up and down) your bowl to help you feel the line and length you need.
- Rivet your eyes on your line and not the target when delivering. Seek for a mark to help you deliver along the line you choose.
- Analyse your techniques, skills and approach when you get home. Concentrate on only the game while it is in progress.

CHAPTER FIVE

In some ways those years leading up to the 1962 Commonwealth Games were among the most important of my whole career. It had been possible to experiment and extemporise in social games or when practising alone but there is a world of difference between that and the competitive game.

Somerset may not have been the strongest county in English bowls but the standard was high and in competing with such a variety of good players I learned much about the knack of winning. This knack – it might even be called a skill – embraces not only a good technique but also an unflappable temperament, instinct for realising what are or are not moments of crisis, and the will to win when faced with difficult situations through belief that one will succeed with the shot one is about to make.

Looking back, my table of successes reflects the progress. Starting at the Somerset Championships, I qualified for the EBA singles in 1958/60, the pairs in 1953/57/59 and the fours in 1956/57/59/61.

At national level, I won the EBA fours in 1957 and the singles in 1960. The latter moved me on to my highest achievement yet, the British Isles Singles Championship in 1961. Those results led to my inclusion in England's Home International team in 1958/59/61/62. Note the missing year, 1960, in my membership of the England team.

Though my record as a skip in the fours, helped immeasurably by my favourite team-mate, my father, bettered my singles performances at first, there existed in those days a widespread, unjustified idea that bowlers who were good with four bowls in singles were often far less effective when cut down to two bowls in fours matches. Despite my record in fours, a few whispers went the rounds that I was one of those bowlers. To me it was nonsense but when I suffered a bad day on the 1960 international team trial it seemed the selectors agreed with the idea.

Anyway, I was omitted, as was Percy Baker, in those days the highest rated player in the British Isles. He had won the EBA singles title on four occasions, 1932/46/52/55, and represented England in fourteen of the International Team Championship series. That one off-day on trial should outweigh a then outstanding record in top class bowls so sickened Baker that he vowed he would never again bowl for England, a vow he kept.

Apart from those four triumphs in the EBA singles, Baker won the pairs in 1950/62 and the triples in 1960; his record of seven championships standing until I eventually equalled him on August 13th 1969 at the Watneys Club, Mortlake. With my father Reg at second man, David Rhys Jones as number three and Bill Elliott leading, Clevedon beat Harold Powell's formidable Farnborough BL team 20-13. Seven days later David Rhys Jones and I beat A Papworth and B Crawley, LBC, Arlesey 25-11, so bettering Baker's splendid record. It was a memorable evening for me, the more so because in overtaking Percy Baker I had carried forward the skill and honour of a truly great man.

However, I am racing ahead. Discarded by the English selectors, I would have been less than human not to have felt extra satisfaction for winning the EBA singles for the first time a few weeks later in 1960. That year heralded the arrival of the British Isles Championships which were contested by the various winners of the events at the English, Irish, Scottish and Welsh championships of the previous summer. Ken Coulson, the 1959 EBA champion, beat JA Connolly, Ireland, 21-18 to become the first name engraved on the handsome trophy and I followed him in 1961 by beating RD Roberts, Wales, 21-6 at Eastbourne.

My 1960 form at Mortlake ensured my recall to the England team for 1961 and it was at Eastbourne that Tom Fleming, Leslie Watson, Syd Drysdale and I were given to understand that we were going to represent England some sixteen months later at Perth in the 1962 Commonwealth Games.

As all of us would need to seek leave of absence for a month, it was essential that we received ample time to make the necessary arrangements. Tom and I were both schoolmasters and it was just another typical English vagary that the Middlesbrough educational big-wigs gave him time off with full pay while the Somerset authorities allowed me four weeks leave but paid for only two of them. Once again in my life, my parents immediately came to the rescue.

Official notification came in April 1962 but the knowing winks thrown our way during the 1961 Home Internationals - incidentally, our four won all their three matches, good justification of my recall - had been augmented early in 1962 and I began my preparations right away. Shedding some weight formed part of them, as did stretching exercises.

Realising that the greens in Perth would be considerably faster than those at home, I sought for all possible information. We knew the greens could be around 16 seconds but realised that they might be even quicker. Leslie was a dab hand at timing greens and many a time I found him quietly sitting with a stop watch recording speeds and analysing performances of bowls.

The Perth rules allowed only four players per country and that limited the programme to, first, the fours, followed by the singles and pairs simultaneously. I was scheduled for the singles and as number two in the fours, with Tom Fleming leading, Leslie Watson at third man and Syd Drysdale skipping.

Because of the fast greens supposedly being prepared, we were all equipped with sets of bowls that ran as straight as the rules permit. Additionally, I borrowed a set of 'straight' bowls from a club-mate, Sam Waite, and when I arrived at Perth my supplier met me with a brand new set. Sure enough, the greens were faster than those at home but only by a couple of seconds or so. The 'straight' bowls I'd carted with me proved unsatisfactory so, to the amazement of most people, I used the new set. They suited me as though by magic.

We left London Airport at 10.30 p.m. on November 6th for the trip of our lifetimes; indeed, in my case, it was my first trip out of the British Isles. The journey, though long and exciting, proved tedious and tiring but it gave me time to think deeply about what faced us, my attitude to and love of the game and of my determination to win the singles. I think all of us were aware that none of the four who won the 1958 gold medal for fours at Cardiff had been chosen for 1962 and the general feeling was 'this may be our only chance'.

Perth turned out to be a beautiful city and the Dalkeith Club, the venue for the bowls, was amazingly spacious and luxurious compared to our clubs back home. Even more pleasing was the unbounding hospitality and comradeship of the residents and the moving rapport that grew among the contestants.

Since bowls was our business, I was eager to see and try Australian greens and, again, my eyes were opened. They were less densely grassed than ours and they ran with all the smoothness of a billiards table. We also cast our eyes at the light-carrying pylons which we were soon to see in practical use because of the many night sessions needed to complete the bowls events on schedule.

Any sign of dampness brought out the 'no play' boards, each green was rested on two days a week and all matches were banned for a whole day each week. The temperature hovered around 100° F throughout the three weeks and my most pleasurable match was a fours under floodlights on a heavenly evening against Hong Kong.

Bowls generally and the need for focusing all my mental and physical energy on the matches virtually abolished any chances of sightseeing but I enjoyed being taken to the small but lovely nature reserve at Yanchep where I saw kangaroos, emus and koala bears in their natural surroundings. I also visited some reputedly breathtaking caves but as a Somerset man I know the Cheddar caves and after seeing them who can be awe-struck by any others?

After more than a week of practice we got down to matches and it seemed certain right from the start that we would pick up the gold medals. Ignoring the abilities of Leslie Watson and the exuberance, bravery and inspiration of Syd Drysdale, I found it a source of great confidence to bowl after our lead, Tom Fleming.

Fundamentally, the lead's duty is straightforward, to deliver his two bowls nearer to the jack and in better tactical positions than those of his opposite number. Maybe his skip will allow him to set the mat wherever he likes and to exploit the length of jack that gives him the best chance of carrying out successfully that duty of winning his match within a match with the opposing lead.

However, the remaining six players have another twelve bowls to deliver and they can, and usually do, set up enormously tricky and complex situations; problems which the skip has to solve. So it is more customary for the skip to call on his lead to place the mat and throw the jack in the best way suited to the four as a whole. Maybe the definitive example of this comes from the 1958 Commonwealth Games when England and South Africa finished with identical records and a play-off was necessary. Norman King was leading under John Scadgell as skip and in the first meeting he convincingly outbowled the South African lead. However, the South African skip was formidable with short jacks but Scadgell felt sure he could outbowl the Springbok skip on long jacks.

Carefully explaining the tactical plan to King, Scadgell asked for long jacks throughout. King obliged and, seemingly, was less authoritative than in their first match. Nevertheless, Scadgell lived up to his prediction; England won the gold medals and the almost

The green at Waratah, New South Wales, Australia in 1975 was several seconds faster than ours at home. Even so, your follow through must remain free. Note my back foot, still on the ground although the bowl is on its way. It shows I have cut down my body flow slightly ... But not my follow through.

imperative requirement for a skip totally controlling the tactics was amply demonstrated.

So the lead's duty is enlarged somewhat. Not only must he outbowl the opposing lead but he must do so with the mat and jack positioned where his skip demands it. This imposes a formidable task on the lead, one he can only fulfil satisfactorily if he is a master of the drawing to the jack shot. There are other, 'ritual' duties for all members of a four but I hope all readers are fully aware of them.

If you are the lead, your first active-play action should be to fix the line of delivery. With that done, the weight of delivery necessary to nestle your bowl against the jack must be determined. Direction is achieved by having all parts of your body, legs, arms and swing compact and integrated in movement. Length demands a sensitive touch. (See my approach to line and length in Chapter four.) However, they are so fundamentally important that a little revision cannot go amiss. On a fast green you can develop touch with the bowl as it rolls out of the fingers. On heavy greens extra force is necessary and that demands a stronger grip. Yes, that brings about some loss of touch but the braking effect of a heavy, slow green is such that even quite a noticeable variation of force may only change your length by nine inches or a foot. On a fast green that same change of force may cause a difference at the head of several feet; perhaps as many as six. But whether the green be fast or slow, strive always for your delivery to be smooth and flowing.

Good weight is the child of correct propulsion and correct propulsion is governed by the length of your swing. So when assessing your delivery, hold the bowl high on a heavy green but keep it low if the green is fast; say 14 seconds or more.

The height at which you hold your bowl exercises some control on the length of your back swing, providing you are swinging rhythmically and not in a series of jerks. This demands variations in the height of your stance at the start of your delivery; it is virtually impossible to stand upright and smoothly deliver a bowl from the low position needed on a fast green. Similarly, it is equally difficult to squat down, hold your bowl high and then deliver powerfully and accurately on a slow green. Pace goes best with grace.

A little experimenting on the green should quickly convince you that this is true and alert you to the definite correlation between height of stance and length of back swing which is dictated by the pace of the green. How high the stance and long the back swing must relate to all the prevailing conditions as judged by the player.

The higher the stance and the longer the back swing, the greater the propulsion. This is not purely the effect of elevation and swing. The follow through of body weight generated by the forward step also has an important effect, especially on the slow greens abounding in the northern hemisphere. At the other end of the scale body weight effect must be minimised.

Whether bowling on a slow green and taking a long step or on a fast green when the forward step is little more than a shuffle of the foot, it is essential that you lean forward over the bowl in order to achieve the correct follow through.

On fast greens the majority of the weight you impart to the bowl must come from your arm and wrist. That in no way gives you licence to stand upright or to pull back from your bowl in

My favourite lead, Tom Fleming, and I practising for and acclimatising to Perth on the green at Gibson Park.

the act of letting it go. Always, but always, think 'forwards'. If the green is ultra fast, let your stance be as low as possible and your back swing restricted accordingly.

Indeed, the principle of correct elevation and length of back swing should always be your first consideration, no matter the conditions. Only in continuously striving for and achieving a smooth cohesion of step and swing (no matter what the differences of propulsion you may use) can you develop a masterly control and consistency in maintaining line and length, so earning respect and fame as a lead.

Let me emphasise yet again that the arm, body and foot must integrate in an overall smooth and rhythmic delivery. My observations while travelling the bowls world is that many bowlers confuse themselves by concentrating on one of these factors while neglecting the others, so becoming jerky and erratic. By concentrating mainly on the length of the back swing and relating it to the speed of action, the foot, if it is in sympathy with everything else, will automatically step the required distance.

If you develop a copy-book delivery, with your head and hand well down and following the intended line, the back foot will automatically rise above the mat … and in a line integrated with the rest of the delivery. Understand that it is comparatively easy to adjust height of stance, lengths of step and back swing etc. while maintaining rhythm and control.

Seeking for changes of length simply by speeding up or slowing down your actual swing is a sure path to failure. Remember, world class golfers swing a variety of clubs at the same pace, using their differences of weight and construction to control each situation. In tennis, too, world class servers swing at the same speed for both first and second services, using spin to vary control of flight and direction.

From this it should be clear that effective, consistent drawing to the jack, either as a lead or in singles, depends enormously on leg control. Tom Fleming, our lead at Perth, established that control by delivering from the front foot fixed with overall balance maximised. The greens were fast – 15 seconds – compared to those in England, and Tom was 6′2″ tall and endowed with long arms. Thus he could always make up for his loss of body momentum with arm leverage. At Perth he broke the confidence of nearly every opposing lead. Back home in Middlesbrough he bowled his way in two successive years to the EBA Championships and on to the singles finals, losing to Ken Coulson in 1959 and me in 1960. That gives him the somewhat sad but none the less great record of being the only man in history to lose the final two years in succession. Maybe if he had begun with the athletic stance he would have earned the extra shots for victory. Who knows? Certainly, his leading at Perth greatly simplified things for the rest of the gold medal winning four.

Summarising Fleming's success as our lead at Perth, he followed implicitly some special points that all exponents of the draw shot should have embedded in their memories.

1. The 'true shoulder' of the bowls line is always inside the 'imaginary shoulder'; the faster the green, the more apparent this becomes.
2. Never follow a left-hander's line of delivery; his bowls always start their paths a shoulder's width (about eighteen inches) to the left of a right hander and that changes the geometry significantly.
3. When taking your stance on the mat, point the right big toe at

the aiming point. Keep that right foot, your elbow, wrist and bowl and its aiming line in one straight, compact line.

4. Glue your eyes to the point of aim throughout the delivery, taking particular care to keep them there until your follow through is totally completed.

5. It is necessary during the stance to keep glancing at the jack and jiggling your bowl while assessing the line and weight of delivery needed. Once your assessment is completed, concentrate completely on the point of aim to ensure any anxious, premature lifting of your head, eyes and body to see if your bowl is 'on line' before the bowl has been released. On a wide drawing rink you will not be able comfortably to see both the jack and your line-showing object; there are no great problems in learning how to keep the head down and forward.

6. Do not unthinkingly maintain the same lengths for a given green. Always be prepared to move the mat with care and skill when necessary, thus changing the line, and keep your eyes open when looking for weaknesses among opposing players.

How factually Fleming simplified my task was clear for all to see. He was always there or thereabouts and, mostly, all I had to do was maintain a good line making sure my bowls finished in the head, usually behind the jack.

As a number two in the British Isles any class bowler would be expected to possess, in addition to straightforward skill in drawing to the jack, accuracy in a range of running-through shots spreading between about twelve inches to several feet over the position of the target. Nowadays, with skips who believe in clearing dangerous heads long before they can become impregnable, number twos must also be adept with the drive.

Apart from many of our matches and my thirteen singles clashes, two things remain clearly in my mind. One was the piles and piles of pills, special foods, and other 'goodies' which almost took over our apartments; they would have needed twice as many men to demolish them, perhaps more.

The other was a friendly chat with the Duke of Edinburgh during his official visit to the Games. Informal and relaxed, he soon revealed quite good knowledge of bowls, possibly from the time he spent at the 1958 Games at Cardiff. It would have been easy for him merely to lend his name but that did not seem to be any part of his make-up. He took care to spend time with us and we were profoundly gratified and stimulated.

Our opening match turned out to be more than a serious international contest. We met the Scottish four skipped by Willie Moore, by no means a placid competitor. However, his personality was almost nothing compared to that of Syd Drysdale whose verve and enthusiasm was splendidly captured by the pen of journalist Syd Donovan. He wrote, 'The scene was quite unlike anything experienced before. Excited players barracking, urging, galloping after their bowls, gesturing, shaking hands, even lying on the rink ... it was as one WA official described it, "a complete circus".

'Star of the show was England skipper Syd Drysdale who had the crowd in fits of laughter. They quickly nicknamed him "the crab" because of the ungainly, weaving action he had as he chased almost every bowl from delivery to its final resting place. There was no set pattern to his performance which heightened the entertainment.

'One moment he would creep off to the left with a little, stuttering run, hands upraised in an ecstasy of concentration. Next moment a crouched pose would see him break to his right, tiptoeing down the path of his bowl, appealing to it, pushing it, though never once actually touching his bowl.

'Once he even went charging down after a full blooded, neck-or-nothing-drive, reaching the other end only feet behind his bowl – a sprint that would have done credit to England's Peter Radford.

'At times Drysdale would finish crouched right over the kitty, his nose almost rubbing against his bowl. Said one spectator "I paid ten shillings to get in, five for the bowls, five for the best circus I have ever seen ..."'

There were serious debates concerning antics specifically barred by Australian rules but, wisely, there was a general recognition of the extra interest stimulated by Drysdale's exuberance. This sometimes clouded his great skill with his bowls. That combination of exuberance and skill put him among the best skips I have ever seen or competed against. A skip must be capable of producing any kind of shot there is ... and with an accuracy that can find gaps or positions which, seemingly, don't exist. His contribution to the gold medals we ultimately collected cannot be measured.

Nor can that of Leslie Watson, who had demonstrated his magnificent touch and deep understanding plus character on major occasions when he skipped his brother to the EBA Pairs Championship at Paddington in 1956. That final made a little history as

Sid Drysdale chasing his bowl. See why they named him 'The crab'?

an all-family affair; the Pullins, father and son, losing 14–16. The low score tells its own story of one inch here, another there – finessing of the highest quality. Filling almost the role of a policeman, Watson almost inevitably rectified any blemishes suffered by Fleming or me and delivered his bowls with mathematical exactitude to any precise position demanded by Drysdale.

Our acquisition of gold might have been easier but for a magnificent wrest out by George Makin, the Australian skip, with the last bowl of the match. The head forecast a 16–13 win for us, only for his wrest out to push out our single and leave Australia with a three and 16–15 victory.

As there were only two matches remaining, our disappointment and anxiety can easily be imagined. Following the Games, I contracted a duodenal ulcer which drove me to bed the following year. But, they say, every cloud has a silver lining and my long spell coincided with the 1963 cricket test matches so my TV set produced innumerable hours of total freedom from bowls.

Following the fours came the singles, with thirteen matches my formidable task. Though I won all of them – the first time anyone returned a 100 per cent, unbeaten record – I was chased to the very end by Watson Black of Scotland and Alan Bradley, the tenacious Rhodesian. My concentration made considerable demands on my self-discipline and my form seemed variable. Nevertheless, it sufficed to overcome Jeff Baron, New Zealand, and Stirling Shield, Canada.

That fortnight of strain and striving took a heavy toll of my physical resources which the immense applause and friendship bestowed on me by players and public alike only overcame momentarily. Undoubtedly all the stress before and during the Games started the ulcer and there was to be no relief when I reached England again.

Before leaving Perth, unknown to me, I had been generously invited by the Clevedon Council to switch on the Christmas illuminations on the first Tuesday in December. It seemed I could reach home in time so, feeling honoured, my wife had said 'yes'. She had forgotten the unreliability of British weather. Our aircraft was scheduled to land at London Airport but was directed to Prestwick, Scotland, before being told to return south to Gatwick. This hazardous journey finally ended at Temple Meads, Bristol, at 17.00, leaving just enough time to be rushed home for a change of clothes and then on to the official ceremonies. It was pleasing to see 1,000 Clevedon faces and to hear their bountiful applause and good wishes ringing around The Triangle before setting off three rockets and switching on the lights.

Even pleasurable events can impose stress. More were to come, including an invitation for me to play an exhibition match during the opening ceremonies of the South African National Championships the following March. Numerous circumstances had ruled out every possible chance of my wife, Ruth, accompanying me to Perth and nothing seemed more tempting to us than a luxurious few days in South Africa.

Problems: how could I again approach the Somerset Educational Department and ask for more leave of absence, especially when it was not for international representation. Probably leave would have been granted but, then, how could I ask yet again for time off for the International Team Championship? And how about my salary? No, South Africa was simply not on.

● If you are leading, your task is to outbowl your opposite number ... but from where the skip (not you) wants the mat and the jack.
● Accurate drawing to the jack depends enormously on leg control so never neglect your leg-strengthening exercises.
● Remove tension with inner calmness to ensure your delivery is always relaxed, smooth and flowing.
● Always be ready to move the mat and jack around if your opponent is less adaptable than you.
● When practising for an unknown green, remember it is easier to adjust to a slower green than to a faster one.

CHAPTER SIX

My duodenal ulcer, pressure of work at school and other factors imposed severe limits on my bowling throughout 1963. Meanwhile, signs of international and national developments promised big things to come, notably a World Championship.

The 1966 Commonwealth Games were scheduled for Jamaica where there were no greens and precious little chance of an indoor stadium being built; imagine indoor bowls in the sweltering heat of the West Indies. There were rumours of a World Championship in Los Angeles, California, where a considerable amount of bowls is played. Bill Hay, USA, had been elected President of the International Bowling Board at Perth in 1962 and, for a while, the project seemed a possibility.

At the other side of the Pacific Ocean Neil Benjamin, a determined, go-getting Australian doctor with a great love of bowls, was campaigning vigorously and by 1965 had struck gold, in the form of Ampol Petroleum and Qantas, the major Australian airline. The inaugural World Championships were ultimately born at Kyeemagh, a place adjacent to Sydney Airport and within walking distance of Botany Bay where Captain Cook anchored in 1770.

More of Kyeemagh later. Back in the British Isles indoor bowling was developing rapidly. Reputedly started by William Macrae, then President of the Drumdryan Club, in 1888 on a sawdust covered, cement floor in a drill hall, the standards that propagated the concept of a bowls abundance for twelve months of each year were set at the Crystal Palace in 1906 and Wimbledon in 1909. The indoor section was established in 1933. By the outbreak of World War II there were fifty affiliated clubs. Reduced to thirty-three by its end, those clubs multiplied to 117 by the start of the seventies and topped 180 early in the eighties. The English Inter-Club Championship was launched in 1935 and the International Team Championship – Hilton Cup – followed in 1936. Of course, both were team events and it was not until the late 1950s that ever increasing pressure, notably generated by Arthur Sweeney, then Honorary Secretary of the English indoor game, and *World Bowls* magazine, that a challenge cup for the English Indoor Triples Championship was established.

Despite immense resistance, the English Indoor Singles Championship opened the flood gates for individual indoor championships. There was a restriction of entrants per club so that the entry barely exceeded 200. Allan Spooner won the event, a fact I recalled when I saw him mingling among the crowd watching the 1983 Gateway Building Society National Championships at Worthing.

My inherent liking for an outdoor life and the challenge of ever varying outdoor greens, to say nothing about a need to take time off from bowls, delayed my thirst for indoor play but my somewhat desolate summer in 1963 helped to galvanise me into action. Winning the National Indoor Singles Championship that 1963/64 winter, I managed seven encores by 1977. The first twelve years of that event spotlighted the strength of the Bristol indoor club, with four of its members capturing the singles eight times in that golden era. It is also a measure of the testing practice that was always available.

First selected in 1965 for the England team, I had played in eighteen series by the 1983 series ... and I am still learning new things every year.

That 1963/64 winter campaign helped my match tightness and I retained the indoor title in the winter of 1964/65. I thought I had the final safely sewn up in 1965/66, only for my club-mate, Gilbert Attwood, to produce a remarkable spell of accuracy and take the title. I regained my title in the winter of 1965/66. The year 1965 saw the start of a new partnership, later to prove highly successful, when David Rhys Jones and I survived a somewhat perilous course in the EBA Pairs Championship at Mortlake, scraping home by one shot against Stan Carter and Bob Stenhouse, Wellingborough Town. Bob was later appointed Captain of the English World Championships team and he remains as fine a bowler as he is person. Number two rink on the Watneys finals green at Mortlake always played beautifully and their use of it forced both David and me to produce more high tension shots than usual. Our final against George Scadgell and his lead Rex Glover Phillips proved a little less scary, the more so because of our respective earlier matches. Maybe my victory over George in the National Indoor Singles final four months earlier helped us because of a seemingly daring tactic had come off and earned me a timely, valuable four. Our 24–21 win qualified us for the 1965 British Isles Championships; those Championships are of necessity always staged during the July of the following year and we proudly captured the pairs event.

People down our way in Somerset often profess sympathy for David Rhys Jones, saying that my record over the years has pushed him into the shadows and prevented the public from seeing his full worth as a player. Let me put that right. He shared the pairs title in 1965/69, the triples in 1966 and the fours in 1968/69, a total of five championships before reaching the age of thirty. Since then he has added the pairs (1974), the triples (1977) and the fours (1971), a grand total of eight championships, one more than the seven won by Percy Baker which took me so long to better.

Cynics have been heard to attribute his successes to my play, which is sheer nonsense. Whether it be pairs, triples or fours, it takes all players to blend and bowl well to win major titles. The impossible a skip may do occasionally. Miracles are beyond their capabilities. David has always ensured that I have avoided those miracle situations during our successes.

Our last triumph came in 1983 when we followed up as English champions by capturing the British Isles Indoor Pairs title. Meanwhile, David has been gaining ever increasing popularity as a television commentator. But then, he has such a command of the English language: has any reader found a lead, as I have, who advises me 'I am a little apprehensive of the position behind the jack'? How much more interesting – and cheering – that is than a cursory 'get one round the back'.

By August 1965 my mind was acutely tuned to the prospect of the ultimate, World Championships. Though bowls is still primarily, a British type of game, there were many countries outside the British Commonwealth capable of producing high level skills. More and more I read articles, features and the like in which I was promoted to 'World Champion', and I am sufficiently vain to prefer the real thing acquired by my own play than other people's ratings, no matter how knowledgeable and well meaning those analysts might be.

Many of us had heard of the growth of bowls in the USA and we wondered if their approach differed greatly from ours in the British Isles. Little was known of the Canadians and stories abounded about the legendary South African 'Snowy' Walker, four times winner of the Republic's National Singles Championship.

Remembering Perth, I planned my campaign for weight reduction and seriously worked on physical fitness. Particularly,

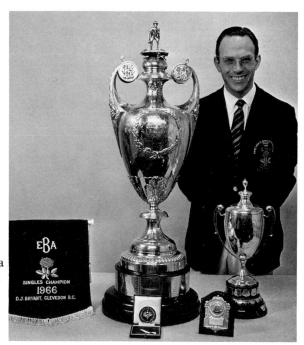

I'm not greedy but sometimes I like a lot, as in 1966 when I won the Somerset, England and World Championships singles events.

The first ever World Championships came into being only because of the drive and determination of Dr Neil Benjamin, Australia, the International Bowls Board President, *far left*. He is briefing the English contingent, *left to right*, Bill Lewis, Cedric Smith, Tom Brown, Mick Cooper, Bob Stenhouse and David Bryant.

I understood the importance of my legs and their strength and suppleness. Flexibility of the back is no less vital to anyone seeking for smoothness and consistency of delivery.

Rumours had it that the greens at the Kyeemagh Club would be faster than those at Perth but that did not worry me unduly. My game has always been well suited to fast greens.

As 1965 drew to its close the prime thought of those rated as contenders for a place was 'will I be chosen?' So it was something of a relief, both to the chosen and those who were not, when the team was finally announced. The members were Robert Stenhouse, Derek Cooper, Cedric Smith, Tom Brown and me.

Bob Stenhouse was then 41 years old and he had packed a whole lot of experience into the eighteen years he had been in the game, including the winning of the 1963 National Fours Championship at Mortlake. Also a keen cricketer, he made many friends in Sydney by spending some time in the nets at that city's world famous Test Match ground.

'Mick' Cooper – no one called him Derek – was forty-two and the winner of the 1965 National Triples Championship. We knew he would fill the role of third man to Stenhouse in the fours and triples.

Cedric Smith, forty-one, specialised in leading and it was that dedication that earned him his place. He was lead in the fours and, with me as skip, in the pairs. He earned his England colours in 1956, a reward for his regular appearance in the EBA Championships, and his articulate, enlightening discussions about the game resulted in him becoming one of the first radio commentators when, belatedly, the BBC began coverage of the National Championships. His liking for Australia and its people resulted in him finding his wife Lorna and emigrating to Sydney after the World Championships. He is now a prominent member of the New South Wales bowling establishment. On the green his minimum curve bowls helped him to impress all those who played against his leading.

Tom Brown emphasised his skill and competitive capabilities by winning the Surrey Singles Championship three years in succession, an achievement that amply merited his choice for the 1964 England team. By nine years the oldest member of our team, he bowled well but not quite with the brilliance seen so often in his home regions. Possibly the climate and his distance from home affected him slightly.

Working on the principle that we would be targets and that defeats – extremely possible when meeting players who have nothing to lose and everything to gain – might diminish our confidence, the EBA selectors thought it wise to split us up for the summer of 1966.

The tactic had been successfully employed in 1962 prior to the Commonwealth Games when Tom Fleming and I had played lead and second in one four and Leslie Watson and Syd Drysdale third man and skip in another.

So we arrived at the Kingsford Smith, Sydney, air terminal with limited knowledge of one another as players. The reception oozed friendship and hospitality. Each team enjoyed the constant attention and thoughtfulness of an individual host who collected us from the Kings Cross Motel around 8.45 a.m. each day and deposited us back there again late in the evening, usually after a communal dinner or reception – or both – following the day's play.

Our pre-championship practice took place on various greens around Sydney, all of which left us stupefied with their vastness and luxury. All gathered their income mainly from 'one arm bandits' which could be found in almost every nook and cranny. Kyeemagh had several dozen and their takings can be judged by the club's need to have a full-time booking clerk from mid-morning until late in the evening. Would be punters often had to wait an hour or more for their spell on an allocated machine.

Personally, I stayed clear of them. With a testing, three matches a day programme I realised there was no nervous energy to be wasted, to say nothing about the extra physical effort of standing by a machine instead of resting and recapturing physical strength and stamina.

The England team under John Coles practised at the Green Leas Club where we were offered three different greens running at speeds of 13, 15 and 18 seconds. Having bowled on greens of the first two speeds, I plumped for 18 seconds, telling my team-mates 'it is easier to move down to a slower green than up to a faster one'.

There were no dissidents. We settled down to intensive preparation and the end justified the means because during our practice sessions we experienced considerable difficulty under windy conditions on such a fast surface, a hazard none of us had met before. The knowledge gained was to prove invaluable during the next two weeks.

The activities began in the morning of Monday 10th October 1966 with the complete teams of the sixteen competing countries. It was a moving ceremony spoiled somewhat by the unexpectedly small crowd. Be clear it was huge compared with our own National Championship attendances but the stands were pretty vast and, consequently, appeared emptier than they really were.

Following the memorable, rotating march of players, their respective flags and the welcoming speeches, play began at 1.30 p.m. with the pairs and triples, continuing for seven days. October 17th heralded the start of the singles, with the fours following one day later.

Cedric and I began tentatively against the Americans Arthur Hartley and Professor Ezra Wyeth, an Australian by birth whose fame embraces bowls and cricket in an amusing way. He has the impressive bowling record of twice dismissing that legendary cricketer Sir Donald Bradman.

During the championships I learned how thinking and planning had secured that triumph and had seen why in his bowling at skip against us. He and Hartley began with a single and held two shots on the next. Pleasingly, I drove them out and we levelled with a single. Two more singles left us level at two-all before racing ahead to lead 11–2, ultimately finishing 22–11 ahead.

It was the start of eleven matches of which we won all but two. Australia lost four and South Africa three matches and any other scoring system would have given England 1, South Africa 2, Australia 3. Because there were two groups of eight who played round robins, with the top four of each group then playing each of the four top teams from the other group, only those four matches per team counting, the finishing order was Australia 1, South Africa 2, England 3.

That format had been contested right from the start of the event but the Australians staunchly adhered to the system 'if teams are level on points, the highest scorer will be given first place'. Australia scored 90 and conceded 81, South Africa returned 85/73 and England 77/73, all of us with four points. The English football league of 'goals for divided by goals against' would not have put Australia first. Instead the order would have been South Africa 1.16, Australia and England level 1.11.

Be quite sure that the system was chosen long before the championships began and there was no question of Australia 'conning' anyone. Simply, it was that country who coincidentally prospered through it. However, I still feel 'we wuz robbed'.

Our matches against the USA, Malawi, Kenya, Jersey and Ireland caused few qualms, our aggregate scores showing 121 shots for, forty-nine against. Our solitary defeat came from Ron Buchan and the aggressive Phil Skoglund of New Zealand 26-18. In the final group matches we defeated Scotland 18-15, South Africa 26-20 and Rhodesia 18-16 but lost to Australia 22-15 and, with it, the gold medal. That defeat and the scoring system hardened my attitude about the singles and I was determined to win.

Before moving on, I must relate an amazing end to the match between Bert Palm and Geoff Kelly, Australia, against Arthur Hartley and Ezra Wyeth, USA. In bowls pairs matches each man delivers four bowls, making a total of sixteen. At the end of one end there were only six of the sixteen on the green, all of them Australian. First in some loose drawing, later in poor driving, the USA pair put all eight of their bowls into the ditch, taking two Australians with them. I simply cannot visualise them doing such a thing on a green running around 13 seconds and with a thicker growth of grass than those in Kyeemagh.

Promptly at 9.30 a.m. on October 17th I met George Behway of Jersey and avoided early stresses by winning 21-12. In my second match of the day Cliff de Rungary, Rhodesia, clung in until the end and he fed me with a valuable lesson of always keeping in control, even if the opponent looks to be in his last days and en route to the mortuary. Cliff bowled splendidly and concentration of a high level with a sharp, never-losing-a-chance attitude by me, was essential. I finally reached 21 with Cliff only four shots behind. My final opponent that opening Monday was Arthur Hartley of the USA and, mercifully, he never established any rapport with the green, so allowing me off with a minimal stress 21-9 win.

Tuesday brought me a thankful day of rest while the greens were devoted entirely to the fours matches. On resumption I played Sandy Houston, born a Queenslander but a Canadian by virtue of emigration. Aged seventy, he was at something of a handicap and even his considerable talent could scarcely overcome the physical problem of stamina. A 21-10 win proved a useful luxury for in the afternoon I met Jack Spiers, also an Australian by birth playing under another flag, Papua New Guinea. Ultimately he finished equal bottom with Houston but there was nothing to forecast that during our match. Leading 18-12 I seemed reasonably safe but then he raised his game and battled end for end to 19–18 to me. On the next end he trailed the jack to lie two but I drew a real beauty to snatch back a single. Another accurate draw gave me a match lie, only for Jack to brush the jack though not quite hard enough to rob me of game. Then came Harry Lakin, Malawi, and a 21–14 victory.

Roy Fulton, who represented Ireland in the 1958 Empire Games, and Len Smales, yet another Australian player resident in and playing for another country, Fiji, came next. Rain prevented play until lunchtime and slowed the green considerably. Neither man, it seemed to me, adapted quickly enough and I won those matches 21–13 and 21–5 respectively.

The third match of the day was postponed, leaving the Australian press time to assess and highlight the prospects of John Hershaw, Scotland, breaking my unbeaten record of twenty matches in Australia, 1962 and 1966. It turned out to be a tremendous tussle which the noted Australian player and writer Aub Sargeant described in the Sydney *Daily Telegraph* 'as fine an exhibition of bowls as has ever been seen in Sydney'. I built up a 10–6 lead laboriously and then came 13 ends, many of them replays after a head had been 'killed', in which only singles were scored. I simply have no idea how many heads swung first one way, then the other during my advance from 10–6 to the ultimate 21–18 after three and a half hours of never ceasing concentration and tactical manoeuvring.

It was by no means easy coping with a strong, side-on breeze and a slow green added to our problems. Both of us used the draw shot mostly, but neither scorned a drive if the situation called for it. I doubt if I have ever seen my scoring positions scattered more often by an opponent's firm or fierce shots, climaxing on the 26th end when I, leading 20–14, drew three bowls within inches of the jack. With one bowl remaining, Hershaw drove and killed the end, drew a toucher with the first bowl of the replay and that held for a single.

I continued to draw with great accuracy, only for Hershaw to produce singles that robbed me of victory – but my break came on the 30th end when he lost the jack and I immediately extended the length of the end.

It produced a superb end in which we both started by drawing. With three bowls remaining I trailed the jack to lie two shots. Compelled to use force, Hershaw was on target to lie one. Now it was my turn. Emulating his method, I also went for a take out which was smack on target and left me with the match winning single for which I had seemed to wait for an eternity. Even then Hershaw's tenacity remained unshaken. After acknowledging the skill and sportsmanship of the match, he said, 'I think if David had missed with that last shot I would have gone on to beat him.'

Thankfully Augusto Pereira, Hong Kong, fell below his normal high standard and so made my 21-8 win something of a relief. Nevertheless, I felt somewhat tired and, unthinkingly, spent a long time outside the club house talking to a London feature writer when I would have been wiser to have settled down in the warm quietly contemplating my evening contest with Maldwyn Evans, a Welsh left hander who was to become World Champion at Worthing in 1972.

The evening was cold and windy and I don't think there was anything wrong with my play and concentration. Possibly I suffered a little from a reaction to my morning marathon and then a further match in the afternoon. We had over 2,000 spectators crowded around the green cheering for every good shot especially from Maldwyn because he appeared to be the underdog. Some underdog. He bowled magnificently and from the very first end I could make no impression on him.

The British *Daily Telegraph* summed things up thus: 'Bryant persisted in playing the forehand on the southward run against the wind. Evans played the backhand, which was taking good draw to enable him to swing behind a short bowl to find the jack.

'Evans had Bryant down 14-2 after 11 ends and looked a certain winner when leading 19-11 after 22 ends. In a breathtaking comeback Bryant won the next five ends to trail 18-19.

'On the crucial last end (28th) Evans drew with his last bowl to nudge out one of Bryant's woods and hold two for match.'

It was a wonderful shot, perhaps made a little easier because he is a left hander and, thus, delivers his bowls about eighteen inches over to the left from a right hander taking up the same position on the mat. That eighteen inches changes the 'geometry', so offering different pathways to the jack. As I wrote earlier, there are times when the green or the wind or both plus the characteristics of the bowl will materially assist a left hander.

Make no excuses and have no doubts about it, Evans bowled splendidly and as he showed at Worthing in 1972, he was masterful on a slow green or bowling into a wind. Maybe there will come a day when all ambitious right handed bowlers learn to use their left hand in order to have at their disposal a means of delivering along completely different courses.

That left me with matches against Geoff Kelly, Australia; Bill Jackson, Rhodesia; Phil Skoglund, New Zealand and 'Snowy' Walker, South Africa.

Kelly is a formidable bowler but he suffers from severe nervousness and on one or two occasions he was physically sick prior to going on the green. This alone showed how eager he was to hit peak form; if you are not nervous before a match, you are not ready for fight or flight. He did not hit top form against me and I was thankful for a 21–9 win.

Jackson proved himself a tremendous fighter. Ahead 8–2, I fell 8–10 behind against his unwavering consistency and I remained behind until the last end but one, the 25th, when he lay two shots but I 'killed' the end with a drive. Holding one shot, I drew in a second with my last delivery of the replay to lead 20–19. The 26th end was a corker, the more so because I scattered the head with only two bowls remaining against Jackson's three. A draw shot and then a jack trailer left me with two shots, one of which Jackson tipped with his last bowl but not strongly enough to rob me of victory 21–19.

Our duel had lasted 185 minutes and during some of it cramp in my leg forced me to abandon my forehand deliveries and concentrate on the backhand. All in all, it was a battle which I was quite proud to win.

Now, with two matches remaining I was two wins ahead of Hershaw and Fulton. So they were in with a chance should I lose those matches. I doubt if ever before or after I have bowled with greater concentration and determination.

A fast green and 2,500 spectators crammed around it converted the final Sunday into an exciting occasion and I could feel my inner strength and determination perhaps as never before. Phil Skoglund, the popular, outspoken New Zealander, is no mean bowler and on other days we might have contested a close match. It was not to be for right from the start I knew I was on peak form.

The rink was set out in a north–south direction which was in alignment with a fresh wind. The thoughtful years I had spent developing consistency of direction paid dividends and seldom, if ever, have I produced such consistency in drawing to the jack.

The 15 seconds of pace would normally have meant nine inches from the jack setting up spectator clapping. On that morning I repeatedly drew my shots within two or three inches from the jack and Skoglund could not measure up to such accuracy. With me leading 12-2 Skoglund made a determined drive to get into the match but I remained unflurried and his spell soon ended, leaving me the ultimate winner 21-5. No matter what others might then do, I could fairly lay claim to the title 'World Champion'. 'It's wonderful' I told the press men: 'so much better than being an unofficial champion.'

Thus two weeks of intensive pressure had come to its conclusion. Yet in minutes there was more to come ... but of a different kind. It lay in the person of Snowy Walker, the 65-year-old South African who many critics considered to be a superior player to me.

Long before all the teams set forth for Australia there had been widespread conjectures about the outcome of our meeting. Understandably wishing for an epic climax to the singles, the Championships committee drew up a schedule that kept us apart until the fourteenth and final round of matches. Throughout the first thirteen matches I banished the name Walker from my mind and concentrated on winning each match as it came along. Self-discipline and care headed my actions and, suddenly, I had won the title, so fulfilling my ultimate dream. From the World Championship viewpoint, whether or not I beat Walker was of no apparent importance.

However, ambitious people, I understand, set themselves individual targets and I did not relish lightly the idea of losing to Walker, great player and man though he might be.

Even so, it provided a new problem for I had finished the intensity of those thirteen singles and was unquestionably relaxed and off the boil. Here my sheer love of the game helped because I felt that Walker and I could contest an outstanding match which would show the vast audience just how skilful and exciting bowls can be.

Sheer match winning, intense concentrations and strategy had gone. I was remarkably tranquil and missing that drive for victory with which I had lived for many days. Once more 2,500 spectators crowded the stands and after some careful manoeuvring by both of us, I established an 8-6 lead. Then a spell of my best play took me to 18-9, only for Walker to hit back with a single and brilliant three.

The 18th end produced what surely must be unique in bowls. I established a two shots position and maybe a third which the umpire was about to measure when, wham, a mighty drive by the Canadian fours skip cannoned a bowl on the adjoining rink into our head where it displaced our jack. There was no way of deciding whether or not my bowl had been the match winner. I scored two and, somewhat shaken, continued play.

Seizing the chance so strangely given to him, Walker scored on the next four ends and on the 23rd end set up a two shots, match-winning lie with me left facing a formidable last-bowl situation.

One of his bowls was positioned in front of and slightly to the right of the jack. The other lay behind the jack and fractionally more to the right. A draw shot was on but it looked intimidatingly dangerous so I searched for an alternative. I found it, a drive on to the front bowl so that it crashed on to the back one, both flying out of range and leaving my once third bowl the winning shot.

Maybe, at last, that relaxation coming from winning the title helped to build up power without the muscle tension which can destroy direction. That is conjecture. The fact is that my drive was right to the millimetre, Walker's two bowls were scattered far and wide and my personal pride was saved. One of the strangest matches I have ever played, it will stay vividly in my memory for the rest of my days.

After my first visit to Australia for the 1962 Commonwealth Games I received a number of offers which filled my mind with life in that country. Many clubs made clear their wishes for me to become a member-coach and that would have been lucrative. I would also have been able to continue as a schoolmaster. Living conditions and climate were unquestionably better and I foresaw far greater opportunities for my two young daughters.

On the other hand, Ruth and I had our roots in Somerset in general and Clevedon in particular. She had no wish to leave her circle of friends to live in a strange land 12,500 miles away and there was always parents to consider. Inevitably, I agonised for a long time but, in the end, Somerset and the family held sway and I put the idea of emigration out of my mind.

Thus the inaugural World Championships came to an end, the Ampol-Qantas sponsorship had turned up trumps and, immediately came the question 'where next and when?' The USA manager/player Ezra Wyeth had already been in touch with home and he reported a strong likelihood that the next series would be staged in Los Angeles in July 1968. His efforts came to naught and there was a six year delay before the second series lifted Beach House Park, Worthing, Sussex into the highest levels of the game. They were preceded by the 1970 Commonwealth Games at Edinburgh. In between, I received many invitations to the ever growing number of International Masters tournaments springing up around the world, especially in Australia.

Those would be time consuming and costly of my salary as a teacher. Additionally, each trip would reduce my chances of elevation to school headmastership and it was difficult to visualise anything above Deputy Head; and even that would have seriously cut down my activities as a world class bowler. The years from 1966 to 170 and beyond were troublesome. Though World Champion, I understood that there were still many things to be explored but they needed time and an absence of inner conflict.

The temptation of bowls increased through the rapid advance of the indoor events headed by the National Indoor Club Team Championship, colloquially the 'Denny Cup' and soon to be supported by a full quota of individual National Championships.

- Physical fitness and strength lead to better bowling. Supple legs, a flexible back and a reasonable weight are normally advantageous.
- Major championships and tournaments can severely test your nervous system. So keep calm inwardly and cultivate quietness.
- A compatible team of five is considerably stronger than five self-centered stars. So always play a positive part in maintaining tranquillity and enthusiasm.

CHAPTER SEVEN

Kyeemagh marked a further, definite mark in my career. The opposition had proved to be as strong as I had expected but it was the great variety of players that excited my mind and kept me constantly thinking. True, I had won the singles and, in my own mind, also the pairs although the surprising format of that event reduced Cedric Smith and me to third place.

Nevertheless, it was all too clear that standards were bound to rise, especially because the World Championships had stimulated bowlers all over the world and, clearly, there was bound to be a sharp increase in the number of international events that invited world stars to attend and participate. It was no good me staying put with my then current methods and ideas. Refinements of technique and tactics would have to be the order of the day.

Malcolm Allison, the controversial but dedicated soccer coach/manager once said on radio, 'when tiredness creeps in skills seep out' and that is something I have seen all too often on the bowling green. Make no mistake about it, three and a half hours of fours or a singles that carries on for two hours or more is severely testing, as much or even more so on mental stamina than on physical freshness. Consequently, I am convinced that a sound, simple delivery will stay more faithful in the closing crises than one which has strange or unnecessary kinks.

For example, I have heard it advocated many times that the palm of the delivering hand should 'look' straight up the green. This means it must be turned from its natural, hanging position by ninety degrees. This is an unnatural position which causes strain, especially when tiredness and/or stress come stealing in. That is harmful to consistency and costs shots. Even after a year of intensive practice swinging the arm in such a position, the strain would, in my opinion, still be felt when the situation least wanted it. A serious, competitive bowler cannot tolerate such a thing; it is essential that he has a relaxed and flowing delivery.

Apart from strain, there is another factor. Let your arm hang naturally at your side. You will find that the upper part of your arm is parallel with your body but the part below the elbow tilts slightly outwards. My advocacy of a compact, 'everything working in one line' theory demands that the arm must remain close to the body throughout delivery. This cannot be, except by letting the elbow actually brush the body and that is a sure road to jerking.

This is not plain theory. I tried this out myself on many occasions and, through that experience, developed a method that eliminated the weaknesses and made the utmost use of the good features of the two differing hand positions. This was to hold my bowl with a natural finger grip and with the palm of my hand at an angle of sixty degrees to my side. Starting from my shoulder, this turning of the hand ensured that my delivery came from a straight line lever (my arm) extending along the line I wished to propel the bowl; I am assuming the absence of any momentary flaws. With this grip and position the delivery flows naturally and there are no problems.

Meticulous, determined practice helps in getting your bowl away consistently and on an even keel. Additionally, I learned to tilt my bowl inwards at an angle around thirty degrees from the vertical. That tilt did not end up as a wobble because the bowl I was using then was elliptical rather than round. It was also narrower than lignum along its vertical plane and this made it a shade more difficult to hold than a lignum, but the shape intensified centrifugal action and the tilt quickly rectified itself. The degree of tilt also varies with the positioning of the thumb. The actual running surface of the bowl was parallel to my fingers, which were inclined slightly to one side, i.e. on the bias side when playing the backhand and the non-bias side when playing the forehand.

All those theoretical disadvantages, if, indeed, they were disadvantages, were significantly outweighed by the ease of my swing and absence of any strain. I remain convinced that it is far better to hold the bowl and let the hand make that easy, natural angle of sixty degrees to the side, than to distort the wrist beyond that point in order that the palm of the hand can 'see' the line of delivery.

If something should force me to bowl with my wrist in that position it would take me many months to develop any sense of it being 'natural' and even longer to arrive at my present standard of performance. Indeed, I doubt if I would ever reach it.

This is no idle theory. I tried delivering in that way many years ago when I was suffering difficulties but this was one of my many experiments that did not produce the hoped for results. At that time I was delivering my bowls with a distinct wobble, a flaw

The late Tom Brown, of the 1966 England World Championships team, always let his arm or hand 'see the ball' as it went up the green. I find it less of a strain to let my hand turn inwards at both the start and stop of my swing.

which I tried to eliminate by turning my wrist outwards. Certainly this cured the wobble but at the cost of a demoralising loss of control of length and direction. Gradually I returned to my natural swing and the wobble disappeared. Subsequently, other delivery problems arose but, so far, highly disciplined, carefully thought out practice has always eliminated the problems – not the showing of the palm of my delivery hand to the shoulder.

Let me make two points before going any further. There are many fine bowlers who deliver that way. Clearly, they have overcome the difficulties I have experienced and revealed. Yet I must wonder if they would have been even greater players if they had used my system for eliminating or reducing arm strain in the way I have described.

My second point lies in the extremely fine details that frequently decide who is the winner rather than the runner-up in world championship levels of competition. An inch here, half an inch there, a few differences over the full spread of a dozen or so matches can exercise immense effects on the total outcome. My own justification of adhering to my natural delivery lay in the first major world event I contested, the 1962 Commonwealth Games in Perth. I scarcely admitted to myself the ambition of winning two gold medals. From a technical viewpoint, my delivery method did the trick.

In bowls, as in any other human activity, early progress is comparatively simple but then grows increasingly difficult as one moves towards the higher levels of play. Every tiny detail becomes extremely important and that, for me, is why the natural, sixty-degrees-inwards delivery is the best. Understand that I have never pulled out a protractor and actually measured such angles. The figure may well vary a few degrees either way for you, depending on your anatomical make-up. The target is to attain a relaxed, compact swing when delivering.

The forehand and backhand of most bowlers vary a little and I am no exception. I tilt my bowl with the bias on the forehand and my swing is very slightly curved or round-arm; I seldom if ever hook. My swing remains on-line with the direction of the bowl long after it has left my hand; then only Divine intervention can impose any effect. Such hooking goes hand in glove with anxiety and consequent upward-jerking of the head. That ruins the integrated, compact delivery which can project bowl after bowl precisely in the direction one aims.

Thus it is important that one develops a clear, mental picture of one's delivery so that the 'hiccups' which inevitably invade from time to time can be diagnosed and eliminated. To that degree, one's practising should be, if possible, even more concentrated than when one is supported by the intensity of competition. Practice offers chances of developing not merely a sound technique but also a total awareness of how that sound technique works.

As in driving a car, most of the time thought seems non-existent and one's mind is ready to correct instantaneously the flaws and dangers which occur. So in bowls, one needs an unencumbered mind to be aware of all that is going on on the rink and to conceive the tactics apposite to any special situations.

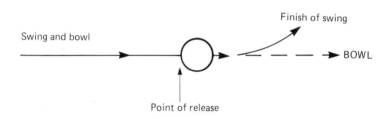

Line of swing and bowl in normal delivery

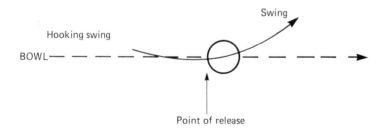

To ensure that you understand precisely what is meant by hooking, please refer to the diagrams on this page. With the normal delivery the arm and bowl are 'on line' before and for a long while after release, even though the arm may ultimately curve around the body.

In the case of a hooked delivery, the arm is actually curving before and at the moment of release. The end of the swing may not look different but in the case of the hook, the possibility of actual release coinciding with the swing momentarily being on the right line are disastrously unlikely; repeatedly, the bowl will start 'thin' and then swing across the front of the jack. The most obvious feature to the onlooker is the player's elbow straying from his side. Probably one is less likely to hook with a crouch or semi-crouch delivery than with an upright delivery. Not only is one more likely to step off incorrectly when coming down than when one sets the foot first for a crouch delivery but there is also a greater likelihood of hooking.

With a semi-crouch start and controlled leg action the whole tendency is to go forward, not across.

I believe my forehand and backhand look similar but, in fact, the backhand swing feels slightly freer, straighter and nearer to the body. Both are very much under control and are so mechanical that I can apply full attention to finding the right length and direction. This has proved immeasurably valuable in top level competitions.

There is a subtle difference, in that the bowl has to be reversed in the hand when changing from forehand to backhand; the small disc is always innermost. In the past, particularly with lignum vitae bowls, which are almost spherical, and others of similar ilk, the differing contours of the two sides were more easily recognisable. Today, when 90 per cent or more of flat green bowls devotees throughout the world are using composition bowls, the difference between the two sides is minimal.

Providing you ensure that your bowl is held correctly, with the fingers parallel to the running base and the little finger carefully positioned, there should be no great difficulty in acquiring complete competence on both sides of the rink.

Adhering to all these principles during a Saturday afternoon roll up or friendly match is not too difficult. Remembering it all at 18–19 down in the county final and with an opponent holding two shots can be a vastly different thing. Consistently accurate bowling demands that your arm is not stiff but relaxed with, perhaps, a slight bend in it. Although I have seen many good bowlers pulling up their arms, not merely in critical situations but also in ordinary matches, I cannot recommend such an action. I cannot see that the pulling up serves any useful purpose and I consider the habit as a needless, extra hazard.

Bad wrist action is another frequent cause of trouble. Many

bowlers curl up their wrists at the last moment in a scooping action. This should not be. Also avoid twisting your bowl on delivery. Some bowlers add a slight flick of the wrist when releasing the bowl. Maybe an occasional slight flick of that nature will prove successful but that flick can so easily become exaggerated, with costly loss of direction the result. It is just possible that a tiny flick *could* give a bowl a couple of extra turns and so slide it past another bowl to go in for shot. However, in high grade competitions, consistently clustering 75 per cent of one's bowls closely around the selected positions means one is playing the percentages that are favourable. Such solidity may not excite spectators as much as an occasional 'bobby-dazzler', but it wins matches.

Because of that, I must, yet again, emphasise my total belief in the virtues of a simple, efficient, flowing delivery, completely free of kinks, scoops, flicks and other exotic embellishments. As a born experimenter, I know they sometimes look good from the bank and that tempts one to try them. If you wish to win rather than look pretty, never give away to that temptation.

I arrived at my normal delivery quite early in my career. I was taken by the important relationship between the movement of leg and arm and, early on, realised that consistency relied, to a great extent, on the steadiness and length of my forward step when coming out of my crouched position. Actually, it begins slightly before then because in sighting the situation I squat and from that gently change into a crouch, forward shuffle and release of my bowl. If that technique is to be effective, my legs must be strong and supple. Unfortunately I can visualise that as I grow older I will be unable to retain those essential factors. Certainly, any bowler who decides to adopt that delivery style will be well advised to pay close attention to his legs.

The extent of my rise, the distance of the forward shuffle of my left leg and the length of my back swing are closely integrated and related to the distance of the target and the pace of the green. Dropping a 'dead toucher' smack onto a jack twenty-five yards away on a 15 seconds green demands only the slightest movements. On a medium-paced green my rise from squat to crouch and the length of my forward step have to be higher and longer, that is if I am to retain the same cohesion of movement.

On very heavy, long-grass greens considerable force is needed, even for drawing shots. On such greens I sometimes revert to a basic, athletic delivery. But whatever the green or the situation I strive consciously for cohesion and flow. They are the children of relaxation with tension and stiffness the enemy.

Whatever the delivery, the follow through remains constant. It will vary its speed in accordance with the length of the back swing and consequent force of the forward swing but the follow through must still be a long, flowing continuation of the swing as a whole.

There can be no question of it being a factor of its own. One must never start a swing quickly, then pause and finally go through slowly. Obviously, after the bowl has left the hand there is a slowing up. It must be gradual and lasting over the full flow of the swing.

One can see how the swing should be executed by studying the pendulum of a clock. First it goes back. Then, after an almost imperceptible pause, it starts its downward swing, gradually accelerating to maximum speed at the bottom of its path and then slowing down as it swings to the full extent on the other side.

Except on fast greens, when the back swing must be short, the pendulum principle remains ideal but even when the back swing is curtailed, the follow through should be extended as a crucial factor leading up to a smooth, gradual stop.

There is nothing fundamentally different about the deliveries I have just analysed and because of this I believe I am able to achieve minutely fine distinctions on touch and length.

In terms of feeling, my delivery is that of swinging. One sees many bowlers who eliminate this use of gravity as the force, instead relying on muscle power to propel the ball. My experience over the years suggests that muscle power is more vulnerable to the tensions that arise in the green compared to a primarily gravity based technique.

Returning to the follow through, it is not only the arm that is involved. The whole body must be allowed to flow through with the arm. That is why it is an unwise practice to strive to keep the back foot firmly planted on the mat. Let it swing right up and banish all fears of foot-faulting. Better, if necessary, to stand a few inches farther back on the mat, so that the back foot will rise over it, than to strain to keep the back foot down, with the consequent disruption of balance. The back foot should be allowed to rise as the bowl is released and then, as the arm extends on the follow through, the back leg automatically lifts and straightens.

The firm planting of both feet in the fixed stance delivery prevents this body flow and is one of the weaknesses of that delivery so far as all-round play is concerned, though it can prove advantageous in ultra-fast greens found in New Zealand and parts of Australia. Then the difficulty lies not in generating power but in minimising its use.

There are substantial differences in the relationships between back and forward swings with several other types of delivery. Some players seem to keep their arms continuously moving while others swing back and then pause for a long while before swinging forward. During this interval most users of the system plant their two feet and weight so that the delivery that starts out looking like the athletic type is, in reality, a full crouch.

However, the arm movement cannot be disassociated from body flow and so long as the overall delivery remains smooth and without any trace of jerk, the pause, or absence of it, between the back and forward swing is not too critical. Leonard Kirton is one name that comes to mind when thinking of a fine example of such a delivery.

In all deliveries the left arm – if one is a right-handed bowler – is used to sustain balance. Mine brushes on to the front part of my left leg, just above the knee, at the critical moment of actual delivery. Other bowlers, though they are in a minority, let the left arm fly freely throughout delivery. This does allow pivoting of the body in an anti-clockwise direction and so increase power. Indeed, I recall that in my earliest days, my left arm flew freely. However, this disrupts the compactness of delivery which I believe to be a prime factor in consistency of delivery.

Bjorn Borg practised five hours a day, day after day, in order to develop his tennis strokes to such a pitch of mechanical consistency that he never had to think about them when involved in matches. His detailed thoughts of stroke play filled his mind when practising and that is precisely when any ambitious bowler should be giving his unwavering concentration to details. Practice makes perfect ... of whatever it is one is practising. If that something is mechanically unsound, it is an unsound delivery that is perfected. Replacing that with a sound technique will take three or four times as long as it does to learn correctly from the moment of starting. So it might be said that important championships are really won in solitary practice on wet and windy evenings when no one else has the drive and determination to get down to improving.

Geometrical considerations help a bowler who takes a long forward step to be more accurate in line than one who takes a much smaller step. That longer step, when taken after the right foot has been carefully aligned with the desired line of delivery, is a stabilising factor in the straightness of the swing itself and, consequently, in maintaining a good line for end after end.

There is only one place to look when delivering a bowl and that is to a point along the aiming line. It is essential to maximise one's concentration on that point and to fix one's unwavering eyes on it. This drill, for drill it should be, must be followed for so many weeks, months and years until it becomes completely automatic. After a time one sees the arc as being just a pathway to the jack, or whatever the target may be.

One then begins to pick out guides on the green; perhaps a variation in the colour of the rink or a bare patch or even one solitary blade of grass across which the bowl should travel. All these little things become fixed in the mind, leaving ever more room for conscious thought about strategy, tactics and their application.

One should always bowl at the imaginary shoulder or mark, never at the jack or other target, save in the case of drives. Undoubtedly, one can bowl at and hit a target more easily along a straight line than find a target at the end of a curved line. But the whole challenge of bowls lies in assessing correctly and then delivering a bowl meticulously so that it finishes its arc of travel precisely where one hoped. Nay, expected, because ultimately one learns to 'read' arcs as surely as one does the print in a book.

One looks at the jack, assesses the length and then fixes one's eyes on the imaginary shoulder or mark. I believe that one of the last things to go through the mind before the actual moment of release is length. I am sure that one can learn to isolate a target and deliver bowls right over it time after time. Equal accuracy of length, as distinct from direction, is more difficult to acquire. It becomes less difficult when one has micrometric control of direction.

Finally, in this deeper analysis of delivery, comes the follow through which, in some ways, can be linked to bumping. A well taught, reasonably supple young man should never, but never, bounce his bowl when delivering; never launch it up the rink in mid-air.

That skill should stay with him throughout youth and middle age, onwards to the autumnal years of life. Hopefully, even then he will remain sufficiently supple to green his bowls smoothly because doing so provides a sweetness all of its own. However, old age, arthritis and other impedimenta may win the battle, at which stage there may be a need to change the style of delivery. Normally, the change is from athletic to crouch, even though it is not so well suited to heavy greens as the athletic. This must be accepted and is not so dreadful that one thinks about giving up the game. Sure, the athletic delivery looks more flowing and graceful but onlookers and players forget that grace when watching bumper after bumper clattering up the green. Undoubtedly, bumping is worse and more of a handicap than the occasional short bowl emanating from a crouch delivery.

Bumping is no prerogative of the aged, even though stiffening knee joints, aching backs, girth and other annoyances may be major causes. Over anxiety is in no way reserved for the elderly. Teenagers and players in their twenties are just as vulnerable. Defeat – or victory – is near, one is anxious to see just where the bowl is going, up jerks the head, the body follows suit and, bingo, the delivery is wrecked before the bowl leaves the hand. This fault also devastates follow through.

With a good, flowing delivery the body flows with the swing and the shoulder is well over the hand at the moment the bowl is released. Concentrate on body flow, hold on to the follow through and get well down; then there will be little danger of bumping.

On the other side of that coin lies the 'rubbing' of one's bowls; catching the ground slightly before release. This is not unusual. I err in that way quite often, usually because I am stiff, particularly after a long car drive. This usually wears off after a few ends but 'rubbing' can be caused by bad movement.

If this starts to happen during a match there is little one can do. Strive to relax and bowl naturally; ensure that the bowl is being held correctly; concentrate completely throughout the delivery thereby eliminating anxiety and putting all negative thoughts out of mind.

If the fault persists, it must be shut out of mind completely. Maybe some definite flaw in delivery has crept in but the middle of a match is no time to start meddling with one's normal delivery. Meanwhile, strive for relaxation and continue to concentrate on the tactics. When the match is over go out on the green with four bowls and a jack and practise delivering thoughtfully until the fault is cleared. This may well be helped by mental rehearsal, or visualisation as it is known in the USA. This entails 'seeing' in your mind the shot you are going to make, followed by its execution. Make the pictures as vivid as possible and when they are right, follow with the actual delivery itself.

During the match it may pay dividends to walk to the head to analyse the position of the bowls and to decide which will be the best shot to attempt. The situation when closely viewed is liable to differ from the one seen from the mat forty yards or so down the green. In deciding on the best shot, visualising your making of it and establishing inner calmness with the aid of deep, yoga-type breathing gives you the best chance of succeeding.

Using such time in squarely facing the challenge, and then attacking, generates confidence rather than fear so do not fall into

Despite weight and size, the late Bert Keech used to ground his deliveries superbly, one of them (a drive) converting defeat into victory for Yorkshire with the last bowl of the 1946 Middleton Cup final. That legendary shot earned him selection by the BBC for the first ever television transmission of bowls in 1954. The Paddington IBC supplied the venue.

the common trap of seeing a difficult position and rushing at it in an uncontrolled hurry.

Developing that kind of attitude and, tournament by tournament, finding that I could discipline myself to face challenges ever more successfully, added the valuable, ever increasing knowledge of 'being there before' whenever I faced difficulties. That experience in itself added authority to my play in those busy years between the first World Championships and the 1970 Commonwealth Games at Edinburgh.

They were also time consuming years, with several visits to Australia, representing England in the indoor internationals in 1966/67/68/69/70 and outdoors in those same years. Indoor Bowls continued to expand and many weekends of matches earned me the English Singles Championship in 1966/67, 1968/69, 1970/71 and 1971/72.

Outdoors, I had long tried to go through the Somerset Championships to qualify for the National Championships in all four events, ideally to make a clean sweep of the finals. In 1968 I qualified in three, happily winning the fours with Dad alongside me on the green. Sadly, his health was failing and he was unable to go forward to the British Isles Championships which were staged in the following month.

Luckily, I qualified for all four National Championships the following year, 1969, winning the pairs and, again with Dad there, the fours championship. The 1968 final is one I will always remember because the only time we led was after a four on the 21st end put us 21–20 ahead of Walter Phillips' Boscombe Cliff quartet.

In the 1969 final Bill Elliott, David Rhys Jones, Dad and I beat Harold Powell's Farnborough British Legion team 20–13, a proud score against such an outstanding player and man as Powell.

That year the British Isles Championships were contested at the Mount Florida Club, Glasgow, on Saturday 13th September. This time Dad was able to play and things went our way, culminating in the most precious moment of my life. We reached the final of the fours but no one expected us to offer much opposition to the crack Welsh four skipped by the respected and skilled Gareth Humphreys. Maybe because of that we all avoided tension, and to everyone's surprise we won with great ease.

The Commonwealth Games at Edinburgh took precedence over all else so in the 1970 Somerset Championships I had to scratch from the singles and give way to a substitute in the fours. Because bowls did not figure in the 1966 Games in Jamaica, this was my first chance to retain the title I had won at Perth in 1962. Somewhat to my disappointment, the structure of the England team removed my chance of also retaining the fours and I was to spend the early days of the Games watching from the greenside. In so doing I learned much.

Both at Perth in 1962 and Kyeemagh in 1966 I met the world's best on fast greens. One look at the Balgreen turf alerted me to many dangers. However, I had sampled Scottish greens earlier in the month when skipping for England in the International Team Championships at Queens Park BC, Glasgow. With Harold Powell leading in two of the matches and Arthur Whitehead in one, David Rhys Jones at number two and Harry Kinnersley at third man, ours was a strong team. Though Jock Thomson and his men of Wales carried us to a one shot win, we had more to spare against our Scottish and Irish opponents and I felt my match tightness could not have been much better. The length of the Balgreen grass dismayed me, even though I knew it would be cut closer as time wore on. When Phil Skoglund saw the greens and then nearly blew a gasket I realised that, at the worst, I should enjoy and exploit my greater experience of slow greens.

Play in the singles began on Monday 13th July, the other participants being: GA Kelly, Australia; HW Clayton, Canada; J Bradley, Fiji; WC Woodward, Guernsey; EJ Liddell, Hong Kong; D Gosden, Kenya; RS Ewing, Malawi; PC Skoglund, New Zealand; R Fulton, Ireland; AW Lapsley, Papua New Guinea; R Motroni, Scotland; R Fulton, Northern Ireland; JD Wilkins, Wales; N Bryce, Zambia.

It was a strong field and throughout my thirteen matches I never really felt confident or certain of my touch and, consequently, I never enjoyed any feeling of being right on top form. On reflection, I probably over-reacted to the green because the only defeat I suffered was at the hands of Bob Motroni, a Scot who excels on heavy greens.

Overt evidence of my worry shone out when, in one match, I concentrated so strongly on the green's idiosyncracies that I forgot to check my bowl ... and promptly sent it down the green on the wrong bias, then to suffer acute embarrassment when it curled steadily on to the adjacent rink instead of towards the jack.

Apart from Motroni, I met with difficulties before overcoming

Fulton, a man who learned how to cope with heavy greens in Ireland. At the end of the six days my record in World Championship and Commonwealth Games singles was played 41, won 39. It looked good on paper and maybe it was vain of me to feel any dissatisfaction. Even so, I realised that there was still much to learn. That was to be driven home to me in the 1972 World Championships at Worthing ... but now I am racing ahead. In the interim other problems had to be faced and solved.

● When competing in a strange or new event, take care to read and understand the 'small print'. Then adjust to any differences which are new to you.
● Be glad if you suffer from pre-match nerves. It means you are mentally ready for action. Just fix your mind on smooth, imaginary shots and 'see' them scoring point after point.
● Beware of chill when contesting a marathon late in the afternoon. Make sure you keep your legs, arms and hands warm.
● If you are scheduled for two or three matches a day, avoid long conversations or interviews until you have finished all matches. They sap your mental energies more than you think.
● Reaction often follows an important or exciting win. If possible, go off alone for ten minutes or so of calm, relaxed practice before your next match.

CHAPTER EIGHT

Winning the Commonwealth Games singles resurrected many of the feelings and ideas that had flooded my head after Perth and then Kyeemagh. High amongst them was the temptation of emigration, especially because of the climate, freedom and the opportunities I was promised if I moved to Australia.

So 1971 became crisis year, particularly because an invitation to compete in the Banyo Masters tournament at Brisbane over the Easter period included my wife, Ruth, and our daughters Jacqueline, then eight years old, and Carole, who was six. This fabulous event was sponsored by Errol Stewart, whose generosity and hospitality we will never forget.

Nor will I forget the experience of the Australian system of playing 31 up in singles instead of the 21 up stipulated by the IBB. Nine top Australians participated, with play beginning on Monday and finishing on Friday. All ten players contested the round robin format and when the Friday arrived I had already lost to John Snell, Stewy Shannon and Artie Booth. However, my five wins had left me 44 shots plus, while Shannon, the league leader with six wins, was only up 36 shots.

Putting aside all thoughts about the matches of other potential champions, I tackled Keith Dwyer of East Brisbane with fixed determination to win ... and handsomely if at all possible. This meeting followed my morning 31–24 win over the genial Australian giant Barry Salter.

Finding the greens faster than during the morning session, I quickly found the length, my control never wavered and I won 31–23. So now all depended on Shannon in a neck and neck match against Barry Salter. It hovered first one way, then the other, until Salter reached 22–20. At this stage he suddenly unleashed a series of terrific drives smack on target, reaching 29–22. He then nicked Shannon's toucher off the jack with another fast drive, drew a second scorer, Shannon than unleashing a drive which just missed its target.

So the last round ended: Bryant, six wins, plus 52 shots; Shannon six wins, plus 27 shots and Soars six wins, plus 21 shots. Soars had won the title on the previous three years so, one way and another, I felt that in leaving London on the Saturday, starting play in Brisbane on Monday and, without having much time to adjust to climate, jet lag and so on, winning the Master's title, I had more than emulated my previous performances in Australia.

The friendliness and hospitality we met and the wonderful life-style that would lie before us if we made our lives in Brisbane strongly tempted us to abandon our Somerset roots, our parents and friends but our basic feeling of being English again held sway.

The early seventies were to prove to be my most consistent years, especially in my record-breaking hat trick of EBA Singles Championships. Perhaps fittingly, the first win in 1971 topped Percy Baker's record of seven EBA championship wins, four of them the singles, and I felt considerable pride in bettering what had been a tremendous record by a splendid, gifted man like Baker. It is a good feeling to win, a better one when the field is strong, and best of all when one surpasses a giant and that giant is among the first to offer congratulations ... genuinely. Percy Baker is a bowls legend who honoured me with his constant friendliness.

In those three EBA singles finals I defeated John Blewett, Pen-lee, 21–18; Bob Robertson, Middlesbrough, 21–16 and Ian Harvey, Marlow, 21–12 – but I am running ahead.

That fateful 1971 was in many ways swamped by the immense efforts made by Ralph Bentley, then the EBA President, and his fellow senior EBA councillors to raise the £65,000 calculated to be essential for the promotion of the second World Championships. England had been accepted and sanctioned by the IBB and most bowls addicts believed it would be relatively easy to find sponsors willing and eager to back the project. Bentley, professionally a skilled and successful accountant, shared this belief but was sadly disillusioned by a string of refusals to the plans he put before a host of nationally famous, potential sponsors.

Finally his patience broke, but not his determination, and at a dynamic meeting he said, 'I am fed up going, cap in hand, to sponsors and being turned down. I have worked out a plan for all counties and players within them to raise the money without any help.'

Each county was given a target and all exceeded it, so that, ultimately, there was money left over for refunding. I, like many other bowlers who had helped in the drive, felt uplifted by such an outcome and, on reflection, that brave independence did more for bowls than if some multinational giant had dipped its hand in pocket and pulled out that £65,000 as a gift.

Well in advance, the EBA announced the England team and the dates were to be June 5th to 17th. The venue, Beach House Park, Worthing, was to be improved by the building of an extra club house, complete with offices, dressing rooms, etc.

Bob Stenhouse, who had been England's chief skip at Kyee-magh six years earlier, was appointed team manager of Norman

Percy Baker shows no disappointment that I have beaten his record of seven English Championship wins.

King, Cliff Stroud, Ted Hayward, Peter Line and David Bryant, seemingly a very powerful team. Altogether eighteen countries affiliated to the IBB competed.

The organisation and management did British bowls proud but there was one traitor in the midst, the weather. It was dreadful, with the greens disappearing under water on three occasions. Consequently, Jock Munro, the outstanding British greenkeeper, was unable to crop the greens as he would have wished and there was a lot of nap to combat with.

It is always easy to be wise after the event but I realised that the bowls I had chosen were over biased for the conditions and that presented severe problems. They were satisfactory on short length jacks but whenever an opponent pulled back the mat I simply could not find the middle of the rink. This sapped my confidence and in many matches I was almost totally devoid of that valuable asset.

Maldwyn Evans the only man to beat me in the inaugural World Championship singles in 1966, mastered the greens better than anyone and he had assured himself the winner when there was still a round of singles to be contested. Left handed, thorough and patient, he maintained a high standard of play. His overall record ran: played 15, won 12, lost 3, shots for 289, lost 222, points 24. Richard Bernard, Scotland, came second with 22 points. Tommy Harvey, South Africa, Barry Salter, Australia and Jim Candelet, USA, all scored 20 points, finishing in that order because of their points ratios for and against. I finished sixth with 18 points, having lost to Eric Liddell, Hong Kong 16–21; Bob Henderson, Papua New Guinea, 14–21; Harry Lakin, Malawi, 20–21; Maldwyn Evans, Wales, 6–21; Jim Candelet, USA, 19–21 and Tommy Harvey, South Africa, 17–21. My only consolations were wins over Dick Bernard, 21–18 and Barry Salter, 21–10.

Sadly, Cliff Stroud, Ted Hayward and I were no more successful in the triples, ending sixth with 18 points; the title going to Bill Miller, Clive Forrestor and Dick Folkins with 24 points. Cecilio Delgado and Eric Liddell, Hong Kong, took the pairs and our solitary touch of gold was experienced – superbly – by King, Stroud, Hayward and Peter Line who won 13 and drew one of their 15 matches to finish five shots ahead of Scotland. Scottish all round solidity earned eight points and captured the Leonard Trophy (best record over all four events) from South Africa who scored seven. Scotland went on to win the British Isles International Team Championship, England coming in second.

The severe lessons I learned in those World Championships alerted me to the steps I had to take if I was going to retain my EBA singles title and, following that, the British Isles crown. My corrections proved right and one year later I completed that hat trick of English singles titles and then magnified it by winning the British Isles Championship for the third year in succession. Despite the disappointments of the World Championships, those years, 1971/2/3 must stand as my finest spell of top form consistency.

Commonwealth Games 1970, World Championships 1972; bowls now seemed to have a formula for a major international set of championships every two years and thoughts during the 1972/3 winter and 1973 summer frequently turned to 1974 and who would be representing England and the other home countries in the Commonwealth Games at Christchurch, New Zealand from January 25th to February 1st 1974. England went the whole hog by choosing separate players for each of the three events (triples was still not included). Our line-up was: Bob Robertson, Harry Taylor, Ted Hayward and David Crocker: fours. John Evans and Peter Line: pairs; David Bryant: singles. Finally, despite various threats of withdrawals, bowlers from fifteen countries eventually took to the greens at the Woolston Workingmen's Club.

Prior to that, bowls, as an important sport, received a tremendous accolade and I felt humbly honoured when singled out from the 347-strong England contingent to be the country's flag-bearer for the 1974 opening ceremony at the 30,000 capacity Queen Elizabeth Park stadium. Marching round with that flag sent many tingles up and down my spine. It also set me thinking about the vast number of experiences that had fed my mind with the knowledge and skills I would need to deploy during the coming eight days. And perhaps this is a suitable place to consider the intangibles which had proved so valuable over the preceding fifteen years.

Based on a little known fact of bowls mechanics, I have come to realise and often to wonder just how much 'soul' exists in bowlers who consistently win through in situations which force them to add, perhaps, an extra inch of length to better their previous 'second wood' into a match-winning shot.

At Woolston we would be playing on greens that had been timed around 19 seconds in the mornings, rising to 22, 23 or even higher in the afternoons. To lay a dead toucher on a jack thirty yards from the mat on a 20 seconds green it is necessary to reduce the speed at which the bowl leaves your hand to a meagre eight feet per second. To add as much as an extra foot of length necessitates something like a one in 10,000th morsel of extra strength in one's delivery. How many of us can even judge one part in ten of extra strength?

Such reasoning must, surely, make one think in wonder about the human-body mechanism and its ability, match after match, to turn defeat into victory through corrections of previous deliveries by an inch or even less. Logically, it is impossible . . . yet it happens far too frequently to be categorised 'lucky'.

That, maybe, is a good starting point for analysing the techniques, disciplines and attitudes, the courage and the determination, the patience and philosophy, which enables those who shine in the extremes of pressure met in major championships still to produce such magical qualities of triumph.

Seemingly, it takes more personal integration of skill and mind than can be summoned in the six seconds or so between stepping on the mat and releasing a bowl. Since many singles last around two hours, during which 100 deliveries per man will be made, he will be mat-active for only ten minutes out of an overall 120. That leaves 110 in which one can either work to a disciplined, off-mat routine or stand around with an unthinking, perhaps worrying mind. In a nutshell, one should learn how to make maximum use of time *off* the mat as well as *on* it.

Most people seem to believe that personality, temperament, character and other factors which show in match winners are inborn qualities. No doubt some inherit better abilities than others in developing such qualities but personal experience has convinced me that one can, through experimenting, experience, determination and a sound philosophy of life, acquire the self-discipline which is the solid foundation of match winning.

I have a personal experience which shows clearly how I learned to isolate my mind from all but the task in hand. It began in the thirteenth round of singles at the 1962 Commonwealth Games in Perth. My opponent was Ian Barron of New Zealand and victory was essential, not only because it would ensure the gold medal, irrespective of what happened on other rinks, but because I had a strong personal incentive for beating Ian and thus winning the Games without a defeat.

If you imagine my concentration was more intense than ever you are wrong. On the adjoining rink J Watson Black of Scotland had only lost one match and he was chasing me hard. My eyes should never have left the rink on which I was playing. Instead I found myself paying as much attention to Black's progress as to my own. Fortunately my touch and direction were good and I was producing two, three or even four good bowls each end while Ian, though less consistent, was slipping in too many shot stealers for comfort. Ultimately Black lost his match and allowed me to enjoy my last few ends more than any I ever had.

It was not a solitary misdemeanour but when a similar situation arose in the 1974 Games at Woolston there was no question of my eyes and mind roaming over to the rink on which Cliff White, Australia, was playing. The years had taught me that there is nothing I can do to change what is happening elsewhere and that I must give full attention to my own match, accepting all other outcomes, good or bad, with the thought 'I gave of my best. I could not have done better.'

This time there was no agonising, only unwavering concentration which earned me a convincing 21–8 win over Percy Jones, New Zealand. White went down to Harry Lakin, Malawi, 18–21 – remember Lakin beat me in the 1972 World Championships – and when Ruth, who had set her alarm clock for 5.30 a.m., tuned into the early news bulletin she learned that I had secured a clear cut win in the 1974 singles and, thus, won the event in 1962, 1970 and 1974 (bowls did not figure in the 1966 Games in Jamaica). You will, I am sure, understand and appreciate how bouncily Jacqueline, then eleven, and Carole, nine, hurried to school, happy that Dad's absence from home had, at least, countered their loneliness with success, not just for the Bryant family but for bowls generally.

The intervening years between 1962 and 1974 had taught me, unforgettably, that periods of intense competition and concentration demanded complete periods of rest from time to time. This, I understand, was first postulated by the eminent King's physician Lord Moran during World War I in his classical book *An Anatomy of Courage*. Winning at bowls, or any other game for that matter, does demand varying kinds of courage, specifically on the green in going for one's best shots without fear yet knowing that they may not always succeed. Failure is an occupational hazard which, if it is not swallowed happily, must be accepted with an attitude 'it happened this time. I will strive to improve my techniques and temperament so that next time I will win.'

The importance of that attitude cannot be overstated because there can be no courage of that nature if you allow yourself to fear defeat. One may not like defeat but that is no justification for fearing it.

Concerning rest after spells of intense competition, I find it is mental rather than physical stamina and tranquillity that needs refurbishing and for me that means a spell of fishing. Back home at Clevedon I have discovered a number of peaceful havens to which I flee whenever possible, sometimes with my daughters. Fishing requires a kind of uninvolved concentration which allows quiet meditation without losing that awareness of a 'bite' and the energy and cunning which lands the fish.

You cannot rush things when fishing. Everything has to be carried out meticulously. Patience and calmness are essential and these, of course, are helped by the tranquillity of the places where I normally go to fish. This provides an important similarity with bowls. If you try to rush the fish or hurry your shots you simply don't get anywhere.

Achieving success demands calmness under the pressures inevitably linked with skilled competition. Years of practice and tournament play provide experiences which can be fed into one's 'know-how' bank. Mostly one has met the situation and learned how to cope in the past. Yet how easy it is to forget completely the way to counter with that situation. Indeed, I would say that the prime task is to remember to remember. That is where calmness is so essential. There is a positional, adverse problem at the head. OK, don't wonder about it from the mat. Walk up the green to survey the head from close quarters. Take your time, not merely by studying the positions but also in summoning calmness, confidence and courage before delivering your next bowl.

The time you take belongs to you ... but it won't help the opponent's nerves. As long as you are using the time to improve your own performance, then it is justified and essential that you do so. However, players who deliberately waste time to disrupt their opponents are resorting to a form of gamesmanship which I cannot condone. A true sportsman wishes to win from superior ability, not from spoiling tactics.

Some tournaments and championships impose time limits but these do not include World Championships and Commonwealth

Games. If there is no time limit you are at liberty to take as long as you wish before delivering each bowl. I have a reputation of being a very slow player and I confess that I have participated in many pairs matches which have lasted more than four hours. In six-rink Middleton and Denny Cup Championship matches I am the last to finish probably eight times out of ten. I make no apologies for this. One plays games to win and giving anything less than the limits of one's skills demeans the opponent and breaks the spirit of good sportsmanship; what true sportsman wishes his opponent consciously to give less than his best?

I am not alone in using time until my mental and physical equilibrium seems ready for action. Mal Hughes used this system

Mal Hughes, one of the world's greatest skips, is
skilled and patient in using time to calm himself when
the pressure is heavy.

with heartening success when he and George Turley won the EBA Pairs Championship in 1983 following a nerve-testing final.

Over the years I have devised various ways of escaping out of trouble and these have proved successful so many times that nowadays, though I may worry a little, my mind never overheats or stops thinking altogether. In such situations belief in one's chosen shot is compulsory even though time has shown it does not always work. This is an occupational hazard which must be faced and surmounted without any loss of confidence or belief in self. Each successful escape from trouble is yet another proof of capability. Positive thinking buries that proof into the mind, so adding each time a fraction more self-belief and reducing inhibition a little the next time a crisis shot is needed.

As time moves on, thoughts about the success or failure of any vital shot gives way to total awareness of critical situations and how one can best overcome them. This allows 100 per cent applied concentration to the actual execution of each delivery.

There is no escape from such situations. They have to be faced squarely. In golf you can often shake off such tensions with one mighty drive. In football, rugby or tennis you can burn up tension and nervousness by running around at top speed. In bowls there is no such escape. You can deliver two superb bowls to establish a potential match-winning lie, only for your opponent to run the jack so that he then has a match lie and you have only one bowl remaining. This can be infuriating and frustrating but there is no way out other than by facing the problem fairly and squarely, building up inner calm and determination and then confidently launching your positional regaining bowl.

This is where a sound technique is worth its weight in gold. The better it is and the more you have ingrained it through hours, months and years of meticulous practice, the most chances you will have of success. You will be able to face the situation knowing you have proved your ability in such situations a hundred times or more. You will be able to stay free of panic while analysing the various options, sensibly select the shot most likely to succeed and then nervouslessly deliver your bowl, thinking neither of success nor failure but only that you have mustered all your skills and done your best.

You can do no more and, consequently, you should be able to accept the outcome free of extreme emotions. This is, indeed, the moment when you learn to live in the present not the past or future.

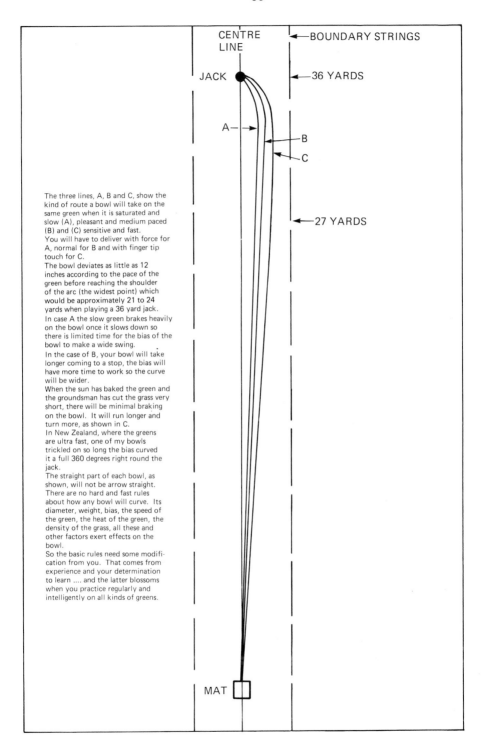

CENTRE LINE

◄─BOUNDARY STRINGS

JACK

◄─36 YARDS

A─

B

C

◄─27 YARDS

The three lines, A, B and C, show the kind of route a bowl will take on the same green when it is saturated and slow (A), pleasant and medium paced (B) and (C) sensitive and fast.

You will have to deliver with force for A, normal for B and with finger tip touch for C.

The bowl deviates as little as 12 inches according to the pace of the green before reaching the shoulder of the arc (the widest point) which would be approximately 21 to 24 yards when playing a 36 yard jack.

In case A the slow green brakes heavily on the bowl once it slows down so there is limited time for the bias of the bowl to make a wide swing.

In the case of B, your bowl will take longer coming to a stop, the bias will have more time to work so the curve will be wider.

When the sun has baked the green and the groundsman has cut the grass very short, there will be minimal braking on the bowl. It will run longer and turn more, as shown in C.

In New Zealand, where the greens are ultra fast, one of my bowls trickled on so long the bias curved it a full 360 degrees right round the jack.

The straight part of each bowl, as shown, will not be arrow straight. There are no hard and fast rules about how any bowl will curve. Its diameter, weight, bias, the speed of the green, the heat of the green, the density of the grass, all these and other factors exert effects on the bowl.

So the basic rules need some modification from you. That comes from experience and your determination to learn .... and the latter blossoms when you practice regularly and intelligently on all kinds of greens.

MAT

Peter Line won gold medals as a skip in the 1970 Commonwealth Games and
the 1972 World Championships. He is one of the minority who use a limited
backswing when delivering and let the left arm float so that body flow is not
encumbered.

Development of the attitudes I recommended depends on a lot
of thinking and acceptance of logic. Your increasing understanding of those intangibles must go, step by step, with unflagging,
intelligent efforts to perfect technique and to increase, almost
match by match, knowledge about greens, tactics, equipment –
indeed, everything connected with the game.

Those chosen for the 1974 Commonwealth Games knew the
greens would be much faster than any we had ever met and we
had conditioned our minds to accept the necessity of adapting our
styles and methods. Yet only when we began to practise and play
did we comprehend all the differences.

For example, drawing to a centrally positioned jack on a 13
seconds green entails delivering the bowl well out to the edge of
the rink; to the string maybe. A 22 seconds rink produces such a
wide swing – finishing at right angles or even travelling back down
the rink on to the back of the jack – that one has to send the bowl
half way across the adjoining rink. So in concentrating it is imperative to be aware of when players on that adjoining rink are
delivering and where. Experience of several crown green matches
being played simultaneously produces comparative chaos for those
who meet it for the first time. At Woolston it was by no means
uncommon to see bowls from the next rink curving their way
down a path just being assessed for one's own delivery.

Time also enters the situation. At Worthing during the annual
Gateway National Championships the greens usually run at about
12 to 13 seconds, with numerous singles matches taking two hours
and twenty-four or more ends. That means 192 or so bowls traversing the green. At 22 seconds per journey instead of 12 that

means an extra 1,920 seconds (thirty-two minutes) of watching bowls journey from mat to jack.

In the case of pairs or fours, a 21 ends match usually takes 336 individual shots. Ignoring the spin-offs caused by such speedy greens, one is assured of an extra hours play simply because each bowl is taking around ten seconds from mat to head, I am noted for being a thoughtful bowler who takes his time. I recall playing a National Pairs final with Roger Harris on a 16 seconds green at Mortlake which took 270 minutes.

At Woolston, therefore, they were only able to play two rounds of matches a day, one beginning at 9 a.m. the other at 2 p.m., this comparing with the three rounds a day programmed at Kyeemagh, Worthing, Edinburgh and so on. Yet even the afternoon session, starting five hours later, was often delayed because of the numerous dead ends in the previous round. I can remember finishing my singles match only to find our fours competing their second end which, like the first, had been replayed several times.

I have already given figures of how gently one must deliver a bowl on such fast greens. At Woolston we also met with strong winds each day and they were capable of totally straightening out a draw shot or, conversely and as I saw, of making the bowl completely encircle the jack before coming to rest. Luckily, the strong wind was constant rather than gusty so that there was not much point in waiting for a pause and then quickly getting a bowl on its way.

There is also, for some, a psychological effect. At Worthing it is commonplace for a player to draw a couple of bowls per end, sometimes more, within six inches of the jack. On a 22 seconds green it was pretty good to have just one of four bowls finish two feet from the jack. Yes, one understands this intellectually but in the realities of play one becomes accustomed to lots of bowls nestling near the jack and one tends to want to keep within that six inch mental limit.

Experience has proved that my squat, crouch, step and swing delivery system is both adaptable and effective. My step was just a tiny shuffle and my back swing almost non-existent but that, and what the media kindly called 'cool and unflappable Bryant forging away in between puffs at his pipe', gained me eleven wins from thirteen matches and the gold medal.

I've already written about my final win over Percy Jones. Simultaneously Clive White, the silver medallist, lost to Henry Lakin and then said, 'I think my trouble was that I kept looking across at the other rink and once David opened up a big lead I started to lose interest.' Shades of me in 1962.

Even if he had beaten Lakin 21–0 and also finished with eleven wins, I would still have topped the table because of a much greater shots for–against margin. Clive admitted, 'I would have loved to have been square with Bryant in wins. It would have looked so much better on paper.' I felt the same way about finishing with that one extra win.

Willie Wood, the Scottish motor mechanic, won the bronze medal with nine wins and four defeats. I was one of his victims, by 21–11, and my other conqueror was Clive White, 21–19. John Evans and Peter Line came in second to Jack Christie and Alex McIntosh in the pairs. Both duos won eleven of their thirteen matches but the Scots drew one of the other two and so scored 23 points against England's 22.

This was a just reward for McIntosh whose skill and standing, I feel, are not always realised in the UK. Apart from being a fine technician, he has the kind of temperament and attitude that can see a beautiful scoring position ruined by an opponent's fluke shot without, outwardly anyway, showing any negative emotions before going to the mat and calmly restoring the situation with a superb shot.

An external appearance of calmness carries no guarantee of total calmness. Often one is suffering and only that unwavering self-discipline built up by years of attention to detail enables one to override it.

Probably inevitably, this inner tension accumulates and there is only one way to deal with it, rest. In my case it is fishing and to regain post-championships tranquillity I managed to sample the New Zealand variety before joining my team-mates and returning home.

Gardening, too, is a pleasant way of refurbishing one's inner strengths though not always one's physical condition, as I discovered some years after Christchurch when moving our garden shed. That is in no way helpful to the suppleness and freedom from pain when delivering a bowl. Tending to my roses, that's another thing. They look so beautiful, smell marvellous and are a complete joy. In reaching the highest levels of sport one works for years on techniques and tactics and learns to be calm and tough on the green. There is one other ingredient, soul or less tangibly, emotion. Or even feeling. My 'escapes' give more than rest. They teach me 'soul'.

- When tiredness creeps in skills seep out. So always have a little carbohydrate food and a thermos flask of hot tea in your bag on the bank.
- Play to win ends, not to please the crowd.
- Through intensive, intelligent practice, help your subconscious develop a clear picture of your delivery. Then you will be able to draw on it when 'gremlins' occasionally cause you troubles.
- Tension tends to 'choke' deliveries. So take care in crises to let your arm and body flow right through and your head stable when you deliver. Keep it in mind.
- In a two hour singles you will only apply active concentration for around ten minutes. Teach yourself how to make utmost use of those other 110 minutes of passive concentration.
- The higher you climb, the more vital it is to maintain technical excellence. That demands regular, high-level practice.
- Accept that high class players will wreck many of your finest shots or heads. That is an occupational hazard that you must ride . . . and then hit back.
- Human beings have limited competitive stamina. Exceed it and your form crumbles. So mix your tournaments with a complete change for a few days now and then.

CHAPTER NINE

While we were doing out best for England in Christchurch the EBA administrators back home were busily completing the last details of, perhaps, the Association's most important operation since its inauguration in 1903, the switch of the National Championships from the Watneys Club in Mortlake, London, to Beach House Park, Worthing, the venue of the 1972 World Championships.

Prior to a move to Watneys for the 1958 Nationals, the Paddington Club, London, had gradually become known as the 'Mecca' of English bowls. There is no doubt that the club made an enormous contribution to the game. I, for one, will never forget it because it was there in 1957, its last year as venue for the Nationals, that I won with my father and Roger Harris and his father my first English Championship, the fours.

However, times change and there were various problems in having a London venue, among them the difficulties of maintaining impeccable greens in a major, cramped city. The decision had been taken, many promising venues had been closely scrutinised and analysed and, ultimately, Watneys had been chosen.

The company's back-up programme was, in those pre-sponsorship days of bowls, too good to pass up and it remained that way from 1958, the year that fine player Harold Powell won the singles, through to 1974 when a monster business take-over brought the Watney-EBA association to an end venue wise. In fact the new controllers continued to give generous support to the EBA right through to the 1980s, not the least of which was the 1,000 cans of beer given to the four who ran up the biggest winning score on the opening day each year. Most bowlers, me included, enjoy a pint after play – some even during it – so the excitement each opening day can be well imagined. Funnily, in two successive years it was won first by a man contracted to a rival brewery who therefore could not accept his share, and then by a teetotaller – but I digress.

Frankly, I believe the main green at Mortlake was the best I ever played on in the British Isles. Certainly my results there justify my belief and the confidence I enjoyed when competing

The 1969 EBA fours at Mortlake bring back many happy memories, topped by our win over Farnborough British Legion in the final. *Left to right*, Bill Elliott, Ted Websell, my father Reg, David Rhys Jones, me, EBA President John S. Mill, Willie Stewart, Harold Powell, the England captain, and Ben Galfskiy. I never dreamed we could win this title for the second year running.

there. Apart from winning the National singles five times, I also won the pairs twice with David Rhys Jones; the triples in 1966 with David and Bill Elliott, and the fours three times; twice with my father added to that trio, the third time with John Knight as his replacement.

I hope and think I never became big-headed over those years at Mortlake. Certainly I can recall two defeats; one by Mick Gallagher, the other by a virtual unknown from Kent, Bill Milton ... by 21–4! Maybe more than any other game, a player of limited experience can occasionally walk out on a green and put down a champion. That does little harm to the champion, thrills the underdog and puts a small quota of belief in many other players' minds that they, too, might produce similar results and this inspires them to try harder to improve.

David and I qualified for the pairs and, with Bill, the triples in that first year at Worthing. Reaching the semi-finals of the pairs, David and I beat D Roberts and L Bates of Denham and then B Gedney and F Smith of Burton House, Lincs., each time by 17–

14. They were long, hard battles won as much by our mental stamina and concentration as by our technical and tactical skills in action. Particularly, the Lincolnshire pair were remarkably accurate and consistent, a legacy from their experiences in the Federation code of bowls and its handicapping of the drive.

Seemingly our struggles at Worthing provided us with valuable experience of new situations because we reached a high level of form in going on to win the British Isles title.

As a team member of both the England outdoor and indoor teams in 1972 and 1973 I was involved in a lot of skipping, this during a period when Scotland was dominating the International Team Championships, both outdoors and indoors. Every match England played was immensely important and, without being self-satisfied, the fours I skipped produced very good results. No matter how brilliant the skip may be, he cannot win unless his colleagues are pulling their weight. So if there is one particular factor which must lay high among all others, it is the ability to discover and bring into operation those players' strongest assets, be they technical or temperamental or, even better, both.

War-time research into the performances of RAF bomber crews established that a technically weak member who was not an especially hard trier could and often did have a deleterious effect on other members of the crew. That stress was greatly reduced if he really gave of his best. This has been proved over and over again in soccer, where the absence of a star man and the substitution of someone inferior has led to a much more serious falling away in a team's results than expected.

Players can occasionally be bullied out of below par form into their top performance level but for each success achieved by castigating, humiliating or generally bullying there will be 99 successes achieved through encouragement, support, patience – even an occasional laugh from the skip. That kind of approach must come from empathy, a complete understanding of precisely what the player is suffering at that moment. False, hypocritical attitudes are insufficient. Most men can tell the difference between false and genuine support and the former of those may well worsen rather than help a struggling, out of form, team colleague. This calls for a mixture of psychology, diplomacy, equability under all situations and firm, positive leadership, especially when the going is tough. Indeed, it is often said that 'when the going gets tough, the tough get going'.

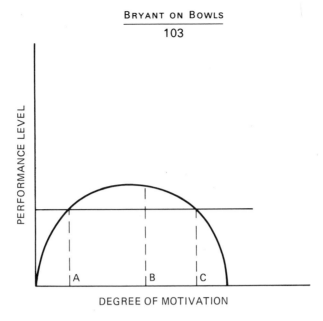

Performance versus motivation. The graph shows the general pattern of
performance against varying degrees of motivation or desire. A skilled
skip will know instinctively or from experience when a man is bowling
very well (A) but can be pushed a shade more and, later, when he has
reached a peak and is starting to fall away (B). That is the moment for
gentle, quiet encouragement.

The ability of the skip to perform solidly when under pressure
is vital. If he can remain calm and pull off some good shots when
coping with adverse heads he will ultimately lighten the pressure
and load weighing down his players and will help them lift their
games. On no account should he fail to keep the opponents guess-
ing about what might happen and to fear a little the sheer tenacity
and equability of the skip competing against them.

This demands that he is a master tactician. Tactics will play a
major part in his role as a leader/player so he must, through
experience, study of the game, a readiness to learn whenever he
plays and inherent leadership, possess profound knowledge of his
craft. That will not be enough on its own. He is the man who
shares the last four bowls with the opposing skip. He is likely to
face situations in which an inch or so this way or that in a
bowls-packed head may convert the shots by anything up to six
or seven on occasions. Knowing about it will not be enough. He
will need the skills and control of the varying shots he is likely to
be called on to play as when he pulls one of these shots off he
must know precisely how to use 'body language' or 'presence' as
it might be called. A player reaches a precise point on the inverted

'U' which measures the mental part of his overall 'ideal performance state'. If he has not yet reached it in a match, then enthusiasm
about his own brilliant saving shot is likely to push him a little
higher towards the top of that inverted 'U'. However, if he is
already on the top of it, that enthusiasm may well push him over
it, so reducing his mentally ideal state. It is difficult enough to
estimate that mental state with one man to control. When, as in
fours, there are three of them, it is a huge problem.

However, Professor Chan Thomas of California who studies
extra sensory perception at his prestigious Californian University
has established strong beliefs that confident concentration on a
player when facing a difficult position does, factually, transmit
supporting strength. That kind of positive support is important
when skipping. In passing, one should note that Professor Thomas
asserts that this transmission is not airy-fairy but a specific fact of
high level physics.

A possible need for supportive mental action can usually be
anticipated before a match when a combination of players has a
long standing relationship. Skip, for example, may well know that
his number two is good on both hands when on a fast green but
that when the rink is heavy and slow his accuracy on the forehand
fades away. This may well be the time to build up or sustain his
self-confidence by signalling for, say, draw shots on the backhand
for a series of ends, concentrating steadily on transmitting success
thoughts to him during his delivery. Of course, this same system
can be used equally well when a player is suffering difficulty mastering a particular hand or shot at any time.

So the number two may be eased back to form and confidence,
only for third man to slip into a bad patch. Maybe he doesn't
suffer that hypothetical weakness of number two but, instead,
starts thinking of ends to come and of winning the match instead
of the end now being played. He needs to be gently but positively
brought back to the immediate moment so that he can harness all
his skills for the bowl he is to deliver in thirty seconds or so. How
is up to the skip. It's his job to know just how to bolster and
inspire each one of his men.

Clearly, then, there can be no rests for the skip. He must be
totally aware of everything that is happening throughout the entire
match ... and when one remembers that a 21 ends fours match
can last three or, sometimes, even four hours, one can understand
why there are so few 'Master Skips' emerging from an abundance

of good ones. To me, skipping a four and finding ways of unifying four men into a happy, integrated, powerful unit is one of the most intriguing facets of bowls.

Returning to factual rather than intangible aspects of skipping, it is extremely important to give sound directions. 'One round here' (pointing) is inadequate. The demand must be positive for many reasons, one being so that a poorish attempt can be reduced in the player's mind by the next demand which might be 'same hand but six inches shorter in strength'. Note that this does not highlight a previous blunder but uses it positively to help the next delivery being spot on. This will find a better head and, no less important, increase the player's belief that he can bowl accurately.

Such positive approaches can become extra effective by knowing the behaviour of the player's bowls. The skip should make it a prime duty to know exactly how each of his four's bowls – eight in all – behave on any type and pace of green. Then he need never fall into a trap like, say, asking a player with straight running bowls to 'curl it round the back to here'.

If he has a left-handed player in his four he must realise that the line to the jack is different because of the width of the shoulder for that player. Sometimes he will be able to take advantage of this and ask for shots not open to right handers. This can be most effective, both in positive scoring shots and in demoralising the opponents. In a nutshell, a master skip seeks always to exploit the strengths of his own players at the expense of the opponents' weaknesses.

A common fault of some skips, I know I experienced it in my teens, is to feel it is imperative always to hold shot each end, no matter what. An opponent's bowl nestling nearest to the jack acts like a red rag to a bull – that bowl must be knocked off immediately. I remember a situation something like that in the first World Pairs Championship when an end finished with only six of the original sixteen bowls on the green, all of them belonging to one pair. Driving paid heavily that time, as it does so often. Many big losses can be prevented by concentrating unswervingly on producing a good second shot; two or three of them, maybe.

Alternatively, it is sometimes equally as dangerous to pack the head too early, thus boosting the ego through the accompanying oohs, aahs and applause from the crowd who are thinking little of the ever larger target being presented to the opponents.

Complacency is an unforgivable sin though it sets in all too

Maldwyn Evans in this picture is about to win the 1972 World Championship at Worthing. He exploits his left handedness to the limit, as I know from experience; he beat me in both the 1966 and 1972 World Championships.

often when one four is racing away from the other. First, you are insulting your opponents if you do not play as well as you possibly can from the first bowl of any match until the very last; after all, would you want an opponent to make you the gift of a shot or two? Also slowing down denigrates the game itself for, surely, you can only honour it by striving for improvement with every bowl you deliver throughout each successive year.

So you are eight shots ahead with only two ends remaining and have drawn two good bowls close to the jack. Relaxing, you forget to protect them with bowls behind the position and with his last bowl the opposing skip trails the jack with his final delivery, changing that potential two into a five for himself.

Suddenly your lead is under a little pressure and, additionally, you are somewhat angry about not protecting the head. The opening lead is well off target with both his bowls while yours are well positioned when the opposing number two is well off course, only to wick off a stray and run the jack into a good position for more shots. Now the pressure is well and truly on. Probably you will scrape home but not with the relaxed mind that usually accompanies big-score wins. In the afternoon the opponents are stronger and each end demands great efforts. At 18-all that nervous energy squandered in the morning would now be a godsend, but when tiredness, particularly of the brain, sets in, skills seep out. So remember, you've never won until you read it on the results board.

It is easier to play at your best when the odds are in your favour. A good skip asserts himself when the reverse is the case. It is difficult for an ambitious third man to realise fully what the skip is suffering and to resist taking on his role, if only with his mouth. I'm all for encouragement and 'having a go' but more often than not it is dangerous for young bowlers to be given responsibility on a rink too early.

Far better for them to experience a long stint as third man where their repertoire of shots should be as varied and accurate as the skips but where they can be spared the skip's heavy responsibility for a little longer while they absorb ever more experience.

Finally, and imperatively, there should be no post-mortems except within the team off the green. Dissent between must be taboo. If it must come out, at least 'close the ranks' until all are back in the changing-room . . . and then no heated dissent!

Post-mortems can be invaluable but only when conducted positively and constructively. Then they can become veritable 'Master Classes' from which all learn and become more integrated in thought and deed.

Summarising, there are nine commands which should be observed:

1. Watch every move on the rink.
2. Sum up the opponents' every move.
3. Sort out the opponents' weaknesses and strengths.
4. Know the strengths and weaknesses of your own team.
5. Inspire your players to bring out their best.
6. Give full encouragement to players, both when all goes well, and, particularly, when they are off form and needing help.
7. Give your instructions on what shot you want.
8. Bring all players into discussions of tactics and strategies.
9. Produce every shot in the book to inspire example.

I am all in favour of young, talented bowlers serving a long 'apprenticeship' as third man to an experienced, admired skip rather than submitting to pressures from club officials to play as skips. So far as shots are concerned, a top class third man should possess just as wide a variety as his skip and the ability to use them accurately and consistently without needing the 'glory now' stimulus of a skip. This is a stiffer test than might be imagined and it may turn out that he does not reach county skip levels until he has developed a keen yet humble personality. Keenness needs no explanation; humility shows a willingness to learn without ever becoming a player in constant need of temperamental support from his skip; furthermore, it demands a total self-control that never allows constant suggestions and orders up the green. No, a good man studies the play and may sometimes quietly make suggestions to his skip, yet without ever taking over command by swamping his skip with enthusiasm. That is why a quiet, determined third man can make life unbelievably easy for his skip.

- When skipping, be clear and positive with your instructions ... and also very confident.
- Know the strengths and weaknesses of your four and exploit their strengths as often as possible. If you have to use someone's weakness, never chastise him for failing; that is counter-productive. Later, over a pint perhaps, feed him a little skilled advice.
- Do not take silly risks when ahead. Keep the ends tight. Being brash often gives away a five, shatters confidence and concentration and leads to ultimate defeat.
- If you suffer a major upset, let your opponent enjoy his triumph ... and later analyse precisely why you lost. The ladder to the top has many rungs, most of them defeats.

CHAPTER TEN

The 1974 Commonwealth Games ended on 1st February and by the time we had returned and re-acclimatised, the British Isles Indoor Championships and the Hilton Cup team event were almost upon us. I was deeply into bowls all the year round by then and I had won the English indoor singles six times and gone on to capture the British Isles title twice.

That had sufficed to keep me in the England team and, once more, I was chosen to skip for Mike London, David Rhys Jones and Ted Hayward. Each country in turn hosts the British Isles events and in 1974 we should have played in Ireland. Understandably, Ireland remained hosts but at the Prestwick Stadium in Scotland, the individual events running to completion on Tuesday 12th March. England's sole win came from AL Rider, I Boys and Les Traves in the triples, the event eventually brought into the individual championships five years after the inauguration of the other three in 1967.

The team event began with an hour of splendid entertainment by the Dalmellington Silver Band and the Ayr Majorettes, so reminding us that although Ireland was our host, the matches were in Scotland and there was no misunderstanding about the number of people we would be playing on the Thursday. In fact 1,143 spectators packed in for the match against England, leaving our team of 24 plus the 'magnificent six' English ladies in their yellow dresses. They clapped and cheered enthusiastically for us and the decibels output per lady must have challenged the world record – if such a thing exists.

Though they became known affectionately as 'The Canaries', when it came to our meeting with Scotland their vocal efforts were completely drowned by the Scottish contingent who, seemingly, were inspired by 'The Canaries'. So England's 24 plus six were matched by the strong Scottish team plus its noisy back-up of 1,131 partisans.

How strongly this affected the Scottish bowlers cannot be quantified. Suffice it to say, they won on five of the six rinks for an overall 140–87. Probably because of my many years of self-discipline and concentration, I might have been able to support my team in a close contest. Instead we were routed by Rennie Logan's strong four 22–12. It was a sad day for us and sounded a warning for future series.

Simulation of such situations are, I know, part of the curriculum at the Angela Buxton Champion Tennis Player's Academy, and are broken down by psychological analysis and countered by special 'hazard courses' in which players are subjected to every annoyance possible. They are then made to analyse them quietly in order to develop resistance and control. This has been proved successful and it might well be brought into bowls advantageously.

It is difficult to know precisely where one is going wrong so I was relieved when that knowledgeable and authoritative official-critic, former international Graham Howard, wrote in *World Bowls* magazine 'David Bryant was the one Englishman who played like the champion he is.' He also wondered 'has Peter Line completely recovered from playing so well on the fast New Zealand greens because I observed a slight imperfection in his delivery. He was not, I thought, following through completely with his arm as he used to. In New Zealand, of course, the fast surface requires a shortened back swing and the follow through is similarly affected.'

I have already dwelt upon this vital part of one's delivery and I sometimes wonder if it is possible to preface a perfect follow through by a wayward, non-flowing back swing and release. Certainly, that thought of an imperfect follow through strengthens my certainty that my crouch, foot movement and length of back swing relationship is a tremendously effective and reliable technique.

Our four won against Ireland and Wales but Scotland were worthy winners. All of us were delighted by an official presentation to Arthur Sweeney of 'a suitable memento of our deep respect of him and the work he has put into our much-loved game.' No history of the indoor game would be complete without acknowledging the role he played. Amongst many services, none bettered the Individual Indoor Championships. The bowls world said they were impossible. Arthur, energetically supported and pushed by *World Bowls* magazine, campaigned that it wasn't and in 1961 they had their way ... softly, softly.

The Singles Championship involved fewer than 200 participants and was won by Allan Spooner of Ascot who visits the EBA Championships each year and often supports me from the green-

John Bell collected a gold medal in the 1984 World Championships fours. He also won the England Singles Championship in 1983. He developed a sound follow through from the start, as can be seen from his competing in the National Championships at the age of eighteen.

Arthur Sweeney, one of the game's greatest developers and administrators, received many awards, among them the first ever 'Castella' here being given by Harry Sherman in 1966. I was thrilled to emulate him later in the year.

side. The pairs followed in 1963/64, the fours in 1966/67 and the triples in 1971/72. All began with small entries.

The EIBA handbook for the winter of 1983 shows entries of 6,969. The number of clubs has grown from 45 to 185 and around ten new affiliations are made each year. More of that later.

Following the British Isles Indoor Championships one tends to start thinking about the summer. The international team trial is traditionally staged on the first Saturday in June and I was pleased to be chosen once more. This paved the way for my position as skip again, this time at the Sighthill Club, Edinburgh.

So, yet again, I was going to face the noisy partisanship of a Scottish crowd yelling for victory. What a week it turned out to be, with heavy rain and strong winds. As I had won the EBA singles in 1973, I competed in the British Isles Championships. Two singles earned me that championship, the final finding me in top form and, on the difficult day, too experienced for Rod Hugh, the 26-year-old Welsh contender. The last end of that final seemed a good omen. Hugh held two shots close to the jack and they looked safe. Again, my acquired-through-determined-practice ability to live only in the moment allowed me to force the head, remove those two adverse shots and follow through for a match-winning double. This showed once more that by forgetting all but the immediate situation and concentrating on how best to over-come it everything else can be driven out of the mind and tension disappears.

In the match against Scotland three days later I found myself skipping against the legendary Harry Reston. A tremendous character and splendid bowler, he was possibly the greatest ever showman to grace the Scottish team. Harry never waited for the crowd's support. Instead, the moment he saw his bowl was on its correct course, he would start calling, 'that's a beauty you've got Harry'.

No one ever found playing Harry simple or straightforward. If his showmanship lit up partisans, his mastery of every shot doubled responses from the greenside and the total effect shattered more than a few opponents. With Prestwick still ringing in my ears, so to speak, I was forearmed. Additionally, when one has experienced a problem and thought about it seriously, the sub-conscious takes over, usually to conjure up methods of coping with it next time.

Whatever the reason, John Evans, Bill Olver, Bob Burch and I all remained calm and composed against Reston, finishing 28-15 ahead as England's biggest winners. Peter Line and Mal Hughes also won and Tom Armstrong only lost by five shots to Jock McAtee. Unfortunately David Crocker's four never got together and in losing by 19 shots to Willie Adrain gave Scotland sufficient shots to win by nine overall.

England finished last that year and examination revealed that rink four contributed to our downfall; Line, Crocker and I each losing in turn for a total deficit of 43. On the day we played Ireland I simply had no idea how to cope with that rink but as my opposing skip Brendan McBrien played superbly, I realise that the fault lay in me and not the rink.

The whole series abounded in English psychological problems which, in retrospect, should not have been. Overall, it demonstrated that, at top levels, intangibles have as much influence on outcomes as straightforward skill on the mat.

One month later Worthing grabbed all the headlines through the switch of the EBA Championships from Mortlake to Beach House Park. Returning to my attendance in two events, the triples and pairs, the first did not last long. Bill Elliott, David Rhys Jones and I drew three never-say-die old-age pensioners from Bexhill; Arthur Allen, 65, Jesse Moseley, 63, and Ernie Berriman, 69, and with an 18-7 lead and seven ends remaining it seemed we would win without needing the full 18 ends.

Theoretically they were dead but nobody remembered to tell them. They held a little mid-rink conference, recalled they had won their county semi-final to qualify for Worthing after trailing 0-13 and decided to 'have a go'. 'We had nothing to lose, anyway', Allen confided to me later.

That decision coincided with Bill suffering a recurrence of injury to his right knee which forced him to abandon his crouch delivery for an upright one which didn't have the easy knee action inherent in that style. So our gallant veterans picked up a couple of threes and 3 twos to go ahead 19-18 and then set up a head which forced me to strive for calmness, assess the situation and then concentrate totally on a shot that would save the day.

Anyone who believes that I am free from nervousness may take it from me that I am not. With defeat staring me in the face I was extremely nervous but self-discipline built up through structured approaches over a great many years enabled the mental-mechanical part of me go almost automatically through my routine. Sometimes it is almost as if I have stepped outside myself and am watching me bowl. Similar experiences many times in the past helped my detached attitude and I pulled out a shot which scored a single and sent us into the 18th end level at 19-all. We had the mat and it seemed, almost the match, but with his last delivery Berriman thwarted us with a brilliant saving single and we were out, first round.

There was nothing we could do about it other than to congratulate our conquerors with sufficient grace to help them enjoy their success. After all, we had in the past lived both with triumph and disaster and, in Rudyard Kipling's words, learned 'to treat those two imposters just the same'.

We also learned how to squeeze the last drop of knowledge out of defeat and, for the first time in my whole career, I worked out tactics for the whole of the pairs event starting four days later. Accepting the variations of the green – really, I had no option and there was no future in pining for the main green at Mortlake – I decided to resurrect my old, straighter running bowls and ordained that David Rhys Jones would concentrate on the forehand, which is his narrower line, throughout the six rounds of the pairs. In fact, Tuesday's and Wednesday's warm sunshine dried out the green, speeded it up and so forced him to deliver the majority of his bowls on the forehand. As I have already said, we went through to take the title. I should add that no matter how many years one has studied and practised techniques, luck can still govern a match. It did for us in our final against Bernard Gedney and Frank Smith.

With the score too close for comfort and the 18th end on its final bowl, I was looking at four Burton House bowls waiting to be counted. I could see a narrow gap and so used a drive. Immediately I saw it was fractionally off course but it cannoned into another Clevedon bowl which, in turn, cannoned into the jack and pushed it over to one of my bowls for a single. The match ended 17-14 but minus that stroke of good fortune we would have been 16-18 and the runners up. In no way am I denegrating the search for skill ... but with humility because Fate intervenes too often.

The 1974/75 indoor season was alive with controversy because of Graham Howard's strong, passionate article in *World Bowls* concerning the hypocrisy in the game and the need for the category 'amateurs' to be abandoned in favour of 'players'. Inevitably, he came under severe attack from many officials but he was also well supported and it could be said that October 1974 was the month in which bowls being open to both amateurs and professionals ceased to be an impossible dream. From then on it was simply 'when will it happen?'

At that time entry into the Individual Indoor National Championships events was limited. Naturally, I competed in the singles and in the other event I chose, the fours, I linked up with close friends at the Clevedon Club rather than any specially strong competitors. This move to what might be called 'fun bowls' also came about because prior to 1974 I had competed from Bristol IBC, initially at the Bristol South Baths – then in 1971 at the new green at Bristol City FC and, because of the size of the section I seemed to be spending many hours driving from place to place. When Clevedon IBC opened in 1974 my travel was substantially reduced as the areas were revised.

However, there was no doubting the rapid growth of indoor bowls. Twenty-three new clubs came into action during the 1973/74 winter and a similar number seemed likely for the winter that began in October 1974. Additionally, the Teesside Masters Tournament that had been inaugurated after the founding of that centre in 1968, had already become not simply a major winter event but the blueprint for others that were springing up around the country.

Staged annually after Christmas and finishing on New Year's day, the Masters brought the best British Isles players to the stadium for competition which was made extremely keen and testing by reducing the singles matches from the 21 up, as specified by the IBB, to 'the first to reach 15'.

Winner of the inaugural 'Masters', I won again in 1972 and 1973, which filled me with a wish to complete the hat trick in the 1974 series. Strong motivation usually lifts my form and this meeting turned out to be a text book example. Beginning in Group B, my victims were: J Burrows 15-3; B Dawson 15-6; E Cossins 15-4. On the following day I continued: K Woodhouse 15-12; GT Fleming 15-12 and R Phillips 15-14. The third series of group matches were just as satisfactory with Alec Jackson 15-7; Brendan McBrien 15-5 and Derek Wier 15-13. That took me to the final in which I used my experience in mastering a difficult rink, so beating the Scottish champion John Fleming 15-2. As McBrien was the Irish champion and Jackson the English Indoor champion, I felt that was not a bad catch in three days.

The next major event was the Hilton Cup Indoor International Team Championship at the Rutherglen Stadium, Glasgow, officially titled the West of Scotland Stadium. Dismayed by four years of Scottish domination at Aberdeen, Teesside, Cardiff and Prestwick, the EIBA gave the selection team extra scope by abandoning the traditional rule that only men nominated by their clubs could be chosen. In my case this scarcely mattered because I skipped for the dependable, talented colleagues Mike London, Norman King and Ted Hayward.

Our opening could scarcely have been more dismal. Down to Jim Donnelly's four 0-11 after only five ends, we clawed back a few shots up to the 15th end when we were four shots behind, only for Donnelly to win 21-14. Altogether Ireland finished ahead on five of the six rinks to win 123-86. Playing Wales, we overcame Lyn Probert's four 26-15 and in the concluding clash with Scotland came from 15-19 to ease out Jock Byres 23-21. Once again, Scotland defeated England 111-99, so taking the Cup for the fifth time in succession.

The 1974/75 winter of indoor play on fast greens was followed by a trip to Cape Town for the South African Masters where Willie Wood, Scotland, also participated.

My previous trip with Peter Line to the South African Games at Pretoria had proved successful as we won the bronze medal in the pairs, I the silver in the singles – Willie Wood beat me for the gold – and England won the team trophy for the best overall performance. The greens had been true and pleasantly paced so our expectations for Cape Town were high.

What a disappointment awaited us. The green was heavy and running at only ten seconds, we had scarcely any time to practise and I finished nowhere, Doug Watson of South Africa winning the gold for the third successive year.

This did not seem an encouraging omen because the 1976 World Championships were scheduled for Johannesburg from February 18th to March 6th and selections were sure to be made during the coming summer.

Despite indifferent results at Rutherglen and the Cape Town Masters the England outdoor selectors stayed faithful, choosing John Evans, Bill Olver and Bob Burch with whom I had won two and lost one in the 1974 series. The 1975 series were staged at Llanelli where the promoters erected a stand accommodating 1,800 spectators. The Welsh enthusiasts give little to the Scots in terms of patriotism, though their deafening shrieks are mingled with a great deal of melodious singing.

So far as our four were concerned, the singing was no less effective as we were overwhelmed by Jim Morgan's four 26-13 after we had trailed 12-0 at five ends and 16-3 at ten. England actually beat Wales 90-88 and my four defeated John McRae 24-16 and C Beck 22-16 in the Scotland and Ireland matches but Scotland outbowled England 91-82, Ireland 94-78 and Wales 99-33 to extend their unbroken supremacy as champions to eleven years. This was way ahead of the previous record, five championships by England, 1958 to 1962.

Naturally, post-mortems abounded and the selectors were criticised for not making better use of their now unfettered freedom of choice. In particular, many believed the weaknesses lay in the number twos and third man but I cannot really go along with that. The emotional enthusiasm of the Scots and Welsh, amply charged by the inspiring support of their always considerable fans, seemed to numb the English players.

Coping with an unashamedly partisan crowd of noisy supporters demands a special kind of concentration considerably loaded with the inner tranquillity found in yoga and zen teaching. To me it seemed that all of us over-reacted too frequently, trying for outstanding shots – and usually failing – when basic solidness would have sufficed and would not have yielded so many threes and upwards.

It was also noticeable that the Scottish players constantly attacked the jack rather than manoeuvred for clever positions. Young sports players are known to cope better with stress than their older colleagues but they are usually less experienced. A winner at the top levels of bowls usually possesses a good balance of both qualities.

Meanwhile, I was ploughing my way through the Somerset County Singles Championship and I again qualified for the 1975 EBA Nationals. This was in some ways a consolation for I had been printed as the English champion in the Llanelli programme when it was really Bill Irish.

Beating David Marchant and Tom Kennedy, Ireland, 23-16 with David Rhys Jones in the British Isles Pairs Championship final had alleviated some of the leg pulling I suffered over that programme gaff but in some ways it could have been an omen.

Reaching the EBA Nationals with the experience of the Worthing greens in 1974 to give me knowledge bolstered my confidence and I was quietly determined to win that singles and make it four times in five years.

No matter how one eulogises about the subtleties of fours, triples and pairs, it is always the man to man 'shoot-out' that packs the stands. 1975 proved to be no exception and the first day bustled with activity. Long years of unwavering self-discipline has enabled me to isolate myself from anything but the match I am playing and I hurried my way through the first three rounds by beating Ted Boyle, Chesham, 21–5; Lyndon Wilkinson, Worcs. Cinderella 21–9 and Ian Pratt, Rowntree Park, York 21–7. Frankly, following all the pressures of Llanelli, I was relieved to have escaped serious opposition and felt confident it would help to have a peaceful night in readiness for the next day.

How valuable this proved to be in my fourth round clash with Bob Jack, the EBA Honorary Treasurer and a formidable player and tactician. A left hander, he decided to stick to the forehand and he did so faithfully. Indeed, during one spell he delivered 33 bowls in succession on the forehand. Though he piled in one four, I eventually reached 20–16, only to suffer a dreadful end which helped Bob to his second four of the match.

Somewhat shaken, I took my time, went through my oft proved 'be calm' routine and held shot when Bob unleashed his final bowl. For ten seconds I suffered agonies but the bowl slid past its target and after 125 minutes of suspense I reached the semi-finals with Alan Ridington quietly having his lunch and getting himself ready for play.

A sound, solid bowler, he was less experienced than me, especially in dealing with the somewhat tricky wind that blows on to the green via the pathway up to the main stand. My control told heavily and I won through 21–12 and prepared myself for stiff final resistance from Bob Gibbins. Like Ridington, a Middlesex man, Bob had played third man to Reg Paine in reaching the fours final eight days earlier and his play had been impressive. I knew accuracy and consistency would be vital. How vital I was soon to discover.

The final needed 23 ends plus one replay, taking in 189 deliveries; the other three were eliminated by the 20th end when I faced a three shot deficit and drove the jack over the string.

This final was logged carefully by Clarence Jones who rated each delivery on a scale: A = excellent, B = very good, C = good,

D = fair, E = poor, U = unlucky.

The breakdown showed:

	A	B	C	D	E	U
David Bryant	13	15	17	30	16	3
Bob Gibbins	10	10	16	29	29	1

On this grading I should have won more easily but six of Bob's A grade shots were his last of an end and they cut out about ten of my shots and earned him a single, so producing altogether a conversion of 16 shots. However, overall I only put down one bad shot in every six while Bob bowled a bad 'un once in every three and this continuous pressure told, dramatically, for after opening the 22nd end with a toucher, he then simplified life for me with seven consecutive poor bowls. Probably he was also undermined by memories of losing that fours final after leading 9-2.

Obviously, my delight in winning the singles for the sixth time overflowed but, in retrospect, I was equally pleased that my years of disciplined thinking and attitude and the conscientious striving

Bob Gibbins, my opponent in the 1975 National Singles final. He made 94 deliveries, me 95. Though I produced three more excellent and five very good shots than Bob, my winning margin was only 21-18. This was a testimony to his ability to produce fine shots with the final bowl of each end. In fact they earned him conversions of 16 shots altogether and made me work very hard, mentally as well as technically.

over the years to blot out everything but the shot I was about to attempt had remained at such a high level over the two days and six rounds. That my tally of National Championship titles had now risen to fourteen was a warming bonus.

Normally I would have turned my thoughts to the coming winter's indoor events but the English Bowling Association had named their players for the 1976 World Championships and we were asked not to enter for any of the indoor championships.

This did not preclude me from going after the Teesside Masters again and it boosted my confidence to win it yet again. The green there necessitates one taking around seven to eight feet of land, which means delivering one's bowls well out to the strings that divide the rinks. Not beyond the strings, as was the case in New Zealand, but still farther out than is usual on English greens.

Not that the pace of the Teesside green had any significance so far as the greens at Zoo Lake, Johannesburg were concerned. Originally we had expected the 1976 World Championships to be staged at the legendary Wanderers Club but as far back as 1972, we learned the South African Tournament Committee realised that the club simply hadn't the necessary space and facilities. It was, perhaps, the first of many decisions taken and an example of the outstanding planning and application which lifted the South African series into a class never before experienced in bowls ... and probably in any other sport. Since many bowlers become involved in administration, the depth and thought they showed is a lesson well worth study.

Recalling the words of the late Ralph Bentley, Secretary of the 1972 World Championship at Worthing – 'you cannot begin planning a day too soon' – the 1976 Committee first met in November 1972 and thereafter, Christmas holidays and the like excepted, they met each month until April 1974, then fortnightly until January 1975, weekly until the Championships began and thereafter daily. In all they met 105 times as a whole; sub-committee meetings must have doubled the figure. Such was the interest created by the 1976 games, club memberships grew by 2,000 in the first six months of that year.

Having eliminated the Wanderers Club, they chose Zoo Lake Bowling Club and immediately went to work on a major problem; three greens were needed but the club only had two. Deciding that the third green would be contributing greatly to international goodwill and that after the championships the green would be

Ralph Bentley, the man who made the 1972 World
Championships come true. His skill and experience were
invaluable to the South Africans and helped them
to promote the superbly run 1976 series at Johannesburg.

valuable to the city, they asked the Johannesburg City Council to
lay this one, which they did enthusiastically.

Bowls is a big spectator sport in South Africa and the Committee calculated that crowds of up to 10,000 would attend on
days when the supposed strongest contenders met one another.
They were pretty accurate because the sixteen sessions pulled in
106,492 ticket buyers, with a capacity of 10,000 on the last day.

They had to be seated, so as well as stands, seats would be
required, 7,500 of them. They were bought immediately, a shrewd
move because their price doubled by the start of 1976. The original
estimate of overall expenditure came to 230,000 rands. This had

to be raised eventually to R580,000. The ultimate outlay came to R440,000 and the income reached R448,257; that welcome surplus went straight to the South African Blind Bowlers Association, much to the satisfaction of everyone.

Careful planning showed that close on 800 volunteers would be needed. Once this was publicised, droves of applications came in and there was no shortage. Payment was both undesirable and financially impossible. Instead many were taken on a trip to Kruger Park Reserve.

Eighteen months before 'D' day it was decided that because of the time proximity, the South African Masters Tournament would be cancelled. The Committee pleaded 'no' because it would serve as a wonderful dress rehearsal and alert officials to things that might go wrong.

Amongst the many things they did learn during that Masters was that it does sometimes rain heavily in Johannesburg. This unexpected warning allowed time for the provision of essential requirements which, surely, would otherwise have been forgotten.

Rain or no rain, the matches began dismally for me as I was stricken down by a stomach bug which necessitated strong medical attention. An injection knocked me out for a complete day and someone had to substitute for me in the first round of the triples. I might well have slept for further days had not the knocking on my hotel room door wakened me. The well-wishing visitor was an old friend of the snooker table, Ray Reardon and his happy, invigorating presence materially helped my recovery. Even so, several days elapsed before I regained full health and during those days I never really got to grips with the greens.

There were three of them and, frankly, they were not up to championship standards, the only flaw in the entire administrative programme. Green 'A' was fast but patchy; 'B' extremely heavy and unreliable and 'C' was heavy but true and by far the best. As with all championships, the ends of the greens ran faster as play progressed, and trampling feet wore and tore the greens.

I won all but one of the matches I played on B and C but never mastered A and lost to Bob Middleton, Australia, 21–13 (good game, no complaints) Kerry Clerk, New Zealand, 21–5 (a nightmarish experience but with no axe to grind) and Roy de Feu, Guernsey, 21–14.

My other defeat came from the hand of Tolova'a Si'inoa of Western Samoa when a rebounding jack saw an unexpected conversion of three up change to four down. A brilliant draw shot when facing game on the last end, earned him victory 21-20 and, as we were to find later, deprived me of the silver medal, leaving instead the bronze.

My only satisfaction during the games was a 21-10 win over Doug Watson, winner of the gold medal in the last match of the series. Even that was not totally satisfactory because by then he was assured of top place and, I imagine, no longer on top adrenalin supply. England also beat South Africa in the pairs and triples and lost by only two shots in the fours. Altogether, England scored 78 shots and yielded 52 for a one and a half to one supremacy.

Unarguably, the organisation was outstanding and the huge crowds, diminishing to dwarf size as they climbed the stairs to back seats in the stands, were something quite new to the UK contingent.

The generosity and hospitality of all the kindly people we met even exceeded that of the South African Games in Pretoria in 1973 and that was a memorable occasion. All competitors agreed it was a wonderful tournament unlikely ever to be equalled let alone surpassed. Certainly the South African players could not have been more sporting, as I was to be reminded when I met some of them a few years later in the Kodak Masters series - but that is another story.

By topping all four events, a superb feat, South Africa won the Leonard Trophy. England, with 56 points - eight less than the champions - took the silver as second-best team, Australia finished third and, surprisingly but admirably, the USA came in fourth.

Because of our abstention of indoor play throughout the winter of 1975/76 we were not engaged in the Hilton Cup. In our absence the EIBA Junior Vice-President Felix Rothon, who was in charge of the England team as manager, brought into operation one or two psychological ideas. These included team workouts behind locked doors and the side-stepping of all functions and celebrations until after the conclusion of the Hilton Cup series at the Rugby Thornfield Club. He also called for a deep study of player's records and produced a shortlist of potential members of the team. Of the younger challengers for places, he said, 'the selectors did not go out of the way to find younger players. They picked themselves by the high, current performances'. His approach demonstrated yet again that attitudes of players as individuals and members of teams are all important. His leadership, seemingly, proved successful with England preventing Scotland taking the cup for the sixth successive year, England supplanting them as champion country.

With the summer season so close, I gave considerable attention to business but it became ever clearer that I had to make a change. Rustlings of leaves among the trees whispered about the game becoming Open in the near future and I was reminded of that when winning the Welsh Brewers Masters singles at Merthyr Tydfil and receiving a £200 voucher as first prize. In the final Peter Santos, Aberdare, offered tremendous resistance but a 21–20 semi-final against Gethin Jones sharpened my form and I enjoyed one of those matches in which one seems to have the right idea and execution on almost every bowl.

That winning streak stayed with me right through to the EBA Championships where Bill Elliott, John Knight, David Rhys Jones and I won our fours second, third and semi-final matches without recourse to a 21st end, only to slump dismally against Reg Cross, Gordon Turner, Norman Kemp and Ernie Barker of Baldock Town. With the score two-all after three ends we built up a five shots position but failed to protect it with a back bowl. Barker seized his chance, collected two shots and a swing of seven. Realising we were but mortals, he and his colleagues dispensed with their awe and proceeded to demolish us 25–8 in only 19 ends. After Johannesburg, Merthyr Tydfil and the early rounds at Worthing, this proved a disturbingly flat occasion. Playing a well-balanced, skilful match is not as pleasurable when lost as it is when won but it can still be exciting. This one could scarcely have been flatter so far as we were concerned.

Having qualified for the singles, I had to return seven days later and before lunch hovered within half an inch of a first round defeat by Jim Ashman, that ebullient skip from Yorkshire.

Therefter enjoying a less nerve shaking run of three matches in which I felt in good control of the game, I met Tony O'Connell in a semi-final which I shall never forget. Three times laying match when O'Connell delivered last bowls of the end, I watched him produce great saving shots on each occasion. Each time I could do nothing but praise him. Then I set up a fourth match lie, only to move the jack myself in an attempt to frustrate O'Connell producing yet another save. By that stage we had just gone into a fourth hour and on the 33rd end I wavered, so allowing him to deliver two potential scorers. With his fourth bowl he made it three, I failed to save the situation and for the first time in 185 minutes O'Connell took the lead 21–20.

Earlier, he had won from 5–19 against GC Richards of Northants and in the final Bill Hobart reached 10–4 before O'Connell worked the crinkles out of his arthritic neck which had been aggravated by his earlier marathons and osteopathic treatment on the first day. Even with treatment, he was severely handicapped when striving for power. That he won the whole event was yet another chunk of evidence that if a player simply refuses to be beaten, then he cannot be beaten. In sports jargon, the phrase is 'staying with your opponent'. I believe that over the previous eighteen years I had gained a reputation for possessing that quality. It is often more difficult to close down a match when in the lead but what can one do when on three occasions the opponent has only one bowl remaining and each time unleashes a superb shot? Maybe it had been stupid of me to move the jack in a match-winning position but there are limits to the amount of patience and calmness of any man. By and large, though, I did not lose the match through any lack of skill. He won it through his own brilliance.

If there was any lesson to be learned from that semi-final, it is that one must first develop, then acquire via unruffled concentration and absolute inner tranquillity, the self-discipline under any and all situations, so as to control every moment of every shot in all the matches one ever plays. And probably the best way to acquire that quality lies in tuition when suffering hazard training. That is all-out practice when every conceivable annoyance is inflicted on oneself. Inflicted at a moderate pace because learning how to manage difficult positions is an intellectual process. The answer is well known to most educationalists; in learning anything new a person must be relieved from outside hurry and hassle. Coping with difficulties is a skill that can be learned ... if the learning area is small, individually orientated, and those concerned are firm and knowledgeable.

Throughout my life setbacks have always stimulated me in thoughts and the desire to use the lessons learned as steps to further advancement. In that vein, the 1976/77 winter provided just the challenge that sparks my enthusiasm. My name was already engraved six times on the English Indoor Singles trophy although in the last four winters four other champions had captured the title. Surviving the sectional rounds, I eventually began the last four rounds at the March indoor club where a 21–18 win over Mal Hughes, the 1974/75 winner, told me my touch and direction were in good condition. The next two matches, the semi-final and final, took place at Spalding where I beat EM Boyle, Desborough, 21–14 and then waited for the conclusion of the David Cutler, Tony Allcock match which was producing a feast of top quality bowls.

Both these young men were past winners of the National Under-25 Championship and Cutler had the special distinction of being the youngest ever winner of an EBA Championship, the triples with C Yelland and Bill Olver, St Austell, when David was only 18 years and 11 days old. He and Olver had won the EIBA pairs three years earlier.

Both are formidable competitors because of their temperaments and I knew that no matter who won, I would need every scrap of my skill and experience. The extra length of their manoeuvering, with David the winner, gave me half an hour or so extra time to add depth, as it were, to my preparation for the afternoon final.

Pressures of international competition prevented me from competing in the years 1974/5/6 and the mere return after those three years was, in itself, an extra stimulant. Donald Newby, the owner/editor of *World Bowls* magazine, reported the match in some detail, parts of which read 'Cutler played well and showed a fine

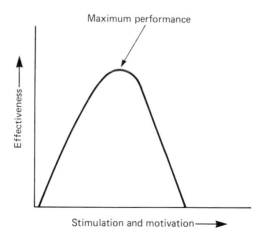

The "inverted U" pattern of performance v motivation and pressure

Maximum performance

Effectiveness

Stimulation and motivation

sense of tactics befitting a being from the Inland Revenue! But Bryant played better, curling in front of the jack, beside the jack, behind the jack and blasting in the occasional rocket. Everything Cutler did, Bryant did better' ... 'Bryant gave the impression that he intended to let nothing stop him from winning his 13th national singles title' (six EBA, seven EIBA).

Victory qualified me for the British Isles Indoor Championships at Cardiff where Leon Stanfield, the Welsh champion, never got into our semi-final despite vociferous support from his lusty local fans.

There is for each individual an optimum balance between relaxation and determination to win. It can be shown graphically in the shape of an inverted 'U'. Too low on the left, upper side of the 'U' shows a need for greater bolstering and that poses no great problems. However, too much effort or external motivation pushes the point over that inverted 'U' and down the other side. That is the situation we have all suffered; the harder you try, the worse you seem to play.

That seemed the situation with Leon and he collected only seven shots. And so to Andrew Prentice, a 62-year-old Scottish colliery manager, who suffered no supporter contingents to push him over the 'ideal performance state' of that inverted 'U'. A dour man, he was also a hard man to beat. We played on rink two at Cardiff and it is not the easiest stretch of green in any of the major indoor stadiums. This resulted in me taking many walks up to the head for close surveys of situations. I also tended to take the forehand side when bowling away from the stand. Sometimes I stepped off the green after examining the head. After a while I realised that Andrew was copying just about all I did.

In a way, it was quite flattering and when the score reached 10-all it seemed he was in with a chance. Then I scored a two and then, after a measure, another two which pressurised him and helped me to a 20–10 lead.

No quitting by Andrew. Scoring a single, he immediately switched to short jacks before I scored a single to win 21–14.

In between the earlier rounds I slipped away for a few days to Teesside where a plethora of 'first to score 15' matches tightened up my concentration considerably. In good form, I won the title for the fourth year in succession.

During 1977 my wish to represent England in the 1978 Commonwealth Games scheduled for Edmonton motivated me to make considerable efforts in maintaining high standards of performance in the EBA Championships which begin, of course, with the various counties championships; Somerset in my case.

Still striving for county perfection by qualifying for all four EBA Championship events. I managed two, the triples and the singles. The former was with John Knight leading and my staunch friend, David Rhys Jones at number two. Apart from a close third round contest with J Davey, B Bick and JJ Burns of Melcombe Regis, 17–15, we cruised fairly comfortably into the final with an overall 95 shots to 52 over five rounds. Actually, the tightest bowling came in the semi-final in which we beat Peter Robinson, Alan Johnson and Ken Thompson, Haxby 18–8. An average of roughly 1.5 shots per end suggests tight clusters of bowls each end and that was the case. Happily for us, we generally seemed to produce the one shot that nestled an inch or so nearer to the jack. On the whole, the score did scant justice to the losers. Our final win over Eric Fricker, Brian Lee and Norman Chalk was more comfortable.

Though by 1977 I had learned to concentrate my mind fully on what I am seeking, on or off the green, my thoughts dwelt often on Jock Munro, that world famous greenkeeper of Beach House Park. He is no mean bowler himself and, consequently, along with Brian Pryce and Eric Parsons (the former Chelsea winger) he qualified via the Sussex Championships and then skipped his men to the fourth round before losing to the Haxby trio.

Jock's greenkeeping skills are well known and I have spent many hours listening to his expositions on greens and have become an admiring friend. This time I was amazed by his stamina and I followed him, round by round, with sincere interest. How good it would have been to have enjoyed a semi-final contest. It would certainly have been remarkable when one considers Jock's forty-eight hours from Wednesday evening to Friday evening.

Beginning with his customary evening session attending to the four Beach House greens, he was back attending them at 6.30 a.m. the following morning, prior to taking his men on to green 'A' for their first round match at 10 a.m. Victory entailed another 200 minutes or so action, again successful, followed by a quick change into working clothes for the evening shift on the greens. Friday found him back on them at 6.30 a.m. as a prelude to another six hours or more play. I've seen bowlers tired after four rounds of matches in the EBA Championships but Jock kept

Jock Munro, the famous Worthing greenkeeper, is also a formidable player who has qualified for the 'Nationals' on several occasions.

going. That he skipped his men so far and then to compete so tenaciously until the end proved him to be a superman. It was also an emphatic reminder that he was a bowler who knows from personal experience just what class of green is needed at championship levels of play.

Winning my first round of singles, I found myself opposing a good friend, Harry Taylor. A member of the 1974 Commonwealth Games team, he and I had spent many hours practising together and I had been impressed by his skill and analytical attitude. This was probably helped by his professional environment as a University lecturer.

Let me emphasise how strongly I advocate 'casing' my opponents whenever possible before matches. I look for their technical proficiency, general approach, favourite and weakest shots, the bowls they use and the way they track on the green.

Taylor is in complete accord with this and in our second round meeting he put it to good use. According to *World Bowls*, he decided he was unlikely to beat, with normal tactics, a man who had won the event so often before. So he set out with a plan to destroy my fluency with variations of length when in control of the jack, 'I kept moving the mat a few inches and slightly changing the length of the jack,' he revealed later.

Now, one of the additional virtues of a pre-planned match strategy is that one starts with a positive idea which can combat and
overcome nervousness simply because the mind is fully occupied
attending to specific aspects of the game. It is fairly well known
that the human brain can only cope properly with one thing at a
time so the chances of nervousness taking control are diminished.
In turn, this supports confidence and on that basis alone I consider
that even a bad plan can be more helpful for victory than no plan
at all. This is also magnified by the way pre-planning simplifies
use of that proven assistant, mental rehearsal; one can sit in an
armchair prior to the match and develop a vivid series of mental
pictures showing with great clarity just how the match will be
controlled and played. Do not think that mental rehearsal is a
lazy man's tool. Developing and sustaining the depth of sharply
focused concentration is even harder work than a similar time
spent delivering bowls on a green. As with all aids to improvement, it is the quality of one's practice and not the quantity that
brings about the greater progress.

How much Taylor's play on the day was brought about by the
actual tactics and how much through inner confidence bred by the
plan cannot be measured. Factually, I scored only on six ends of
the twenty we contested, those six yielding two fours, two threes,
a two and a solitary single.

Taylor went on to the semi-final where he lost to the ultimate
champion, Chris Ward, 21–18. Ward demonstrated one of the
skills learned in the Federation code by holding Taylor to singles
and then pushing in threes himself, a good illustration of the value
of draw shots.

- There's big money at stake. Forget about it, concentrate on
  playing the very best you can and, paradoxically, you will
  win more often.
- Work out a flexible match plan well before you start to play.
- Over-motivation hampers skills so develop your personally
  best relaxation versus will-to-win mental balance and make it
  work for you.
- Live completely in the 'now'. Total concentration on each
  second prohibits negative thoughts and eases tension.
- Stay calm when fortune seems against you, so preventing
  your opponent from winning the next end as well as the one

that has just finished. Forget about feeling sorry for yourself; your turn will come.

● If the crowd is noisy and partisan, concentrate on your breathing and stay calm. On no account be tempted to risk an 'I'll show you how super-shot'. That's asking for defeat.

● No matter how long the match, believe you can keep trying longer than your opponent, stay unwaveringly patient and hang on until he breaks down.

CHAPTER ELEVEN

Although outdoor teams are selected by the EBA, it is reasonable to believe that they do pay some attention to the EIBA. The 1977 National Championships had yielded me one title, the triples, and a quarter-final place in the singles. Having won the Commonwealth Games singles in 1962, 1970 and 1974, I hoped the EBA would again choose me for singles in the 1978 Commonwealth Games scheduled for Edmonton.

However, inevitably I suffered a little uneasiness until the team was chosen soon after the start of the 1977/78 winter, indoor season. Seven men plus a manager, Bob Stenhouse, were chosen, namely Bill Irish, Charlie Burch, Chris Ward, Jim Ashman, Mal Hughes, Bob Robertson and myself. All were world class bowlers and I knew also that they were good companions. Two days after receiving his invitation from the EBA Chris broke his arm when, as a goalkeeper, he spectacularly saved a penalty. If anyone panicked, it wasn't Chris, for two days later he represented Norfolk in a Liberty Cup match; he broke his left arm and had to bowl with it in plaster.

It was an extremely sad winter for me because of my father's illness. Nevertheless, I entered the EIBA singles, working my way through the preliminary rounds. The crisis arose a couple of days before the seventh and eighth rounds at Atherley; my father undergoing major surgery before going into intensive care. Phoning on the morning I planned to leave, the hospital advised that I withdraw and of course, with a heavy heart, I did. He died a week later, a wonderful man none of us close to him will ever forget. If there can be any contentment at such times, mine was the vivid memories of his friendship and our abundance of happy, tranquil hours spent together on the bowling green; never had the 1969 British Isles Fours Championship trophy seemed more precious.

In those first four months of 1978 there was still a mass to be done. On January 1st I began an intensive campaign of dieting, training and yoga to melt away 18lbs of superfluous fat by the time the Commonwealth Games at Edmonton began. As much as losing weight, I realised my need for improved flexibility of my knees, vital to accurate, consistent delivery. We all knew far in advance that the Edmonton greens would be as heavy as those we suffered in the 1976 games at Edinburgh. Heavy greens take heavy toll of one's stamina, strength and, consequently, enjoyment. To magnify all this, there was the prospect of three matches each day. Singles in that class of play average around two hours per match, or six hours or more each day walking around the green. That is an awful lot of time, even for a young, well-trained athlete, to be on one's feet.

During the average single a player will walk or run a minimum of two and a half miles and pick up and propel some 30 yards,

The EBA Triples champions of 1977. *Left to right* David Rhys Jones, David Bryant and John Knight.

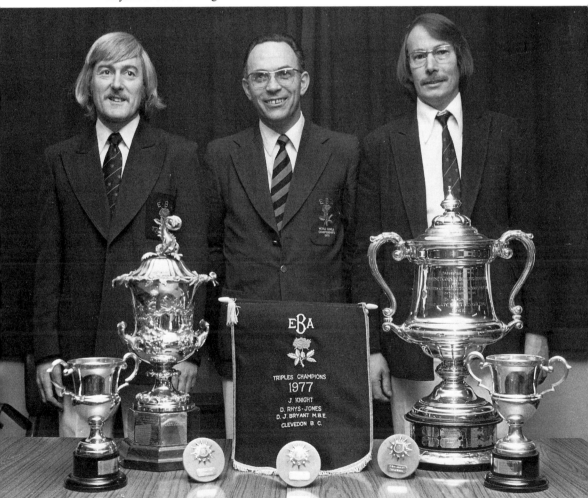

336lbs of composition. In the EBA Championship one contests three singles a day, making a grand total of seven and a half miles of walking and the shifting of over half a tonne of composition. Bowls like that is hard work and tiring. When tiredness creeps in, skill seeps out and that sets up all kinds of mental anguish. The game may look simple from the bank. It takes on another character when experienced on the green against a determined competitor. However, the other side of that coin is that most competitive bowlers enter tournaments to test and challenge their capabilities and skills. Added together, those two sides provide something of a signpost to good, fulfilled health.

It was this kind of reasoning that enticed the EIBA selectors to choose an England Hilton Cup team of men who averaged only 38 years of age. Six years earlier the average age had been 58. The object, of course, was to overthrow Scotland, monopolists of the Hilton Cup for six of the previous seven years. What a match it turned out to be. Let me use statistics to show just how close it actually was.

In Hilton Cup matches six rinks are used, with four men for each team. Ignoring replayed ends and those which occasionally involve only 15 of the 16 bowls that are delivered on each end, the match will consist of six individual clashes in which 336 bowls will be delivered, two by each man on the rink. Six rinks make a total of 2,016 bowls, 1,008 by each team.

I think that, logically, one would expect most matches to be decided long before those last 16 bowls came into the count. Actually, something like 10 per cent of matches lie in the balance until the last one or two of that gigantic 2,016 bowls are delivered. The Scotland v England match came on the first day of the series and I finished in one of those nerve-shattering – to players and spectators alike – situations. I was skipping against Willie McQueen and when we went into the final end Scotland were leading by three shots overall. When my turn to deliver came, my three team-mates had established two shots. With two bowls in hand and the head facing me, I felt confident of drawing that vital third shot.

Bowling first, McQueen failed and then with his last bowl of the match produced a superb drawing shot. There seemed no way of disturbing it and staying in the count. The only thing to do was drive and scatter everything but my bowl went through, Scotland scraped home 121–118 and that set them up for beating Ireland

and Wales and so they retained the Hilton Cup.

That year, 1978, coincided with the 75th birthday of the English Bowling Association and as part of the celebrations Kodak signed a five year contract to promote their new famous International Masters Tournament to which they would invite eight men judged to be the crème de la crème of the world's top competitors. Apart from me, the line up was David McGill, Willie Watson, Ireland; John Russell Evans, Wales; Bob Middleton, Australia; Dick Folkins, USA; John Malcolm, New Zealand and Bill Moseley, South Africa.

Part of the plan involved a pairs event staged at seven different venues scattered around England. Each man partnered all the others twice, once as a lead, once as a skip and the scoring system made it possible for any player to obtain the highest number of points, thus to be identified as the Pairs Master player. The singles event was held back for Beach House Park, Worthing.

To spread popularity as well as placate viewers who felt robbed by the small number of hours of TV bowls, especially when compared with the saturation coverage of many sports events, BBC2 produced a series of six sessions, concluding with the programme that identified the top 'Master'. What a grand bunch of people they all turned out to be: players, administrators, officials, everyone who travelled the country in a luxurious motor coach. I love talking bowls and those rides plus the many meals and pints we enjoyed taught me a remarkable number of new ideas and stretched my mind to its limits.

The pairs event revealed just how good a player Bill Moseley was. Beginning with a defeat, he lost again on his fourth match and then won eight in succession before reacting and losing the last two. This gave him ten wins out of 14 matches and left him 31 shots ahead of McGill and me, both of us with 140 shots. The rules defined that there were 10 points for a win plus a point for every shot up in each game and, in the case of equal ties, the winner of the greater number of games took the higher position. Both Moseley and I had ten wins to our credit and McGill only eight. So Moseley's greater shots score put him ahead of me, and my two wins more than McGill won me second place, putting him in third.

Those positions embraced both leading and skipping. As a lead Moseley scored 110 from six wins, I scored 65 from five wins and McGill scored 73 from three wins. As skips the figures were:

Four formidable competitors in the Kodak Masters. *Above left to right* David McGill, Barry Salter, *below left to right* Bill Moseley and Russell Evans.

Moseley 61 from four wins, Bryant 75 from five wins and McGill 67 from five wins.

On these statistics Moseley finished first as a lead but in skipping none of us headed the scores. That honour went to Russell Evans who topped my 75 by one shot, his 76 points coming from only four wins. Playing as lead to Evans, we met Willie Watson (Ireland), and Moseley and felt we had integrated impressively in beating them 20–17. At that time of my career many critics wrote or spoke that I was a better lead than skip. The figures supported my faith in myself as a better skip than lead.

Following our whistle stops around England, the best part of a week at Worthing came as a welcome break. We were allowed a day for practice and then came the matches themselves. The eight participants were divided into two groups of four in which all played all, the first and second going forward to the semi-finals. In my group I faced Watson, Malcolm and Moseley. Middleton, McGill, Folkins and Evans were in the other group. Prior to the start Donald Newby polled all the competitors, now also a gang of close friends, on who they thought would win the Masters. Almost to a man, they went for me. I was flattered and, in a practical way, pleased because such a belief sent me on to the green with a slight psychological advantage. At that world level even the tiniest advantage is useful.

Home officials were less confident. Examples: Eric Crosbie (Chairman of the sub-committee) 'when it comes to the singles at Worthing David Bryant will be supreme.' Hylton Armstrong, England team manager, and Bob Jack, the finance officer: both went for McGill in the pairs and Bill Moseley for the singles. Gerald Scott, tournament manager: 'I have the idea Bill Moseley will take some beating.' Chris Mills, publicity manager: 'Bill Moseley is the "dark horse" for the title.' Ken Drury, general factotum: 'McGill or Moseley'. Chris Ward, the reigning England national champion: 'when David gets them down to Worthing he will beat them all.' Happily for me, Chris was right.

My wins and scores were: Watson 21–18; Malcolm 21–11; Moseley 21–19; McGill 21–14; Folkins 21–12. The Moseley contest stretched me to my limits as he seemed safely home when leading 19–10. Defeat would not have stopped my place in the last two rounds but personal pride of performance generated immense will to win.

Moseley favours the South African semi-fixed delivery which

begins with an accurate placement on the mat of the right foot in line with the intended line of delivery. That position settled, the left foot is then placed partly down the delivery line parallel to the right. This stance ensures a higher percentage of well-grassed deliveries. As the bowl is delivered, the left foot moves forward to complete the step and a good follow through is possible because the stance is semi- not totally fixed.

Moseley continued to bowl accurately and with good control of length. Gathering in those last ten points was probably the best performance of my bowling life. With near ferocious awareness and concentration firing me with intense will-to-win, I began my climb back; in fact, I scored ten points in succession to win and head my section.

The semi-finals and final were less traumatic, with wins over David McGill 21–14 and Dick Folkins 21–12 after he had, somewhat surprisingly, eliminated Moseley 21–17.

The Masters left me match tight for the Somerset singles, the Middleton Cup matches and the British Isles Team Championship at Uddingston, near Glasgow, one month later. Alas, our hopes were dashed in the opening match of the three days, England versus Wales. As a whole, the new-look English team lacked lustre and were rich in inhibitions. Winning on three of the five rinks, we lost by only two on the fourth. The defeat overall came from the heavy deficit on the fifth rink but I believe the selectors learned from an experimental but understandable fielding of a four of whom three were new internationals. It is quite a mental strain playing one's first ever game for England. A mixture of two established and two new representatives might well have minimised the tension for the newcomers and so won us that vital rink.

The internationals had hardly finished, it seemed, when we found ourselves on the plane for Canada and the XI Commonwealth Games at Edmonton. I had begun my training on January 1st, believing that one can never begin one's preparation for a major task too soon. Mine was, I think, somewhat special because Precious McKenzie, the amazing, New Zealand weight-lifter and I had both won gold medals in our events three times running in the Commonwealth Games. I knew without being told that he hoped to beat me in our unique race to become the first man ever to win his event in four consecutive Games. There was no question of me wishing for him to lose. Sport should be above such petty jealousy and I was totally sincere when I wished him good luck.

Luck, in fact, enabled him to beat me in that race because the weight-lifting event took place one week ahead of the bowls singles. In the end we both won and so share a record of which we are both proud. I must confess that sometimes when I am alone I console myself for being unable to win my medal before him with the thought that I do have a fifth at home, the Fours Championship at Perth in 1962.

Undoubtedly Precious trained and planned just as meticulously as I but our techniques differ greatly – though not our attitudes and mental discipline.

Mainly, in seeking for suppleness I must also retain physical strength. And if any reader believes, deep down, that bowls is really an old man's game, please ponder on the workload that got me through. There were 16 competitors which meant playing 15 matches. Each match varied in duration but one and a half hours is a fair average, as is 20 ends per match. That means delivering around 1,200 bowls a distance exceeding 20 miles in total. Each bowl weighs three and a half pounds and to move that weight on a green timed, at best, 11 seconds and all too frequently nine or so, I can guarantee that one must either be strong, supple, sensitive of touch and sound in stamina or else written off among the players low down the league table.

A strictly adhered to diet of fruit and vegetables and of sliding quietly out of bed to put in an hour's yoga on the bedside rug

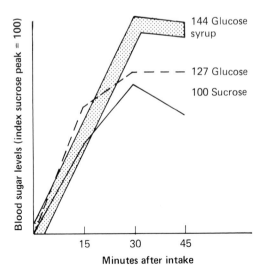

The figure shows the superiority of glucose syrup as a source of blood sugar, compared to both glucose and sucrose.
    Mean rise in blood sugar levels after taking glucose syrup, glucose, and sucrose by mouth.

Long matches or strong pressure produces tiredness, even though few bowlers realise this tiredness. Its most dangerous effect is on a special factor of concentration, awareness. In the case of bowls, this means assessing a head and not realising its implications; that would not happen if you were fresh.
Glucose syrup has been proven its superiority to glucose and sucrose in restoring blood sugar levels and, thus, mental awareness.

(After Butterfield et al (1964) by permission)

produced the required target; the shedding of 18 pounds and a return to the body tone which I find vital.

Forewarned is forearmed and I had discovered almost as soon as my selection was confirmed that we would indeed be playing on heavy greens, two of which had only been down a couple of years or so. Thinking conservatively, I planned for a nine second pace in the mornings, rising to ten or so after a little sun had dried out the overnight moisture.

It sounded very much like Edinburgh all over again and there I had won the event using bowls I had subsequently sold to a friend, Len Snell. A good friend, as I discovered when I asked him if I might borrow them for Edmonton; he was, clearly, greatly pleased ... and more so when they arrived back in his possession.

My campaign began well, David McGill providing me with my third successive 21–7 win. It could have ruined him for the rest of the event but David is a really tough competitor and at one stage he seemed a possible silver medallist. This chance fell away and David finished in fifth place.

My momentum continued smoothly except for a defeat by Arthur McKernan, a dangerous player with the disturbing habit of sending down two loose bowls and then coming up with a real killer. However, there were no ill effects and with one match remaining I was in the same position as when I played Snowy Walker in the last match of the inaugural World Championships at Kyeemagh; so far as the outcome was concerned, it did not matter whether I won or lost. My position was secure.

At Edmonton my last opponent was the formidable Welshman Russell Evans. Unquestionably a world class bowler, he is also a close friend of many years standing. This in no way changes my attitude when we meet in competitions – and we do so fairly frequently – which is to honour him and the game of bowls by striving with all my skill and experience to win.

However, the mental effort in winning 13 out of 14 highly contested matches, with a supreme honour and prize at the end, is immensely taxing. Pride alone made me wish to win but from my position of security my maximum 'bite' may well have been a little less fierce than in matches which were far from 'dead' so far as coming out on top was concerned.

Unfortunately for Kerry Clark, the popular New Zealander, my defeat by Evans meant he scored two more points than Clark ... and Clark had a better shots for and against record. So Evans

Kerry Clark, New Zealand, who dropped to fourth place
to Russell Evans, Wales, after Evans beat me in his final
match.

took the silver medal while Clark had to be satisfied with fourth
place. Inevitably, almost, the next day brought forth accusations
of the British Isles sticking together and of me losing on purpose
so that Evans would win the silver medal.

A similar situation arose in the 1976 World Championships
when South Africa's Doug Watson was safely 'with gold' when
we met in the closing match. My affinity with Watson was not on
the same level as mine with Evans but I tried with everything I
had to win. In the first case I was not mentally exhausted while
against Evans I was worn out with the strain of so many wins on
greens which could scarcely have been worse for my game. The
press may have had a go at me but in my heart I believe Clark
was fully aware of the situation so that his disappointment was
not due to a belief that I had 'tanked' my match with Evans.

So despite that fourth gold medal for Commonwealth Games

bowls singles, I did not find any great wish to live in Canada flooding my heart and brain. Unlike my previous trips to Perth and Christchurch, the friendly crowds at the Village gates were missing and although the Canadians were enthusiastic about the Games, it was somehow different. The Rockies proved to be breathtakingly beautiful but one's emotions need also to be awoken by people and that, sadly, never arose.

My return to Bristol soon banished all that because within two days Ruth, Jacqueline, Carole and I were immersed in furniture, great boxes of crockery, cutlery and all the other things one accumulates in a home one is leaving. Thankfully, we were on our way back to our real roots in tranquil Clevedon twelve miles away. What a rush that was, with the EBA National Singles Championship looming within a day or two.

There was added excitement with the sponsorship of Embassy cigarettes for Indoor World Championships entering the game in the February of 1979. The Monklands Club in Coatbridge was specified as the venue and the Embassy contract covered five years. The signs of yet more things to come?

Rushing home from an ultra-slow green on which I had used borrowed bowls, to moving house and then on to Worthing for the National Singles Championship and 13 to 14 seconds greens hardly demonstrated text book preparation. However, one occasionally has to cope with such upheavals and 40 years or so of continually applied self-discipline and the development of tranquillity when under stressful conditions stood me in good stead. And there was one immense plus. As a family, we Bryants were now back home. It was a pretty good feeling.

The intensity of the summer season had precluded me from reaching the National Championships in more than one event, the singles, and even that had seemed extremely unlikely. However, I did qualify so, once again, the pressure was on, primarily from self pride. I had won at Edmonton and, clearly, pride motivated my attempt to capture the EBA Singles Championship for the seventh time. My start was promising, four rounds costing only 27 shots against my 84, an imposing three to one ratio.

That took me to the semi-finals where I met David Brown, a competent left hander whose accuracy and consistency caused me considerable trouble. However, my own control slightly bettered his, forcing him into situations where his draw shots and yard ons did not appear suitable and left only the drive as a viable defence.

Signing autographs is one of the routine tasks at Worthing, be it during the
Masters Tournament, the Worthing Open or the National Championships.

This is, of course, a basic tactic: use your own best shots to attack your opponent's weaknesses. His own words after the match justified my play. 'I'm not really an expert with the firing shot', Brown admitted, 'I'm really a draw bowler and the yard on is my story. I figured David's shots were too close and my only chance was to burn the end and do better on the replay. I guess I'll have to practise my firing shot.'

Thus I reached the final for the loss of 43 shots and faced a match against one of my Somerset friends, Charlie Burch, who had also participated in the Edmonton Commonwealth Games. Charlie was then 58 years old and he had conceded 87 shots. Thus his matches must have taken something over 50 per cent longer than mine. Apart from any physical tiredness, those struggles should have sapped his mental energy.

In actuality, they seemed to have honed his approach and skills to a new high. In our only previous meeting he had won and that must have supported his natural ability to remain tranquil whatever the situation. Calm and unhurried, he shrewdly varied the jack between 30 and 38 yards from the mat and stuck resolutely to finesses. Using the draw shot as the foundation, he adorned this with gentle jack trailers, promotions and occasional in-offs that would have done credit to Steve Davis on a snooker table.

On the day, his bowls were taking about nine inches more land than mine and I simply could not find the line for the jack at all – shades of the 1972 World Championships on the same green. I tried the backhand but the way my bowls stuck out showed me that was no good.

Charlie went out wider and still came in so perhaps I should have given the backhand another run but I couldn't afford to change hands. I was giving too many shots away.

After a long run I managed to get the jack and I promptly moved the mat well up the rink. I got it with a two, promptly scored another two and then lay three shots; things were looking rosier. But there lies the reality of the game. One can be sitting pretty when, wham, the opponent produces a devastating shot that changes the position immediately.

His destroyer was a dead draw on the forehand, his bowl winkling a way through mine to score a devastating single. I am used to dominating the play, win or lose. From that shot onwards Charlie controlled the play and I never looked like breaking it. He went on to win 21–11 and so was king for a day. A day unique in the National Singles; not only were the finalists both from Somerset but the EBA President of the year, Roland Moore, was from the same county and tradition always has it that the reigning EBA President marks the final.

What a day. Naturally I was deeply disappointed in defeat but that failed to destroy my warmth that two such fine gentlemen had reached a high that will remain ever engraved in their memories. Typically, Charlie took over the microphone to give thanks for all the 630 or so competitors in the Nationals and then said modestly, 'Despite this win, David remains the greatest singles player in the world and it is a thrill to have beaten him. I never thought I could ever win this title but I've always had a go at it. I got to the quarter-finals in 1971 and the semi-finals in 1974.'

Someone once pontificated 'nice guys come in second'. That match is but one of many that convinces me of its stupidity. As in so many contests of that class, it needs a nice guy to admire the best in his opponent, to acknowledge his finest shots and, by retaining tranquillity through absolute absence of fear or jealousy, produce even better shots than a worthy adversary.

One saying is attributed to a famous American football coach, Vince Lombardi, 'Winning is not important. It is everything.' I had heard it and, somehow, had never quite related it to an outstanding coach. Not until 1982 did I learn what he actually said, the evidence coming from his best friend, advocate and lawyer. A famous sportsman himself, Lawrence Krieger was there and he asserts that the actual words were 'Winning is not important. Winning *with honour* is everything.'

Two words but they turn the whole meaning through 180 degrees and, to me anyway, explain why the said Mr Lombardi was a great coach.

This attitude is beautifully communicated by Sir Henry Newbolt in, surely, an immortal eight lines of poetry:

> 'To set the cause above renown,
> To love the game beyond the prize,
> To honour, while you strike him down,
> The foe that comes with fearless eyes;
> To count the life of battle good,
> And dear the land that gave you birth,
> And dearer yet the brotherhood,
> That binds the brave of all the earth.'

It is difficult to tell but maybe that August day in 1978 saw the last days of belief in playing bowls and winning against the best there is. They can beat you or, alternately, feed you the crumbs which give you growth. From 1957 on to 1962 and then through to 1978 my attitude, self-discipline and respect for my fellow players had steadily grown like a mental flower. It was soon to withstand the most radical changes in the entire history of the game.

- Bowls championships are won on the practice green and in your mind. So begin your preparation for any special event six months in advance.
- Media reports can often cause you hurt and worry. Stop reading the papers when in a tournament; save them until it is over and then read what they write.
- 'Nice guys do win'; they can admire an opponent's good shot ... and use it as the inspiration for a better one.

CHAPER TWELVE

It began with the English Indoor Bowls Association who had always abided by the laws of the game as specified by the International Bowling Board. However, the growth of the indoor game produced a few situations which revealed a necessity to draw up laws more suitable to indoor games. For example, it had been discovered that jacks conforming to IBB laws moved far too easily on impact because of the faster running pace of indoor surfaces. So trials were carried out which led to the adoption of jacks twice the weight of those used outdoors.

In studying the laws the EIBA took special notice of IBB by-law 1, paragraph (c) where they read 'In all cases where the value of prizes in Championships, Tournaments or other competitions is stated in terms of money, the responsible authorities shall award prizes in kind and not in cash ...'

The wording of that sentence, in their opinion, allowed Premium Bonds to be 'in kind' and so it became permissible to give them as prizes. Since Premium Bonds received one day could easily be converted into cash the next, bowls was now an Open game in all but name. With the start of the 1980/81 winter all pretences were discarded and the indoor game in England joined golf, tennis and many other sporting activities in a freedom that allows amateurs and professionals to compete against one another. However, the rules banish even those categories and instead call everyone simply 'players'.

Once again living within five minutes of the Clevedon Club undoubtedly helped my bowling and my early matches in the EIBA National Singles nurtured the confidence that took me right through to the final. In it I beat Alan Windsor 21–13 after Mick Gallagher, who had put me out of the EBA singles once in the past, threatened to pull off an encore in the quarter-finals. Intense concentration and a couple of good shots in the last end carried me through 21–20.

That win qualified me for the British Isles Championships in Scotland in March and on the 13th I met John Watson, the brilliant young Scottish champion. He had beaten me in two previous encounters and he produced some threatening form in the early ends. Then, as his supporters began thinking of a third win, I found my touch and some of my best drawing to the jack for a long time took me from 9–8 to 21–14 and a final with John Greer, Ireland. He had decimated George Hindmarsh, Wales, 21–4 in his semi-final and when he raced to 7–0 against me I could sense the murmurings.

Earlier I stressed the importance of patience and calmness when everything is going right for an opponent. Years of self-discipline, yet again, enabled me to put the theory into practice and he had to work very hard for that lead. A two broke his run and another narrowed the score gap. My control and accuracy took over and I followed by scoring a further 17 shots while holding him to three for a 21–10 win, so getting my name on the John Coles trophy for the fourth time in thirteen years.

The British Isles Championships and the International Team Championships were staged at the magnificent Aberdeen Stadium that year and I felt in good form and control as winning skip in the matches against Wales and Ireland and my hopes for the championship deciding match against Scotland were high.

Tom Lang was the opposing skip and his chances seemed to be reduced when two of his players were dropped and substitutes put in. Far from seeming like players at sea, they clicked from the start and were leading 10–3 after ten ends. We cut this down to 15–18 by the end but how I wished I could have scraped one or, better, two more shots because Scotland made good a 21 shots deficit to beat us 109–108 and so won the Hilton Cup for the third year running. Considering that we had only scraped home against Ireland by one shot, we could scarcely feel hard done by. Yes indeed, those matches on consecutive days were vivid reminders that in six rinks match play one careless loss of a single or a two can, and all too often does, change the whole outcome of the match and possibly the entire championship.

Before the English and British Isles Championships were played I passed another milestone by winning the inaugural Embassy World Indoor Singles Championship at the Coatbridge Club, Monklands from January 10th to 14th. Staged by the Imperial Tobacco Company, the event met with considerable criticism because the entries were by invitation. Sanction was given only on the condition of a more open entry in succeeding years. Nevertheless, the 1979 line-up was something of a who's who in bowls.

In line with the general pattern of such major events, the

knock-out format was scrapped in favour of two divisions in which all played all, the winners and runners-up going through to the semi-finals. One section comprised of Gwyn Evans of Ton Pentre, the Welsh indoor champion; Jim Blake, who finished third; George Alley, the New Zealand champion; Bruce Matheson, Canadian champion for the previous five years; and Eric Liddell, Hong Kong and current holder of a World Championship gold medal for pairs.

In my section the challengers were Bill Farrell, the USA champion; Tony Dunton, the EIBA singles champion; Errol Bungey, holder of five Australian championships; and Jim Donnelly, Ireland, who might well have beaten me in the final had I not motivated myself to topmost form in the critical stages of that nerve-testing match.

My training in self-discipline paid a handsome dividend in the semi-finals because Jim Blake, inevitably cheered by the Scottish crowd for every good shot ... and some not so good ... stayed right with me until 17-all. Here my learned ability to remain inwardly calm despite the immense tension of such a match, enabled me to produce one of the best fours of my career ... and possibly the most welcome.

The final was even more memorable. A fortnight earlier I had failed to reach the last sixteen in the annual Teesside Masters and, to some degree, I had been fortunate here to scrape through my section and qualify for the final stages. However, we all know about the legendary rising of war horses to the smell of battle and I had long realised that my most effective attitudes to high level competition came from my intense enjoyment of pitting my skills against those of noble opponents. This, added to the challenge of a new World Championship, set the adrenalin flowing and I approached that final with considerable expectation, the more so because I had beaten Donnelly 21–18 in our sectional match.

Donnelly had shown a great feeling for the rink chosen for television transmissions and he matched me bowl for bowl through 24 ends and for almost two and a half hours.

The majority of the capacity crowd that witnessed the 19th end acclaimed it as the best they had ever seen. Having thought about it frequently since, I can only attribute it to the wonderful spirit in which the game was played – namely two players on top form who had a high respect for one another in every way, both thoroughly enjoying their match. Perhaps I enjoyed it a little more because my 21–14 win made me the first Indoor World Champion.

Soon after in a television interview, Steve Davis made the following statement: 'I cannot play when I am hating anybody. I can only play at my best when I respect the other player.' I wholeheartedly endorse those words. A professional in any sport has to remain cool and unemotional in the application of his skills. Whilst any surge of incentive at a critical period can be stimulating, when it has to be sustained over a long period it can be draining and instrumental in disastrous results. A momentary stimulant makes champions but no player can produce near miraculous shots end after end. These outstanding achievements are peaks during a game which win matches.

The many different greens, indoor surfaces and countries I had sampled over the previous years, often when contesting 'blue riband' events, had magnified my long-standing wish to design or help design and produce a bowl that I could use with full confidence under any conditions. There had been a time when I possessed three sets of bowls and would choose the set I considered would suit me best under the conditions I was about to meet. I understand that in the crown green game some professionals own as many as twelve different sets. Even when I thought about borrowing my old set for the Edmonton event, I had the feeling that, really, I should be able to find a general purpose, satisfactory set that I could use at all times. That day was to come but there were other obstacles to overcome before my wish was fulfilled early in 1983.

Though the first four months of 1979 kept me busily engaged with indoor events, my mind strayed from time to time to Frankston where the next World Championships were scheduled from January 16th to February 2nd 1980. The good news revealed that twenty-one countries would be competing but the bad news was that the Australian Government had ordained 'South Africa, Rhodesia and Transkei must not be accepted.' That saddened me because I had made many friends among bowlers from the first two of those countries, several of them at world class standard. We also learned that our hotel would be some twenty-four miles from the venue – but that the road to it was superbly beautiful.

Happier news came with the statement that Bill Moseley was being invited for the Kodak Masters of 1979. Other participants in this event, all sharing my joy about Bill, were Dick Folkins, USA, the runner-up; David McGill Jnr, Scotland; Russell Evans,

The first Indoor World Championship had its less serious moments, especially when the snow came down. Some competitors had never seen it before. *Left to right* Bill Farrell, Jim Blake, Errol Bungey and me.

Wales. Barry Salter, the Australian who came near to winning the 1972 World Championship Singles, would be renewing his skills on the Worthing championship green and Willie Murray was nominated by Ireland. Phil Skoglund played for New Zealand.

The newly adopted policy of giving Premium Bonds as prizes was surely responsible for forcing the game into rapid adoption of Open bowls and that direction quickly showed in a number of ways. In this case Kodak increased their cash input from their £8,000 for the inaugural Masters in 1978 to £28,700 for 1979. The BBC's contribution rose from £4,000 to £4,700. They were onto a good thing, it seems, because the viewer ratings for the BBC2 'Jack High' programme, all based on the Masters, produced a staggeringly large audience.

The growth of bowls as a spectator sport was demonstrated over the Easter weekend when I finally managed to win the Dundee Masters from a prestigious field of thirty-two contestants from the British Isles. Over 1,000 enthusiasts packed into the stadium for my final against John Summers from Edinburgh. As at Teesside, matches are cut down to 15 up and that can be traumatically short. John looked dangerous when leading 13–12 but, as I have written earlier, 'having been there' is a tremendous asset in such situations. Possibly part of his mind was telling him that he was on the verge of a major triumph. My attitude was one of survival, of isolating each delivery from others past and future, and mustering confidence in my proven ability to retain tranquillity and patience in such crises.

I also had the knowledge, acquired through long years of disciplined work, that technically my delivery technique could scarcely be bettered. All this allowed me to focus 100 per cent of my mental and physical strength on each bowl I delivered and so, raising my game at the crucial stage, I was the first to reach 21.

Suffolk's Sole Bay Indoor Club brought the indoor season to a varied and exciting finish by repeating the Continental Week of 1978 but on a larger scale. BDNW, the firm of four which included me, promoted and directed operations and a great number of people attended but perhaps we were ahead of the times because the enormous amount of work that we and many others put in failed to increase British exports in the way we had hoped.

As in 1978, the Kodak Masters began in May with the eight participants making a whistle stop tour of the UK to show regional bowlers what world class means. In 1978 the eight interchanged partners whilst competing against one another. This time the competition was supplied by the best bowlers in each region in turn. Close on thirty English internationals provided some really tough opposition. Each of us contested ten matches, McGill, Skoglund and Moseley finishing one, two and three.

The singles were staged at Worthing where the old 'A beats B, B beats C, C beats A' conundrum could have rated any one of the eight men the winner . . . or the loser. Consider: Skoglund beat Stansbury who defeated Folkins who avenged 1978 against Bryant who nosed out Moseley who overcame Murray who surprised McGill who beat Salter who took everything back to square one by defeating Skoglund.

In fact Barry Salter and I, with McGill and Moseley, were first and second in the relative sections, none of us with a clean sheet of wins.

The plan put me against Moseley in one semi-final and McGill against Salter in the other. And if anyone thinks that was easy for me, then he is mistaken.

Moseley is an outstanding exemplar of the so-called South African clinic delivery, the key point of which is probably the careful setting of the right foot as the direction guide. His overall system, backed by his calm, unflustered temperament makes him a formidable opponent. Two of the most vital shots of my whole career will, I fancy, stay in my memory for the rest of my bowling life.

The first came when he was leading 15-7 with three certain and possibly four shots clustered round a full length jack. In such a situation positive thinking must be in command. The chances of a drive killing the end or improving my situation or score were virtually nil. As I saw it, I had no choice but to beat his bowls with a perfect jack trailer with the chance of a five or six conversion.

Like Jack Nicklaus, perhaps, when first sizing up and then preparing for a long and critical putt, I surveyed the head, visualised the shot as calmly and vividly as I could and when I finally established total inner calmness, delivered my bowl. Completely right in line and strength, it gently picked up the jack from Moseley's cluster and ran it into those two of mine; what a difference 9-15 was against 7-18 or 19.

This started a recovery which took me to 19-18, once more to face a formidable head in which he lay three shots and potentially match. Here a drive looked to me to be the only chance and, as before, I took all the time I needed in establishing inner calmness and exact direction. Finally thundering my bowl down the rink, I saw from the start it was well on track and it thumped the jack out of the rink for a replay. Minutes later I won. Even so, I felt that, overall, Moseley had been the sounder bowler on the day but there are four bowls per player on each end and on this day I produced two killer shots that swung the score by eleven or twelve shots. To win a major title, then, accuracy and consistency are an ideal foundation but the nerve, skill and experience for an occasional 'miracle' shot makes one the champion rather than the runner-up. I believe the saying is 'those who dare, win'.

McGill beat Salter in the other semi. Our final took place in unpleasant, continuous rain that drove most of the spectators under any cover they could find. In golf they say 'never up, never in' and in that match McGill was liberal with short bowls, at that class of play anyway. That, helped somewhat by relief from my win over Moseley, helped me to a 21–11 retention of my title, a certain amount of satisfaction, a feeling of achievement and a welcome collection of beautiful prizes. McGill finished second and as he had taken first prize in the pairs he had scored more points than I had overall. Moseley came in third in both events.

The Kodak Masters continued in similar vein in 1980, 1981, 1982 and 1983, at which stage Kodak called 'enough' and the EBA were faced with the need for another sponsor but with a glittering product. Long before the 1983 staging had taken place Gateway Building Society stepped in. With the British Isles Championships and International Team Championship under their wing, they became the biggest bowls sponsor in the world.

Moseley won the singles in 1980 and 1981, McGill completing a hat trick of seconds, so pushing me down to third place in both years.

Kodak waited for decisions on all the 'buts' and 'maybes' which the arrival of Open bowls created before introducing in 1982, money prizes: £5,000 for the winner, £2,500 for the runner-up and £1,000 for the winner of a match between the two losing semi-

Perks of the job for David McGill and me! With Miss Kodak after the presentation of prizes at the 1979 Kodak Masters at Worthing.

finalists for third place. 1982 turned out to be a lucky tournament for me though I later demonstrated another mental strength that is vital in top level sport of any kind ... to grab without hesitation and with determination the important chance that comes one's way at these levels.

Over the years Israel has sent over quite a few good players including Cecil Bransky. Born in South Africa, he took to bowls in 1968 and won their National Singles in 1972. Emigrating to Israel in 1981, he immediately won the first Israel Masters and was their obvious nomination for the Kodak Masters. I discovered this at first hand during the early morning session on the second day when he clung on like a leech to win 21-20. That looked like curtains for me but in his previous match he had lost by the same score to Peter Belliss.

That solitary point was to prove conclusive for it held Bransky to one win and two defeats. In a morning match overlapping mine and only two rinks away Belliss completed his 100 per cent run of wins by outbowling McGill, leaving him with one win and one defeat and a deficit of two shots. I then had two defeats but by beating McGill by three shots or more, thanks to his minus two situation, I would finish second in our group and so qualify for the semi-finals.

The motivation could not have been stronger and was the best medicine to cure me of the inconsistent form I had shown since the start of the summer season late in April. Full of determination and will to win, my concentration never wavered for a moment and confidence flowed through me. McGill is in no way short of that characteristic and he is full of fun and highly skilled so my 21-10 win could scarcely have been more satisfying.

The momentum carried me through to the next morning when my semi-final against Moseley, the holder, began with four ex-tremely close singles leaving the score two-all. Play continued in that vein but consistency and opportunism earned me a four on the eleventh end and I immediately moved the mat far up the rink, so setting up a short jack but in the faster region close to the ditch. That foot-trodden area allowed the bowls to trickle to a stop slowly and so enabled me to exploit a situation far less com-mon to Moseley than to me.

This proved decisive in my 21-11 win and Moseley confessed afterwards, 'I was playing beautifully until then but once he moved the mat forward I couldn't do anything. David bowled brilliantly and I never found the line.'

In that match I helped myself by choosing the right tactics. Someone, somewhere helped me in the final against Snell who had taken 21 ends to beat Belliss. Snell had stayed in top form throughout his previous matches and he gave notice of continuation with his very first bowl, a dead toucher right in front of the jack. Shock tactics seemed to be the best move so moments later I thundered a drive down the rink, the bowl ditching the jack for a single to me. Unperturbed, he maintained his brilliance and he later revealed that his plan was simply to play me off the rink.

Every end touched the heights of world class play, with Snell just ahead of me 9–7 after ten ends. Then came that breakthrough – though not in the manner I would have chosen.

Walking or running up the green is not permitted in Australia but Snell had bowled a lot in England and had gradually fallen into the habit. Technically, he was not giving me possession of the green the moment his bowls came to rest but there was not, could not, be any question of gamesmanship from a man of his quality. I was aware that the umpire, Gerald Scott, had spoken to him but in all honesty, his walking did not affect me in any way at all.

The reaction from Snell was most dramatic, a four followed by 3,1,2,2, this setting up my ultimate 21–12 recapture of the Masters title. Strangely, before the match Snell had told me how much he enjoyed the freedom of English play and I believe he had also discussed it with Scott. He said afterwards, 'Although I felt the umpire had a perfect right to warn me about giving possession of the rink to my opponent, I couldn't stop thinking about it and every time I went to walk up again I had to stop in case I upset him again. I am not trying to make excuses but it really played on my mind. Once David got hold of the mat and gave me shorter length jacks I lost my rhythm and that you cannot do against him.'

My one fear when exploiting short jack tactics came from his drives. He used five in all and four of them worked. Luckily, the fifth came on that vital eleventh end and it missed.

There are two lessons to learn from that match, both of them about attitudes. Snell had not put me off by walking up the rink but the umpire decided he was infringing the rules and so issued the warning. Against such a fine fellow as Snell one could have easily felt sorrow and so lost a little concentration. Rules are made to be observed and one is diminishing the umpire, an important official and a human being, by allowing oneself to be disturbed by a ruling. Concentration must continue at the same level reached when the opponent delivers his bowl. Secondly, such an incident is likely to disturb a player slightly and that is the moment to apply full pressure, perhaps by a small change of mat position or a small reduction of jack length. Big changes can be seen easily. Small ones may show less when an opponent's concentration has been disturbed by an unusual event.

We were playing for a £5,000 winner's prize against £2,500 for the runner-up. That is a big differential but it should always be the game and not the prize that one should strive for in competitions. Apart from the ethics, loving the challenge of a worthy opponent is the surest method of reaching higher levels of skill.

Kodak's sponsorship ended with the 1983 series but there are many other reasons why I shall remember that year's matches. As winner three times in the previous five years – Moseley won the other two – I was eager to retain the title. Additionally, I had started using my custom-made Drakelite bowls at the start of the 1982/83 indoor season and this was my first serious test with them outdoors. My belief that a suitably designed and produced bowl would free me from changing in accordance with the green was fully justified with victories over two formidable rivals, Burnie Gill and Willie Wood.

Gill had reached the final of the Embassy Indoor World Championship earlier in the year and Wood had taken over my position as Commonwealth Games champion but I reckoned my match tightness was in no way slack. The Wood match contained a special factor as my decision to become a professional in 1980 had precluded me from extending my 'four times champion' record in the 1982 Commonwealth Games. Thus in beating him I told myself I was surrogate champion.

However, a brilliant newcomer arrived in place of Omar Dallah as Hong Kong's representative, namely George Souza. He beat me in the sectional round robin and so qualified to play John Snell in the semi-finals while I faced Peter Belliss. Both of us won comfortably, Souza by 21–13 and I by 21–8, ending with a pleasing three; just the thing to remember in a final scheduled for the afternoon.

Then came the drama, a freak hail-storm that sent everyone rushing for cover and submerged the green in a thick, white carpet of pebble-sized hailstones. Thanks to an immense effort by Jock

Becoming a professional made me ineligible for the 1982 Commonwealth Games. Commentating was the next best thing, especially with Cedric Smith. We had won the bronze medals in the 1966 World Pairs Championship and Cedric then decided to emigrate to Australia.

Munro and his willing helpers, the melting hailstones were swept off the green and the final eventually began; the positional play-offs were abandoned.

I've experienced many major finals and seen some pretty dazzling performances but I cannot recall one in which there have been so many precise, brilliant jack trailers and wrests.

Souza opened with a toucher that earned a single. Four more singles and a two moved the score to 5–2. Souza, after six ends and on the seventh, yet again drew a shot right by the jack. Back

I went into my 'facing trouble' routine and, taking my time, trailed the jack for a three. Maintaining the momentum, I followed with another three and a couple of singles. Further draw shots, jack trailers and a wresting shot worthy of a place in any bowls text book which robbed Souza of two and scored me three, helped me to an 18–14 lead. At this point it started to rain and the next three ends saw Souza level the scores at 18-all.

Then came the downpour to end all Worthing downpours and, seemingly, that was that. Any chances of further play seemed quite impossible, Souza and·I had a little conference and decided to share the first and second prizes – £5,000 and £2,500 – and go back to the hotel. But we had reckoned without the BBC and their 'Jack High' staff who explained that they simply had to have a finish. So twenty minutes later we returned to the 'lake' and in conditions which would have been adamantly refused by cricketers, tennis players and maybe even golfers, Souza scored two singles and I one. So to the 28th end and with a potential three – goodness knows how – victory seemed mine. Inscrutable as ever, Souza chose to draw and, incredibly, his bowl splashed its way round my three for a single. For the first time in three days play Souza broke into a run, hands in the air, a broad grin on his face, for it was, surely, his shot of a lifetime.

I had played that end remarkably well considering the conditions. It seemed certain I had won, only to be beaten by an outstanding shot that left me with only one thing to do ... congratulate Souza generously, knowing that I had not lost that final; he had won it with some superlative and courageous shots. Such defeats are occupational hazards and must be accepted as such. There have been finals in which I have bowled myself out of similar dangers. There have been others when I have not, and even more others when my opponent should have staved off defeat and has failed or been unlucky.

You don't have to like or enjoy defeat but you have no alternative but to accept it. Graciously, if you can, because that is the way to banish fear of defeat and thus open the way to daring to win by using one's best shots and tactics positively and with the belief that they will score.

● Never fear defeat because if you do you will never dare to use your best shots to win in a crisis.

- A true professional in any sport must remain cool, unemotional in the application of his shots yet be sensitive enough to raise his game in a critical situation.
- In golf they say 'never up, never in'. In crises many more bowls are short and thin than wide and long. Arm tension is usually to blame. The tighter the situation, the more the need for a relaxed delivery.
- Be meticulous in giving your opponent possession of the green the moment your bowl stops running. Otherwise the umpire may warn or penalise you and spoil your attention and concentration.

CHAPTER THIRTEEN

Returning to 1979, the impending arrival of Open bowls and the knowledge that television producers would soon be looking around for programmes alerted the forward thinkers of the game to the need for more action and drama. Broadly, the average singles match varies in time from just over an hour to almost three hours. During the average two hours of play the shots may be excellent but the drama remains small. Not until the score reaches something like 16-all does the real pressure arise. Reaching that score will have taken 75 per cent of the total time, probably even more. And even at 16-all there is no knowing how much longer the match will last. Two more ends may finish it but with a ratio of two singles for every two or three, six or seven ends are more likely. So the time span can spread from twelve minutes – the average end of a single lasts just under six minutes – to forty minutes, perhaps more if there are many walks up the green to study the head. So if the BBC have scheduled the news or other programmes for five o'clock, they and the viewers want a definite result just before that time; we all know how infuriating it can be when a programme is cut off just as Gower is nearing his century in a cricket Test Match or Steve Davis is half way through clearing the table in a snooker match.

Three experiments were tried around the country, namely Target Bowls, Match Play Bowls and 'Sets'. As the name suggests, the Target game has a large, shooting type target laid out on the rink and each bowler in turn delivers his bowls to it. As in normal singles, it is four bowls per man and they all stay in play until the last bowl has been delivered and the score recorded. It is, of course, permissible to wrest or take out opponent's bowls, either positively to help one's own score, or to diminish his. It is quite an enjoyable game though lacking in the ingenious manoeuvering that one meets in the traditional IBB laws game. Television viewers in the West of England were treated to several doses of the game and a tournament was staged on a rink laid over the famous tennis courts at the Palace Hotel, Torquay. A first prize of £5,005 gently topped all other Opens.

Match play seemed to offer more scope. As in golf, the person winning an end scored that hole, just as a golfer is rewarded with the holes he wins. The match can be over any number of ends, with 18 and 21 favourites. Time then depends on how many ends are needed to obtain an impregnable lead such as eleven up with ten ends to go. Experience shows that four up with three to play or three up with two ends to play are fairly commonplace. Thus the timing of a game can be predicted reasonably well.

The third and, to my mind, the best variation is based on tennis scoring and is called 'Sets'. It adheres to all the rules of the game except in scoring. This abandons the historical 'first to reach 21 wins' in favour of sets won by the player who first scores seven. Then it is back to zero for another set. Matches can be on the 'best of three sets' (first player to win two sets) or 'best of five sets' (first to win three sets). At the time of writing there are no hard and fast rules governing sets scoring. Some events use 'first to score nine' as a set and I believe there have been others where a set is 'first to score six'. Now it seems clear to me that the newly formed World Indoor Bowls Council could draw up a set of laws obligatory in all tournaments and matches seeking WIBC sanction. It is particularly important to the indoor game because the realised importance of bowls becoming a major television subject infers the increasing use of indoor facilities. The use of indoor facilities lends itself to the use of custom-designed and fabricated one-rink 'courts' with spectators close to, and in rapport with, the competitors as distinct from, say the National Singles final at Worthing.

The evidence of the superiority of 'Sets' over '21 up' scoring can best be found from an analysis of the 1983 Gateway Building Society National Singles Championship at Worthing – specifically the last four rounds. This championship covers what are probably the most highly rated fifteen matches in the country each year. In 1983 they took 295 ends to complete; in approximately thirty playing hours. In only one of those matches was there excitement through the ultimate loser having the chance of winning by scoring a four on an end being played. That player, Richard Bray, had a second chance. Otherwise, the fourteen remaining matches produced easy rides for the winners.

For a match to be exciting, as distinct from absorbing because of a high quota of skill by one player, there needs to be some doubt about who will win. Assuming that the last four ends of a one-sided match may be watched by friends hoping for a last minute recovery by the ultimate loser, and rating those as 'critical ends', there were sixty of them at Worthing. They took approximately six hours of play out of the total of thirty hours, a meagre 20 per cent of excitement even for spectators with some kind of personal interest.

Now examine the score sheets of those fifteen matches and assume that if the contestants had been using 'Sets' they would

Prior to Open bowls, it was rare to see man playing woman in singles. Mavis Steele MBE and I met on a few occasions for charity but the big step came with sponsorship, TV and the use of sets scoring. This brought parity between men and women.

have come up with the same scores, end by end. This produces a different picture and shows that spectators would have been served with far more excitement in considerably less time, accepting a fact from tennis that winning a set is important to the overall result and, therefore, exciting. To be precise, those fifteen matches would have taken only 217 ends and 127 of them would have been in a state where the set could be won on the end about to start.

The matches would have lasted approximately twenty-two hours and 58 per cent of that time would have provided excitement.

Of those fifteen matches, one could not be given a definite finish as it reached 21-16 before sufficient ends to produce a score for three sets had been played. Of the other fourteen, one loser would have been the winner through sets scoring and seven others would have converted easy wins into matches requiring a third and final set to reach a conclusion.

To obtain most sponsors, television coverage must be guaranteed. Television lives on continuous excitement. Sets provide almost three times as much excitement as the 21 up system in any given match. Open bowls needs sponsors to provide money pools rich enough to encourage bowlers to improve their standards of play. Improved standards of play in snooker, as shown by television, encourage more people to become players instead of viewers.

All this suggests that sets scoring is going to become far more popular, whether or not the traditionally minded try to prevent it. That prophecy was already promising to become a fact by the end of 1983.

So back to 1979 and the end of the second Kodak Masters tournament.

The next item of major bowls interest came with the publication of England's team for the 1980 World Championships scheduled for Frankston, a popular seaside resort adjacent to Melbourne, Australia, from January 16th to February 12th 1980. Four greens providing twenty-four rinks were ready for action and accommodation for 5,500 spectators around three of the sides of the main green had been erected.

Our team comprised Jimmy Hobday, John Bell, Tony Allcock and Mal Hughes for the fours and me for the singles. Bell and Hughes were named for the pairs, leaving Hobday, Allcock and me for the triples. Bobby Stenhouse, who had played in the inaugural World Championships at Kyeemagh, was named as manager. Naturally, we were all elated but I suffered many pangs of sorrow that South Africa and Rhodesia had been banned because the absence of the then existing champion, Doug Watson, and the equally talented Bill Moseley diminished the field.

We understood that the greens would be prepared for a pace of 16 seconds and that suggested difficulties in keeping to a three matches a day programme. Four hour matches seemed inevitable and we began preparing ourselves, physically and mentally, for an extremely testing 28 days of acclimatisation, practice and competition.

The first round of Middleton Cup Inter-County Championship matches had already been played before the end of the 1979 Kodak Masters. Despite my ever increasing involvement in international events, these never supplanted Somerset in my mind; those roots dug deep and the flowers abounded from 1977 through to 1983, with the title in four of them – 1977, 1979, 1981 and 1984 – and second place in 1980 and 1983.

Peter Brimble is one of the world's best skips ... nothing like starting them young. We were fellow England internationals for a great number of years.

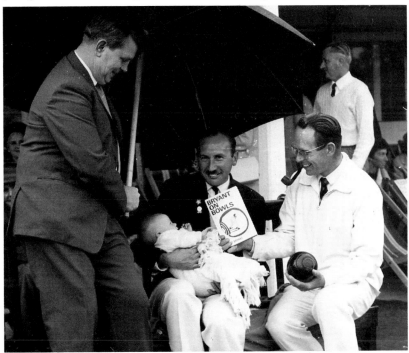

Looking back, that era probably produced in me the optimum balance of the adventure of youth and the experience and caution of age. Certainly I believe my skipping was better over those years than at any other period.

I wrote a little about the art of skipping earlier in this book. Now it is time to elaborate somewhat. Maybe my early days in Somerset County Championship matches laid the foundations, for in those far off days the county sections had Clevedon in a country area where heavy greens proliferated. It is easy to dismiss them and folk who play on such greens as unskilled with limited experience but it is far from the truth. Apart from the general friendliness and fairness they exude, many among them are good players by club standards and as they have enjoyed few chances of finessing on fast, true greens, they have become highly skilled in coping with heavy greens.

A heavy green means quick braking on a bowl. Consequently, it has little or no time to run on and curl round obstacles in winkling out the jack. The traditional lead, almost skittle like, delivers his two bowls in a more or less straight line to a place somewhere in front of the jack and, all too often, too close to that jack for comfort. The natural temptation is to try to beat the shot by curving a draw shot round the scoring bowl and on to the jack. The odds against are astronomical. There is only one course, plug bowl after bowl into the head, seeking protection against a big score and hoping that your third man or skip will find a way out of trouble.

The skip must insist on this … and also have sufficient confidence in himself to tackle adverse heads when his predecessors' six deliveries have not established a scoring situation.

Inexperienced players may well resist such a vague instruction as 'get your bowl into the head' and seek for permission to deliver positively a bowl better than the opponent's. You stand out against this, only to find yourself in the hot spot of three or four shots against you. Clearly, your aim will be to score but in such situations you must have sufficient nerve and patience to go for, and accept, second or even third wood position. In a nutshell, go for the possible and be cautious of a 'maybe' scorer that can, instead, donate the opposition with a four or five.

I know just how much this can go against the grain but champions accept the impossible while scheming how best to negate it on the next end … and the end after that. It is a major test of self-control and discipline. Possibly I inherited the attitude from my father but hundreds of matches on village greens undoubtedly provided the environment that nurtured my basic, inherited 'tranquillity genes'.

Should your lead beat his opposite number in the battle of the leads, your outlook must be equally clear; how can we add more to it? Simultaneously, it must be defended and in this situation I am a great believer in sticking a bowl round the back of the jack just as soon as you have a shot or two near it.

On such greens neither you nor your opponent will gain much with cleverness and delicacy. If there is a cluster of bowls in front of the jack, waste no time. Use your third man or even number two to clear some of them away so that you will have room to exploit your skill after the first twelve bowls have been delivered. You can be pretty sure that if the situation was reversed, the opposing skip would try to do just that. No finesse, just straightforward play ... and if anyone snorts 'its skittles', so what? Never be too proud to use commonplace tactics if the green and/or situation suggest they are required.

Your need for immediate action is magnified when the opposing skip runs the jack; you have to recover the shot and there is no way through to it. The sooner a way can be cleared, the better.

The first four to use the number two aggressively won the Commonwealth Games Fours Championship at Edinburgh. They came from Hong Kong. A Kitchell was number two and skip G Souza had no belief in letting bowls clutter up the head so that he and his third man R da Silva had to manoeuvre in tiny areas of guarded space. No, at the first threat of a packed, adverse head he called on Kitchell to clear the area and right well he did so. The Australians also use that system and it is by no means unusual to see the number two letting fly with a drive; usually with his second delivery because it is difficult to follow a drive with a micrometrically accurate draw shot.

If well executed, this method frees the third man from a 'first drive then draw situation' and so reduces the chances of him going wrong with both shots which would throw an immense burden on the skip.

As a skip I strive always to deploy my predecessors in creating a head to which I can draw with both my bowls. In pairs a skip has four chances of clearing space and then drawing. In fours he only has two deliveries and has to wait out twelve deliveries by the leads, number twos and third men. He is relatively short of space and practice. If he is forced constantly to use a wide range of shots, it becomes dangerously difficult for him to maintain spot-on length. To be in a state to do this he must play a lot of draw shots in order to sum up the rink and to develop the right feel or touch. Getting that feel breeds confidence and so increases his chances of success, no matter what kind of shot he attempts. Only space can set up a head for skips to draw.

Normally, that happy situation seldom occurs. Jack trailers, yard on promotions or trailers and straightforward drives are more customary and that diminishes the feel for drawing. Of course, most of us enjoy one or two days each season when everything tried comes off. Winning top class championships depends on winning on those days when everything goes wrong, or seems to.

Those are the occasions when knowledge and the understanding of bowling, so that one can accurately assess the percentage chances, earns those extra few shots that bring victory when defeat seems more likely.

Knowing how I have surmounted hundreds of crises in the past gives me the inner, quiet confidence which allows me to have positive belief in my ability to pull off the shot I am about to try. I take my time in assessing all the options and when I have made my decision, I take further time calming down any internal flutterings and getting the feel of the right weight I must use by jiggling my bowl gently up and down. I never hurry over this routine and when I finally deliver my bowl I have established belief in success. Often the routine brings success. Sometimes it doesn't but that I accept as an occupational hazard, knowing surely that I did everything necessary and that there is no reason for self-accusation. It is an attitude I recommend to every serious skip.

You may think that the acquisition of inner calmness is a very simple task. I've not found that to be true and nor have dozens, perhaps hundreds, of bowlers I know. Equally, however, it is a skill which can be learned, though not without considerable effort. Mental stamina and determination often cause considerable tiredness but that does not permit relaxation when in the process of building up correct attitudes and techniques that bring about increasing inner calm. Further, the benefits spread beyond bowls and bring special kinds of happiness in ordinary life. Once these attributes are acquired and their maintenance understood, there will be chances of moving down into a lower gear for a while before again building up mental strength for a particular event.

In my case, back in the second half of 1979, the fourth World Championships scheduled for Frankston loomed ever more important and I found it necessary to slow down for a long spell. True, I did give more attention than usual to the business but a change is often the best kind of rest.

Memories of the third championships in Johannesburg, my illness there and how near I came to winning once my recovery was complete, poured determination into my soul. I liked the make-up of our team: Jim Hobday, Tony Allcock, John Bell, Mal Hughes, myself and Bobby Stenhouse as manager once more. As the time drew nearer my tiredness slowly gave way to an eagerness to get into action and a confidence that I would produce my best form.

I truly cherish the thrills and skills of competition and the tremendous admiration and respect it usually creates among contenders who are actually striving to defeat one another. Indeed, some of my closest friends are men who have, in competition, stretched my capabilities to lengths I might well have felt beyond me. The fraternity sometimes approaches a Utopia and is more than an ample reward for the hundreds and thousands of hours I have devoted to the game itself.

July provided a satisfactory end to the summer season in which I won two and drew the third of my matches as skip in the England team at the International Team Championships. One month later Somerset won the Middleton Cup at Worthing which regained the title we won in 1977 and which we were to regain yet again in 1981. I usually know how to bring myself to top form for singles events and had no qualms about Frankston. My results as a skip had been somewhat more variable but in that year I felt I had reached new heights. Thoughts of winning two gold medals, the singles and the triples, filtered into my mind.

Perhaps mindful of the superb presentation of the 1976 World Championships by South Africa, the Australian Committee launched the supposedly conservative fourth series with all the razzmatazz of an Australian Rules football cup final. The Navy band let its hair down, on came a bevy of scantily clad, typically gorgeous Aussie dancing girls and the Governor of Victoria watched with obvious amazement. Maybe all the excitement brought about the one clanger of the ceremony: fittingly he de-

As was shown in the 1984 World Championships, Tony Allcock is a superb competitor in major events. In the four events he contested in Frankston and Aberdeen, he won one gold and two silver medals. I skipped in the Frankston triples and got my wish that he would skip me in the Aberdeen pairs.

livered the opening bowl ... but inadvertently with the wrong bias, so that it sheered off to the side and, amid cheers, disappeared into a ditch. Later he teased gently, 'you'll never know whether or not I did it on purpose.' Then came a parade of the pennants, the release of pigeons, further pageantry and continuous, happy applause from the 4,000 spectators. Thinking back to 1962 and the games at Perth, I recalled how the stress in winning two gold medals led to a duodenal ulcer. Now, eighteen years older, I was only two or three pounds heavier, fit and alert mentally and physically and immensely more experienced in world class events.

The ceremonies over, we began our opening match in the triples against the Australians John Snell, Ron Taylor and Keith Poole.

What a test that turned out to be, with victory possible when Poole delivered the 324th, final bowl of the triples match. On a fastish green that bowl seemed to take hours as it ran on and on towards the jack but it slid by and I knew we were off to a good start. Uncharacteristically, I leapt high with the joy and excitement of winning. Puffing my pipe strongly, I almost camouflaged myself in smoke but, inwardly, I could feel the surge of positive energy. I believed we would win the gold medal but, like Jimmy Hobday, who had led so splendidly, and Tony Allcock, who at second man had eased my play impeccably, I had no realisation of how much that one shot win was going to soften the pressure later on in that event.

Jimmy's brilliance stayed with him throughout and with Tony settling down to a solidity and consistency almost unreal for the youngest man of the sixty participating in the triples, there was an air of confidence about us. My own form was satisfying though we tumbled to the USA in our seventh match and that led to a tremendous battle with Scotland. Like me, Tony was a teacher qualified to handle handicapped children, a task which demands the highest levels of self-discipline and patience. Maybe he was

The 1980 official World Championships dinner. Like giving autographs, speech making is one of the duties of success. In fact, it is a useful lesson for developing self-confidence.

born with that talent, but training, both in his profession and on the green, had raised him to stratospheric standards and he was a tower of strength for both Jimmy and me as, match after match, we won quicker than the Scots and were able to see them finish their matches. On the last morning, with two matches remaining, we had both lost only one match and the Scots had surrendered one extra point through a draw.

We opened against Papua New Guinea and the Scots met Canada. Predictably, we both won and everything depended on us either winning or drawing to take the gold while Scotland needed an outright win.

However, at the start of our match against Papua I could foresee eight hours of unabated concentration, rising to a peak over the last fifteen minutes or so. Thus I set a new bowls precedent by skipping from seats on the bank at each end of the rink. More than that, I let Tony and Jimmy determine our tactics, only intruding when consulted by them.

The bowling was tight with England winning 16-11. That margin enabled all of us to hone our games for Scotland without suffering too much nervous strain. Scotland beat Canada 20-14 and they also escaped any overdose of pressure. So all was set for the key match with me, possibly, the freshest man among the six involved.

Inevitably, the Scottish contingent closed ranks and filled the banks, complete with flags produced by manager Charlie Craig. The fervent waving and noisy cheering did not last long. Our preparation and strategy paid wonderful dividends. Jimmy rose to the occasion magnificently and maintained supremacy over John Summers. Tony, cool as the proverbial cucumber, completely outbowled the formidable David McGill and I had the added incentive of a few England–Scotland defeats by Willie McQueen to avenge.

Beginning with a series of near perfect ends, we raced to 13-2 when the crunch end came. Rallying as they always do, the Scots built up a five shots position and I had just one bowl left. Almost with excitement and, certainly, with all my senses willing me to go calmly through the routines I have revealed in earlier chapters, I lined up for a drive and was relieved to see the jack take off, finally coming to rest several rinks away. The replay saw us collect a further two shots, so completing a conversion of six or seven shots. The boost given by 15-2 in lieu of 13-7 needs no explanation. We moved on to 18–2, that Scottish two having been scored on the opening end.

The 10th and 11th ends produced six shots for the Scots but the next three took us to 20–11 and they failed to stop us scoring on the last four ends to finish as champions with a 28–11 victory.

In fairness to them, the pace of the green suited me ideally and Jimmy rendered yeoman service. But in my view. Tony was the man of the match, as he had been in the run up to it. Indeed, I was so impressed that on our return home I strongly advocated him as an England skip and one year later he became just that.

Moving on to 1983 momentarily, Tony became a highly respected headmaster dealing with handicapped children and I believe the training leading up to the appointment has played an important role in the calmness and discipline he has shown in world and international class bowls. Add to this his unwavering will to win and you will understand why, in the 1984 World Championships at Aberdeen, he skipped in the fours with me leading for him in the pairs.

Back to Frankston and the start of my campaign to annex another gold medal. Repeating the quotation of Rose Kennedy's about accidents – 'they are the result of bad preparation' – I mustered all my ideas, thoughts and disciplines to attain my 'ideal playing state', and again faced the coming challenge with considerable eagerness and confidence.

After all, the philosophical part of games in society is to supplant war with outlets that permit people to measure their skills against their peers. That attitude has enabled me to relish competition and to dare with all my best shots whenever the chips are down.

So with eager anticipation, I waited for 9.30 a.m. on January 25th and my coming clash on rink C1 with Oscar Reymond of Fiji. A 21–8 win launched me on a run of eleven straight victories leading up to a clash with Arthur McKerman, Jersey, whose win over me at Edmonton still hurt somewhat. Alas, he produced so accurate an encore that he won by the same score. As I have said before, humility is a characteristic essential to good sportsmanship and Arthur has certainly given me two jolts that have, I hope, kept me on an even keel so far as humility is concerned.

There was, to me, a slightly humorous side to that defeat and I had little difficulty in putting it out of my mind before my next match. It should have been a tough one because the opponent was

Dick Folkins, the talented American bowler who I had played in the final of the first Kodak Masters. But he caught the brunt of a determined recapture of top form and scored only five shots. In fact, the last eight singles cost me only 88 shots, with an average of under 13 per match.

Strangely, Keith Poole, who just failed to beat us in the triples with his last shot of the opening match, found himself in precisely the same situation against England when he stepped up to deliver the last bowl of both the match and the championship. This time Australia held shot and his two superb blocking deliveries prevented Mal Hughes from snatching victory in the fours.

That win set up a situation which may well never be duplicated. As part of the World Championships programme there is a team event, the Leonard Cup. This goes to the country with the best overall record and at the end of all four events England, Australia and Scotland had each collected 72 points. That necessitated an analysis of shots, a task which took three hours to complete. What a completion; it showed England to be 0.023 per cent ahead of Australia and 0.08 per cent ahead of Scotland. What a finish!

No imagination is needed to understand the joyous trip we made to Hong Kong en route for home. Jimmy, at twenty-eight, was quite young to be a world champion – so what was the 24-year-old Allcock? Such conjectures did not last long because I was scheduled for six matches in Hong Kong, all of which I won to make my record for the complete tour 'played 46, won 44, lost 2'.

There was little time to dwell on it. The World Championships ended on February 2nd and the indoor equivalent was scheduled to start on February 26th. There were the Hong Kong matches sandwiched in-between. It was midway in the month before I returned safely home and it seemed that I had hardly overcome jet lag, the time change and unpacked my bags before I was again on my way. This time it was to Coatbridge, Glasgow and the final stages of my career as an amateur.

- Opportunism is vital in 'sets scoring' matches so be constantly alert for chances.
- In sets scoring matches loss of concentration on just one shot can cost you the set or even the match. The pressure can be enormous so develop your resistance and power to think only in the present.

- On ultra-slow greens it is extremely difficult to curl round short woods and winkle through to the jack. So concentrate on plugging shots into the head to stop a big score against you.
- If there is a cluster of bowls in front of the jack, waste no time. Use your third man or even number two to clear some away so you can have room to manoeuvre.
- If your lead beats theirs and you have one or two bowls near the jack, defend at once with a bowl round the back of the jack.
- Never be too proud or crowd conscious to use commonplace tactics if they are needed.
- When skipping a four, strive to deploy your predecessors in creating a head that allows you to draw on either hand. Minimise your need for 'great shots' to stay level.

CHAPTER FOURTEEN

Until the end of the 1970s Indoor Bowls was a game almost exclusive to the British Isles. The inaugural Embassy Indoor World Championship was auspiciously promoted and presented by sponsors, skilled officials from various Indoor Bowls associations and the competitors. Experience enabled improvements to be made and the entry couldn't have been bettered – ten champions from nine countries undertook the long trip to Coatbridge, near Glasgow – and I was their target.

The ten were divided into two groups of five in which all played all. The two men who produced the best results in each group went forward into the semi-finals. I was in group A, along with Alan Windsor, the Surrey man with a fistful of English and British Championships to his record; Jim Yates, the 1979 Australian Champion; John Greer, three times Ireland's Singles Champion; Ron Jones and Canada's Champion in 1967/74/79. I could sense problems and was glad that I had, once again, borrowed the bowls I sold years ago. They had served me proudly at Edmonton and Melbourne and I hoped they would complete a 'third time lucky' on an indoor green. I am still not sure, even now, if I would have been better served with my own, wider drawing bowls.

I met with strong resistance from Yates in my opening match, as I discovered when leading 9–5 and he pushed in a four that levelled the score. In slightly lower levels of play one special shot each end can often lead to victory. That has never been part of my approach and against Yates my concentration and the way I was able to string together good shots imposed a pressure that helped me to a 21–14 win. The following day I beat John Greer 21–13, so virtually ensuring a place in the semi-finals.

This should have been a splendid tranquilliser but I was still striving to forget the conditions in Brisbane when Ron Jones held a slight edge over me and won 21–14. Normally I meet with little difficulty in finding the right land; length is a far bigger problem. Struggle as I might, I could not shake him off and after 20 ends he reached 18–15. An opportunist three then finished the match and had me wondering aloud if I should have used my own, wider sweeping bowls?

There was no point in dwelling on this and Jones rightly deserved praise for his solidity and perseverance. To repeat, defeats are occupational hazards which should be used for analysis and the correction of the flaws which led to defeat. Then the 'computer' must be cleared and the mind focused on the next match. This meant Alan Windsor and some speedy calculations revealed that I only had to score six shots to reach the semi-finals. In fact the defeat seemed to jolt me into my 'ideal performance state' and I beat him 21–14.

The other group contained John Watson, the Scottish Junior Champion in 1975 and the Indoor Singles Champion in 1978/79. A meticulous and determined competitor, he stood out as an outstanding prospect. The others were George Hindmarsh, 1979 Welsh Indoor Champion; Bert McWilliams, USA Champion in 1976/77/79; John Mears, New Zealand Champion 1979 and the dark horse Philip Chok, Hong Kong Champion 1979 and a gold medallist in the 1978 Commonwealth Games. Until his arrival at the Coatbridge Club he had never even seen an indoor green.

Chok and Watson, Windsor and I qualified for the knock-out section of the Championship, Chok beating Windsor 21–14 and I warding off Watson 21–16. I recall a valuable double promotion shot which staved off Watson's late, determined recovery in the closing stages and realised that I might well be forced to give some encores when I met Chok in the evening.

Right from my earliest bowls days my father had drilled into me the immeasurable importance of mastering the draw shot and, of course, I followed his advice. However, my basic nature has always contained a large quota of 'I wonder what would happen if I do that' which explains why I have developed a wide and varied repertoire of shots.

Impressed by Chok's form in Melbourne and in his previous five matches leading up to the final, the adrenalin flowed and I felt sharp and in the mood to enjoy a major challenge. Naturally, my will to win was at its strongest but my inner wish was for victory over a worthy adversary.

Quickly off the mark, I hurried (for me) to 15–3 and did not forget that a job well begun is but half done. There was no weakening, only a period of machine-like drawing by Chok that severely tested the full range of my shots' armoury. Each end seemed a match of its own as he slowly crept up to 13–15. Perhaps the effort drained him a little or, maybe, my varied play and pressure found a tiny, weak opening. Eliminating everything but the shots I was making, I snuggled three bowls around the jack for a three and, maintaining my momentum, took another three on the 19th end to wrap up the match and retain the title.

It was to be my last major event as an amateur. The English Bowling Association called a special Council meeting on 22nd March 1980, followed immediately by a Special General Meeting at which bowls in England became a game open to both amateurs and professionals. There were, of course, all the provisos that always accompany such a major change; and which quickly melt away. The core of it all was simple; all of us would henceforth simply be 'players'.

There remained one tiny brake, the 1982 Commonwealth Games. Though no special rules had been drawn up, it seemed abundantly clear that only amateurs would be eligible. I had wished frevently to participate in order to try for a fifth, consecutive win in my main event, the Bowls Singles Championship, and so hold that record alone instead of sharing with Precious McKenzie our joint record of four consecutive wins. Something had to go: my family and I could no longer dilly-dally about the future. Bowls was the path to security, happiness and freedom from conflicting occupations.

Four weeks later the EIBA held their own AGM, with President George Brind stepping down from the Presidency following an unprecedented year of office. It had seen an escalation of sponsors, the smashing of the sex barrier through the inauguration of the National Mixed Four Championship and then, on that very day, the AGM's confirmation that the EIBA should 'go Open'.

No game has ever been quicker in seizing an opportunity offered. In less than forty-eight hours the first matches in the first ever sanctioned Open bowls tournament were already being played, thanks to the shrewd assumption of Bill Denny, the Chairman of the BDNW firm.

Bolstered by the injection of £6,000 prize money from that new facet of television, Teletext, Denny, Bill Walker, Donald Newby and I, the members of the consultancy firm, launched the third annual Southwold Continental Week at the Sole Bay Indoor Club, Suffolk. There were several different events, with a unisex Teletext Grand Prix topping the bill. Sixteen men and women participated and as this marked a new era in bowls, their names merit listing. They were Mary Bryant (no relation), Gloria Thomas, Margaret

Pomeroy, Jim Ashman, Norma Shaw, Phoebe Spence, Willie Murray, Brian Thorpe, Lorraine Hawes, David Crocker, Pip Branfield, Bill Hobart, Roy Cutts, Frances Whyte, Mavis Steele and me.

A unisex singles of only internationals and/or national, international or world champions was, in itself, a record. That men and women should compete at that level was almost unbelievable.

Mavis Steele is a bowling legend already and with an enormous record of championship wins and international team appearances. Her contribution to the game was to earn her the MBE and I am sufficiently chauvinistic not to relish defeat by her. I had already played her in a few charity exhibition matches but this time it was for real ... and for a lot of cash, with a first prize of £2,000 and £1,000 for the runner-up.

Full of respect, determination and motivation when we met in the quarter-finals, I took no chances whatsoever, the more so because we were playing only to 15 up. On top form from start to finish, I won 15-2, Ashman defeated Norma Shaw 15-8, Pip Branfield overcame Phoebe Spence 15-7 and Bill Hobart outbowled Margaret Pomeroy 15-4.

So to the semi-finals and Hobart having me in all kinds of trouble. Concentrating on drawing to the jack, he led 11-7 and then 13-10. Each time he held shot, possibly match on one occasion, but, to repeat, the more one has experienced such positions, the better one knows how to cope with the pressure and the techniques of maximising chances of success. Top of the list comes keeping cool inwardly while analysing the situation and deciding on the best shot. Then follows use of time while creating the calmness and detachment needed for delivering a telling bowl.

I have always advocated daring (controlled not wild). Hobart put me to one of the severest tests of my whole bowling life when he pushed the jack into a position where, to me, there seemed no way of reaching it. So, after a long investigation, I surely shook Hobart when I switched to the forehand and, narrowly missing the shot bowl, drew the shot. Truth be told, I was a little shaken myself but also uplifted for succeeding in such a way.

That shot saved me £1,500 for I went on to beat Ashman 15-12 in the final and to collect my first cheque as a professional, value £2,000. That was against the £500 won by semi-finalist Hobart.

Those who resisted the move to Open bowls had mostly given among their many reasons the objection that no one would put up much money for bowls. It was salutary to think that in this first ever Open tournament, staged in a smallish East Anglian seaside resort, my first cheque was double that of Rod Laver's when he won the first ever Wimbledon Open Singles in 1968. However, he and many others became tennis millionaires and although bowls prize money is rising steadily, I cannot see any chances of there being any bowls millionaires in the foreseeable future.

Even so, I still believe a cheque does not provide quite the same incentive as an enthralled crowd for they – with their oohs and ahs, buzz of conversation and general involvement – make one feel the match is important and the atmosphere drives one hard into the match. The reverse of this is felt, perhaps, late on a Thursday night when playing a third round county singles on an indifferent green. Usually it is drizzling and cold and nobody other than the marker is watching. Maybe a couple of disinterested individuals are plodding along a couple of rinks away. I defy anyone to feel an urgency in that situation and that is precisely where disciplining of the mind is essential. This cannot be acquired during an inspired second in one's life. It is learned during the kind of dismal match I have just outlined.

No beginner can possibly equal the skills of a champion but there is no reason whatsoever why he cannot be equally disciplined. This comes from ordered thinking and behaving, memory, determination, patience, respect for the game and total awareness of what is going on and how to deal with it. Methods of dealing develop with experience but the discipline needed to make such things work can be learned, starting from day one as a player.

After the Sole Bay tournament many people asked me about the women and whether or not they were good enough to compete with men. Actually, I felt the scores had not done them justice. Those who competed at Sole Bay had reached a high level of competence, but whereas they cannot meet with many female rivals of equal standards, there are masses of men who are their equals. So the various women's matches and tournaments do not provide enough top competition for them to hone their shots and temperaments to the sharpness of the men.

All four of them drew well but they lacked physical strength. and consequently they were at a disadvantage when jack runners, take outs or hefty drives were necessary. This was the case when Norma Shaw met Jim Ashman in the Teletext Grand Prix. At one end they were on a level but from the other he found the green more easily and so outbowled her. Even so, there were a couple of times when I had to drive and that spotlighted the one general weakness of the women. A man can drive without needing excessive physical force. A woman isn't as strong and has to use force. That, of course, wrecks her accuracy. Thus they miss more often than not.

Probably unisex singles will become more popular and man *v* woman confrontations will increase. They will help to reduce the effectiveness gap but I can only see it narrowing when a few career-minded females decide to embark on a physical fitness campaign similar to the one undertaken with dedication by sportswomen like Martina Navratilova.

Not too many years ago it was possible to succeed without possessing a reliable drive. That is no longer the case. Like all other shots, the drive demands a fluid, rhythmic delivery but it also demands the back-up of physical strength and that physiological factor gives men the advantage. Because there are so many male competition players, they have more opportunities to develop match awareness. Maybe if some major unisex tournaments come into the programme women will have a more equal choice. Perhaps then they will become equally good players.

Perhaps their great chance came at the end of 1983 when the English Women's Bowling Association took the plunge and abandoned the amateur–professional concept in favour of Open bowls. At the worst this should offer a substantially better incentive for competitive play, especially if a few imaginative promoters organise some unisex tournaments.

The arrival of Open bowls had little direct effect on the major traditional events but to the few who were trying to participate in the new events that slowly invaded the game, the work load grew immensely. War-time research proved that there is a limit to the amount of stress that a man can absorb and, in a sporting situation, this means a player cannot remain in a perpetual 'ideal performance state'. Tennis giants of the 1930s and the post World War II eras paced themselves carefully, striving for four peaks each year and competing in about fourteen tournaments.

My programme of money prize events, challenge matches, added to my involvement in the EBA and County Championships, the International Team Championship, the EIBA Championships, the Hilton Cup etc., to say nothing of my coaching courses, meant that I was overplaying. It became necessary for me to make special efforts when competing in things like the Embassy World Indoor Championship, the Kodak Masters and various other 'Masters' tournaments. Rather than describing each one in detail and then trying to unravel the new ideas and attitudes I developed, a summary of my prowess in the existing Outdoor and Indoor traditional events can tell you much.

Representing England from 1980 to 1983 inclusive, I played in twelve outdoor matches and twelve indoor. In each case I skipped my four to seven wins against the loss of five. Outdoors, my shots won–lost, aggregated, were plus 31 outdoors and plus 25 indoors.

This reveals that the wins of my fours included a number of high-scoring matches and very few severe defeats. In fact, my biggest win was by 19 shots against J John and my severest defeat 14 against J Fleming. Outdoors my seven wins aggregated 85 shots for an average of 12.14 and my losses 47 for an average of 9.4. Indoors, the seven wins totted up 57 shots for an average of 8.14 and my losses 32 shots for an average of 6.4. These figures substantiate my belief that in fours, as in singles, a consistent concentration in getting bowls into the head outweighs a strategy of going constantly for brilliant shots.

Individually, my best results were achieved in the prize money events but David Rhys Jones and I won the EIBA National Pairs Championship in 1982 and then converted it into the British Isles Championship.

In singles I won the EIBA title in 1983 though it turned out to be a nerve-testing contest when Cliff Simpson fought back from 13–20 with 1,1,2,2,1 and then drew shot with his fourth bowl. It seemed I would have to beat his good shot when up came one of those strange moments in bowls. For no apparent reason the third bowl I had delivered slowly toppled over into the match-winning position and there was no need to deliver my fourth bowl. As I had not won an English singles title since 1979, this was an outstanding moment in my career.

- Dull matches on cold, wet evenings with nobody watching offer severe tests of your inner drive, total concentration and enthusiasm. Make sure you always pass that test and so increase your self-discipline and control.
- If you feel tension taking control, walk up the green, study the head with full concentration and soothe your nerves by

using yoga breathing as you *calmly* walk back to the mat. Make your mind take control of your body and then play your shot.

● No one can sustain his 'ideal performance state' for fifty-two weeks of the year. So strive for your IPS at the three or so most important events of your year.

CHAPTER FIFTEEN

June 1980 brought me a great honour, one which I felt earned bowls the attention and respect it deserved. It followed the MBE awarded to me for my performances in the 1966 Sydney World Championships. Eighteen years later at Frankston I hit what seemed to me even more satisfying heights by winning first the triples and then the singles at the World Championships. Little did I imagine that the Queen's Birthday Honours List would list David Bryant as a CBE.

Naturally, I felt a mixture of humility and pride, the latter for a number of reasons including the fact that a bowls player had received a higher award than those normally made to those involved in other sports. It also pleased me that I should be one of a fraternity that maintains a high standard of etiquette, good behaviour, sportsmanship and the Olympic ideal of putting the game above the prize, yet without giving anything other than an all-out effort to win.

The switch to Open bowls coincided with an increasing trend towards strengthening the links between the EBA, English Bowling Federation and the crown green codes and, gradually, to a number of events which invited participation of players from all codes; some of which were unisex. These, of course, pleased the Sports Council because they always found it difficult, if not impossible, to share out grants of money to a variety of national associations. These had been doubled because the men and women have always maintained their own associations. By the end of 1983 there were distinct advancements in the sport, but there was still a long way to go.

Despite the action of the various associations in opening the game, there were still doubts and worries but in 1981 the Embassy World Indoor Championship became Open with a £6,250 prize-money pool of which £2,500 was allocated to the winner and £1,250 to the runner-up.

As the winner in 1979 and 1980 I was eager to complete a hat trick and that first prize was an added motivation. Once again, there were ten contenders divided into two groups of five in which all played all. Section A comprised James Candelet, USA; Stewart

Proud as I was to be awarded the MBE following the 1966 World Championships, I felt even more honoured by the CBE in 1980. Neither would have come
my way without the loving care of Ruth and our super daughters.

Douglas, Scotland; Gary Dang, Hong Kong; Derek Bell, England
and Des Moran, Australia. Group B contained David Duncalf,
Canada; John Thomas, Wales; Billy McKelvey, Ireland; John
Murtagh, New Zealand and, as the defending champion, me. All
had numerous national and international championships on their
record sheets and I was certain the going would be tough. I had

a personal debt to settle with Derek Bell as he had converted an 11–12 deficit into a 15–12 win in the final of the Cleveland International Masters a couple of months earlier.

To some degree, that defeat probably jerked me back into top gear. One month later, and as an ideal build up for the World Indoor Championship, John Player sponsored an £8,000 Open Classic at the newly built, superb Darlington indoor facility. Perhaps as a sign of things to come, it is an adjunct and part of Morrisons Supermarkets Ltd. As at Coatbridge, there were two groups, each of five players but among them were Noel Burrows, the crown green champion; Norma Shaw, the English indoor champion and her outdoor equal, Lorraine Hawes.

The surface suited me well once I had adjusted to it and in winning my four group matches I conceded only 18 shots. Mal

Psychological 'warfare'. When driving, I abandon the squat start of a drawshot. Instead, I stand up and hold my bowl well in front as I sight my target. Nowadays I keep my weight forward and rock my bowl up and down two or three times to create a rhythm before actually releasing it. This overcomes a jerk between sighting and delivering. All this tells onlookers what I am going to do and creates anxiety. It seems this drama often has a value over and above the actual shot.

Hughes came in second and we joined Derek Bell and Norma Shaw from the other group at the semi-final stage.

The format brought Norma and I together for one semi-final and the very first end emphasised the one factor which disadvantages women when playing the drive. Norma is superbly accurate in drawing to the jack and her first and second deliveries of that first end left one bowl a couple of inches behind the jack and the other about nine inches plumb in front of it.

I am a great believer in a fast bowl as a deterrent so instead of trying to outdraw her I decided immediately to worry her with a drive. When drawing I use my crouch-type delivery but I stand up straight when preparing for a drive. This is technically necessary, so far as I am concerned, but from a spectator's viewpoint, there is notice of drama ... 'he's going to fire' goes round the green. Taking care as usual, I hit the target precisely where I wanted, so killing the end. There were further encores of that situation and my drives proved decisive. They were, as often before, essential, not only to save shots but as a deterrent against packing the head.

First in the group matches, then in the final, I met Mal Hughes, each time winning 15–2 and on the second occasion earning £3,000 for my efforts. It could scarcely have been a better way of reaching a peak for the World Indoor Championship.

So to Coatbridge; its capacity, cheering crowds; the proximity of spectators, and a good rink made just that fraction faster because of the strong television lights.

Competitions like the Embassy World Indoor Championship, the Kodak Masters, Cleveland Masters and so on adopt a group system followed by semi-finals and finals. Others, headed by the Gateway BS National Championships, go for the straight knock-out system. Each has its particular advantages. The latter because a competitor has only one chance but in the group system one can lose a match and still end up the champion. Consequently, that system demands superior consistency. It also possesses another, more sophisticated virtue, namely the chance of contesting one match in a relaxed situation, thus allowing the 'recharging' of one's mental and physical resources.

Personal pride prevents me from playing any way other than at my best but there is no way in which I can bring up my most intensive determination to win, plus the necessary concentration and competitiveness, in a group match when I have already ensured my place in the semi-finals. Understand fully that I always want to win and I am disappointed when I do not, but I am now also aware of the need to harbour my fullest resources for key matches.

In the 1981 Embassy, collecting a hat trick was one of the most challenging goals in my twenty-four years of contesting inter-national and national championships. After three group matches won by a total margin of 22 shots, my place in the final stages was assured. I had one match remaining against John Thomas of Wales. He is a magnificent example of why people should play bowls for he suffered severe curvature of the spine when only 14 years old. Touch and go surgery hospitalised him for a year and it then took him a further thirteen months to learn how to walk all over again. Bowls began as a learning tool, continued as valu-able insurance against relapses and became an integral love of his life. He has a string of international and national honours to his name, an inspiring reward for his tenacity . . . and justification for the pain killers he has to swallow before each match.

He beat me fairly and squarely 21–16 in my final group game and I was disappointed, though delighted about the pleasure he enjoyed in reaching the final stages. It would be an insult to write that I did not go all out. The reverse was the case but the pressure was off. Whether or not that allowed me time for a 'recharge' I do not know but when I returned to the arena eighteen hours later to play Derek Bell I was positively tingling with match-winning energy and determination. The score, 21–3, against a competitor of Bell's calibre tells me vividly just how well I bowled.

Thomas beat Gary Dang 21–7 in the other semi-final so Thomas and I met again in the final. He started somewhat nervously, or so it seemed to me. Two years of experiencing the atmosphere at Coatbridge gave me an advantage and I built up a 12–3 lead before he settled down.

The gap slowly closed and then a flurry of shots reclaimed my eight shots lead, this time at 18–10. Four fine ends restored Thomas to 17–18, at which point he drew three beauties around the jack and for the umpteenth time in my career I faced a nasty crisis.

I've already outlined how I approach such situations but calm-ness, determination and quiet confidence are so vital that the routine deserves repetition. First, dismiss panic and survey the head calmly, drawing on knowledge and experience in deciding on the shot most likely to rectify the situation. Making full use of

There are many ways of delivering a bowl. Peter Line has won gold medals in the World Championships and the Commonwealth Games and his name appears twice on the England singles championships record board. Relative to mine, he pushes rather than swings the bowl away and his left arm floats freely, so helping body power. His record justifies his method. Jimmy Davidson, here seen winning the England singles championship, is now Director of National Coaching, uses another way to line up his shot.

time, visualise that shot happening whilst quietly creating the necessary inner calmness. Sighting the line and gently jiggling the bowl to gain full feeling comes next, followed by a delivery imbued with all the confidence of hundreds of successful predecessors and the belief that all the skills employed are likely to bring success again.

Time and calmness did not fail me. The target was one of my own bowls and the objective was a trailer to better those three of Thomas and the outcome a single for 19–17. A two on the next end clinched the match, earned me that much wanted hat trick and enriched me by £2,500. With hand on heart, I can truly say that the money came last in my catalogue of joy.

Over the next two years of this championship I was to learn that other players also possess the temperamental and technical abilities to produce killer shots when the chips are down.

In 1982 Embassy raised the prize money to a new record for bowls of £12,000 and increased the entries from ten to sixteen. The latter necessitated a change of format. There were four rounds of straight, knock-out matches plus some play-offs and the outcome provided the kind of excitement that separates the FA Cup and FA League soccer events.

My ability to accept defeat as an occupational hazard came in the quarter-finals after I had survived a 135 minute marathon against John Hosking of Australia. He led 9–5 and looked dangerous, only to lose this early mastery when I scored a couple of fours on successive ends. 'That shocked me' he confessed later.

Teenager John Dunn, the youngest player to win the English Indoor Singles Championship, is one of the best exponents of the push delivery I know. His drawing to the jack is formidably accurate and consistent, as I was to learn after 177 minutes of challenging and absorbing finessing in our quarter-final. Our match produced 20 singles, 6 twos and 3 threes and I hoped the victory would be mine when Dunn delivered his last, 232nd bowl.

Down 19–20, I had scored a single and then delivered my first two bowls close to the jack, a position I endeavoured to protect. Dunn dropped short by a couple of feet with his first delivery and followed with two 'jack highs', so leaving himself in a 'death or glory' situation with his last bowl. Unarguably, it was perfection – a jack trailer that ran six inches with it, so stealing victory from under my nose.

There may be other ways of accepting such things but I do not know them. Of course I was disappointed but what else can one feel but admiration for such a shot, the more so because it came from a teenager born many years after my first capture of a national championship? I would have loved the chance of one more shot but the rules are explicit, four bowls each per end, so someone has the last chance. That this brilliant teenager stayed so unflinchingly calm before unleashing such a superb shot branded him as a potential great prospect and I had no intention of diminishing his pleasure. One feels more at peace with oneself by sharing the joy of a great shot by an opponent ... as well as increasing knowledge and gaining a maturity that allows one to cope with crises, either in success or in defeat.

Such an attitude need not, and indeed will not, weaken one's will to win. Rather the opposite for it destroys fear and, consequently, increases willingness to use one's best and most daring shots when the chips are down.

Perhaps predictably, Dunn reacted in his semi-final and was beaten by Jim Baker, Ireland, who, in turn, went down in the final to John Watson, the thoughtful, intelligent Scot. Watson is one of the best bowlers ever to come from Scotland so I cannot write off his acquisition of the World Indoor Championship as a surprise. That came a few minutes later when he handed his winner's cheque for £4,000 to the Scottish Indoor Bowling Association.

Later, this admirable, philosophical Glaswegian explained his clear-cut action. 'It has always been my ambition since I began playing to represent my country and, recently, to have a place in the team for the Commonwealth Games in Brisbane later this year,' he revealed, 'I cannot deny that £4,000 would have been a godsend to my wife, Linda, and the children but you don't miss what you've never had.'

There were two somewhat bizarre factors in this particular success. One that he was not a direct acceptance but a survivor from the qualifying competition, the other that he was introduced to this essentially British game by his father-in-law, an Italian.

His faithfulness to bowl for Scotland in the Commonwealth Games earned him the gold medal in the Pairs Championship.

One year later, sixteen players from five continents made the trip to Coatbridge for the fifth World Indoor Bowls Championship which boasted an increased, record-breaking prize pool of £13,650. The players included Jim Scott, New Zealand; Philip Chok, Hong Kong and Robert McGaffney, USA - all of whom lost in the first round. Together they made round trips of approximately 40,000 miles but only scored an aggregate of 20 shots. That makes it 2,000 miles per shot, surely a new kind of world record.

They are all fine competitors with enviable records. It seems that this may well be the future's most frustrating occupational hazard and it strengthens my belief that, for the foreseeable future, major international championships should, at least, command some kind of group competition that depends more on consistency over a number of matches than on the 'luck of the day' outcome of straight knock-out draws. The major tennis organisations have evolved a system which incorporates the better factors of both systems as shown in the table opposite.

I arrived at Coatbridge in good spirits and full of determination to recapture the title. However, with nine of the 16 participants past or present holders of World Championship or Commonwealth Games medals, it was not going to be any kind of routine operation.

Wins over John Squires, the Welsh Indoor Champion, 21–16 and Gavin Beare, the left-handed Zimbabwe champion, 21–9 prepared me for the semi-final against Bob Sutherland, the Scottish National Indoor Champion. A former Glasgow Rangers and Stirling Albion footballer, he turned to bowls in 1967 after a severe knee injury wrecked his soccer career.

Always calm and determined, he pinned his flag to the drawing-to-the-jack mast and anticipated that if I resorted to drives, he would still remain calm and not change his strategy.

Beginning with a couple of singles, he then drew three bowls across the jack and there was only one thing for me to do, drive. With two bowls to go, I would have backed myself to connect with one of them but was mortified with two misses, 0–5. Those misses pitched me into deep concentration. Who knows, maybe they were not total wastes as Sutherland lost control of length and I quickly scored 3,3,1,4; a lead which advanced to 18–11 but also saw Sutherland becoming more accurate with each successive end.

Suddenly he scored a four, squeezed further shots in a series of hotly contested ends and eventually I was left with just one bowl and Sutherland holding a match-winning shot.

Two years ago I had produced a killing promotion to wreck John Thomas' match lie. In 1982 I lay game when John Dunn's final delivery ran the jack to beat me 21–20. This time I had a chance of saving but this was the occasion when my well tried and

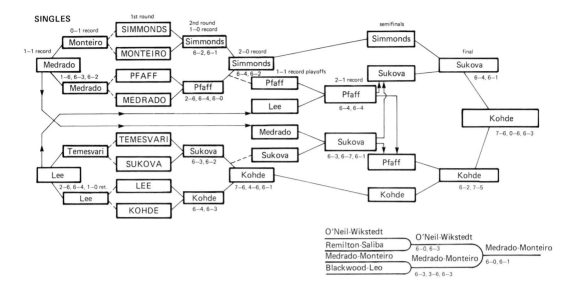

tested routine failed to succeed. My draw shot missed and Sutherland went into the final.

Burnie Gill came through to the final from the other section by beating Clive White, Australia, 21–12 in their semi-final. This was a truly remarkable result for he plays bowls only four months of the year as there is no indoor play in Port Elgin, Ontario. He had never even seen an indoor green before arriving at Coatbridge yet he beat a World Champion Triples player Tony Allcock by one shot in the first match of the event, and he followed with a win over the defending champion John Watson after trailing by eleven shots.

Two such wins probably drained Gill of some of his intense will to win and Sutherland is too thoughtful, disciplined and consistent to allow any opposition weaknesses to go by unexploited. His psychological advantage showed clearly when he led 6–4 and Gill had a toucher, bowl and jack nestling close together in the ditch. Seemingly unperturbed, Sutherland drew perfectly to the edge of the ditch to steal a single. Thereafter he maintained complete control, taking the World Indoor Championship title with a 21–10 win and tumultuous applause from his Scottish supporters.

At that time, February 1983, the World Indoor Championship and the Kodak, now Gateway, were the pacemakers in Open bowls. True, the Teletext tournament, launched on the first day of Open play back in April 1980, must always figure in any 21st century history of the game and that inaugural event was followed by others of varying size around the country. Donald Newby put together an important postal tournament for the 1982/83 indoor season and he received generous sponsorship from Lombard Bank. Richard Roylands, the first winner of this title, received £750 and his club £250, a figure quickly doubled when the second Lombard Champion of Champions was announced.

Nobody can negate the importance of such an event, or others staged at a variety of venues – one quickly recalls Wymondham Dell, Ely, Cumbria, Hartlepool, Cleveland, North Walsham, etc. – but all such events were primarily player orientated. What was missing were some public orientated events along the lines of those that lifted darts and snooker from virtually nowhere to high-ranking positions on the television viewing charts. Thus it was that the entrepreneur of both those operations, Michael Watterson, was brought into the game during 1982.

By then it was rapidly becoming clear that spectator bowls would need some fundamental changes, the most obvious of which was a system that kept the whole of each match exciting rather than just the last three or four ends. In turn, this reinforced the already accepted fact that only singles – the one to one confrontation – could expect to project a magnetic pull on the non-playing television public. Consequently a number of factors emerged. It is necessary to promote major events in venues other than traditional clubs; substantial money prizes are needed to give events an aura of importance; television transmissions are vital (the first two questions put by organisations approached for sponsorship are, almost inevitably, How much do you want? Can you guarantee it will be televised?) and that demands a new system of scoring; world class entrants are imperative; a close relationship between the players and spectators is helpful; British weather is so unreliable that, almost certainly, the major promotions have to be indoors.

One of Watterson's first acts was to order a transportable, one rink green that can be moved from, say, Preston to Brighton in a day or so and be re-erected in any suitable building. Suggestions for venues were the Brighton Conference Centre, Preston's Guild Hall and other, similar places from which snooker and darts had been transmitted.

The facility was completed late in 1982 and I was asked to test it. It played well and clearly met the needs. Rumours travelled around that a major tournament would be promoted at the Guild Hall, Preston and, in fact, it came about in November 1983.

There had been a precedent at Folkestone in 1982 where Triple Crown beer sponsored a £6,000 Classic and TVS transmitted the action. *World Bowls* reported the closing stages of the tournament and spotlighted two aspects of my concentration which they considered worthy of close attention. The sets system of scoring was in use. The article read, 'The first (aspect) is the way he exudes "body language". His dominant "presence" is broadcast by his erect carriage and the quietly confident yet commanding way in which he asks questions about the head. Simultaneously, his "positive, look you in the eyes" use of his head contributes to the positive, inner energy that, added to presence, radiates the general feeling "I will succeed with this shot."

'The second lies in the effectiveness he makes of time spent off the mat and during the intervals between stepping on the mat and actually unleashing the bowl on to the green . . .

'Body language is an important ingredient of mental toughness. It also links with another vital constituent, positive inner energy.'

In detailing how this is developed, the article continued, 'Stand up straight, lift your chest as high as possible, head erect, look straight out at the world boldly and, simultaneously, breathe deeply and slowly, yoga style.

'Almost certainly, that so-simple action will lift your morale, with the deep breathing factor dispersing much – maybe all – of the inner agitation that so often besets one when under pressure.

'The extent to which Bryant utilises these techniques can be identified by watching him analytically – him, not his bowls – next time you see him live or on TV. Part of it can be quantified, beginning with the time he takes between stepping on the mat and releasing his bowl.'

There followed a table of such times covering six ends of my quarter-final with Jim Hobday. The times in seconds were of bowls delivered in order: end 1: 10.41, 10.81, 18.94,* 9.56. End 2: 8.22, 8.53, 12.44, 11.69. End 3: 8.06, 9.06, 8.98, 6.81. End 4: 7.88, 8.31, 7.81, 10.87.* End 5: 21.69, 8.44, 6.66, 7.81. End 6: 7.66, 7.53, 7.03, unused. The two asterisks identify outstanding shots which virtually destroyed Jim Hobday.

'The table shows that Bryant takes as much, or little, time as he needs to adjust himself, mentally and physically, to the shot he is about to deliver.

'It does not tell of the practical way he develops the right "feel" of the bowl for that shot. Next time you see him go into his well known double knees bend, watch him cradling his bowl gently up and down. Like his varying time between taking the mat and releasing his bowls, his "jigglings" of the bowl vary, the number depending on how many are needed to yield the right "feel" for the shot to come.'

The writer of that article noted that on one vital shot I jiggled my bowl up and down nineteen times before straightening up and delivering a 'dead toucher' that produced a large conversion. He also noted that my jiggles varied between seven and seventeen, depending always on my need of the moment and my elimination of all negative thoughts about the opponent or the state of the head.

That section of the article was followed by further measurements and analyses of my final against Chris Ward, one of the elite who have won the EBA Singles Championship more than once.

Waiting for us to shed all nervousness, the analyst assessed each and every shot played by both of us over the rest of our match. Later, the table was scored. It ran:

Player	Excellent shot (5)	Very good (4)	Good (3)	Mode-rate (2)	Poor (1)	Total shots	Full score	Percentage of maximum
Bryant	10	8	22	12	3	55	175	63.63
Ward	8	4	16	12	16	56	144	51.42

Seemingly, my consistency forced Ward to drive on six different occasions; it is rare for him to drive even once in a match.

Five of those drives failed and the sixth forced the end to be replayed.

Apparently my use of the 'land' was more flexible as I used the forehand 29 times and the backhand 26 while Ward's ratio was 38 forehand, 12 backhand, 6 drive.

In terms of the mat, Ward's longest deliberation before delivering was 8.12 seconds ... and the outcome was poor. His quickest time covered 3.53 seconds and it produced a good shot.

This confirms there is no ideal time on the mat that covers all bowlers and suggests that each player should seek an optimum time that allows him to eliminate all negative problems and then deliver before too much delay introduces muscular tension.

Ward uses a shorter, push type delivery, in contrast to my longer, swinging style, so that his on mat–delivery time is essentially shorter than mine. In that final his best shot came from a 4.50 seconds mat–delivery interval.

As I see the future, spectator bowls will concentrate ever more on the use of sets scoring. The reason became clear during the first of the Watterson promotions, the CIS United Kingdom Indoor Bowls Singles Championship staged at the Guild Hall, Preston at the start of November 1983.

Arguably, the entry of 32 players was the strongest assembly of players in the history of the game and with a £16,800 prize money pool the competition was fierce, though almost always friendly. Both the title and the £4,000 first prize motivated me strongly and I doubt if I have ever sustained such a high level of concentration throughout every end of five consecutive matches. Four of them took two sets each, my overall tally was 56 shots for, 16 against. The final was lengthened by making it the best of five sets, my margin in this match ending 21 shots won, eight lost. An added incentive was my defeat by Bob Sutherland for the Embassy World Indoor Championships earlier in the year. All through the week I wished for him to reach the final in order that I might avenge that loss and restore my personal pride as a bowler. There was no animosity about this. Bob is a magnificent sportsman and it is typical of him that at the post-final press conference he said 'I doubt if I have ever bowled so well and lost.'

Any man who can say that so sincerely and generously can never be a loser. He is always a winner because he is complete master of himself and his attitude to life.

I firmly believe that such an attitude is a major factor in reaching the highest levels of bowls and, I fancy, any other sport of similar traditions.

The tournament was scheduled for fourteen hours of BBC television coverage but a strike totally eliminated it all. Despite this, the attendance, according to David Harrison the tournament director and co-director with Michael Watterson, was larger than at their inaugural snooker promotion some years before. Numbers increased all week, culminating in more than a thousand seats being occupied. A 14 per cent sample of this crowd revealed that 62 per cent of the attendances were crown green bowlers, 22 per cent flat green and 16 per cent were not players but inquisitive folk finding out if bowls spectating is a good way of spending time. Overwhelmingly, they said 'yes'.

There were thirty-one matches altogether, they took 2,813 minutes of playing time and needed 475 ends. Compared with the last five rounds of the Gateway EBA National Singles, there was a reduction of approximately 20 per cent time. Excitement-provoking ends exceeded 58 per cent of total time against a maximum, on average, of 20 per cent in traditional, 21 up scoring.

It seems that the sets formula will revolutionise bowls in a similar way to the invention by Jimmy Van Allen of the tie-break in tennis. I wonder if the sets formula will take over, at least in singles, when the 1988 series come along.

Before Open bowls and the birth of my own business, the game cost me a lot of money although I enjoyed rewards in many other ways. There was no question of feeling bitter about the many millionaire stars of other sports because the same opportunities simply weren't there in bowls.

Some people fear that professional bowls and big money sponsorship will demean and spoil the game – but I doubt it. Bowls is not the kind of game in which there will be an influx of unsporting characters. One can sometimes rid oneself of frustrations by 'having a go' at someone, as can be seen most Saturdays in 'Match of the Day' and all too often in tennis and even cricket.

The only way bowlers can surmount difficult or annoying situations is by discipline of mind. Bjorn Borg put it well when he said 'a hot head doesn't make a cool brain'.

People frequently ask me if professional bowls came too late. I hope not. I was the first player to publicise turning professional and only a day or two after the official statement that bowls in England was now Open, I won the first ever Open tournament. By the end of 1980 sponsors were beginning to form a queue. Two years later the biggest prize had risen to £5,000 — £5,005 if one includes a Target Bowls promotion on the indoor tennis courts at the Palace Hotel, Torquay. Usurping a famous tennis centre could well have been an omen.

The tradition of awarding trophies as well as cheques maintains one ceremonial tradition so Ruth will not be spared one of her self-imposed duties, cleaning those cups I have already collected and which, I hope, will be supplemented. Housework and, nowadays, managing – extremely efficiently – a large part of our business absorbs most of her time. Thankfully, Jacqueline and Carole help considerably but Ruth has not yet displayed any eagerness to become a player – 'one in the family is enough' she chides.

Nevertheless, the support and understanding all the family bestow on me adds tremendously to my inner security and, through that, nourishes the confidence, concentration and tranquillity I feel on the green. That, backed by the training and preparation I intend to maintain, fills me with hope that I can stay at world class levels for many years to come.

I was born in October 1931 and now I have passed 50 I recognise that preparation and training must never stop if my hopes are to be fulfilled. The alternative hit home hard in 1982 when, barred from competing because of my professional status, I commentated on the Commonwealth Games in Brisbane instead of competing. What with the long air trip to Australia, putting in a lot of pre-Games rehearsal and then working from 8.15 a.m. to 5 p.m. day after day, mostly sitting down, I went for five weeks without any yoga or other type of training.

Following those Games, I participated in the New Zealand Countrywide Classic and drew Peter Belliss as an opponent. We met on a 16 seconds green with my bowls needing only the gentlest of delivery to travel full length. Even so, soon after starting and without preparatory exercising and stretching, I felt something snap in my leg and almost fell over. Peter came swiftly to my aid but to no avail; I had torn a hamstring. I continued the match but was forced to put my left foot down before delivering instead of moving it forward in cohesion with the swing of my arm.

Though it was extremely painful, I discovered that on so fast a green and with only a slight swing back I was able to maintain better accuracy of line than when I used my normal arm and leg together delivery.

Treatment received when I returned home gradually cured the injury. I was then tempted to change, at last, the position of our garden shed. It was heavier and more troublesome than I had imagined and help was necessary. Help or not, I then tore the hamstring in my other leg. Treatment and yoga again came to the rescue and I was able to participate in the Triple Crown Classic at Folkestone, but torn hamstrings are extremely painful. It will be a long time, if ever, before I will wilfully go into action again without adequate preparation. And as for moving sheds well, I reckon mine has been settled for life.

It is often said that to travel hopefully is better than to arrive. Does that, I wonder, carry through to bowls so that if I ever play

One fine feature of bowls is that handicapped people can play – and to high levels as I discovered when I played with paraplegics at Stoke Mandeville. There are World Championships for blind players.

a perfect match I will feel no further challenge exists?

Maybe there is a grain of truth in that but over the past few years I have discovered another challenge that brings joy not only to other people but also to me. That challenge is coaching and the way I share the joys of many pupils as their skills and pleasures in the game sprout and develop. True, their disappointments mean shared hurts but there always remains the plotting and scheming to lift them over such obstacles. That brings satisfaction as one sees potential being fully realised.

Because of this, I believe bowls to be a wonderful way of life and my ambition is to see it take its justifiable place alongside other major sports. There can be no doubting its rise. I find it personally through the number of people who recognise me and come up to exchange a few words.

Technically, my game is no better now than it was twenty or twenty-five years ago but in those days bowls seldom made news and television presentation was non-existent. Nowadays the public are becoming much more bowls-minded. So now I feel in a position to push the game further and further.

That tag 'an old man's game' is used only by the unenlightened members of the public. Instead, it is ever more gaining a reputation for being one of the few outdoor sports in which the very young, the admirable aged, handicapped men and women and even the blind can play on equal terms. The advent of the National Father and Son Championship grows in popularity each year and in 1983 David Cornwell made history by entering with his eight-year-old son Daniel. At the other end of the time scale, Maxwell Ramsey was still walking half a mile to do odd jobs at the Springwood Club in Queensland, Australia and then joining his friends on the green for a keen game, perhaps in preparation for one of the championships he had entered. His daily routine begins at 5.30 a.m. I learned of his durability when in Australia for the 1982 Commonwealth Games. He was then 102 years old.

Several of the counties affiliated to the EBA are now running junior development schemes and Saga Holidays have been sponsoring National Veterans Championships for many years.

The youngest winner of an adult National Championship is Sally Smith of Salhouse, Norfolk. Then just fifteen, she partnered her mother and friend Hilda Smith in winning the 1981 English Bowling Federation's Triples Championship ... and her mother revealed that it was the eighth year of Sally's bowling career.

Not that I especially want people to play bowls, though I am convinced it is a valuable gate to good health, but I am eager that they recognise the game as one demanding skills just as great as those required in other major sports. Undeniably, it is a game that people can take to in their later years and so pass their days pleasurably. Better, though, that they start at an early age, knowing that it equals golf and snooker in its demands for skills, character and the will to win.

My coaching courses, which are expanding, and the numerous exhibition matches I play aim at enthusing onlookers to play and, on the whole, I believe they are successful ... but not always as much as I would like. No matter a player's proliferation of skills, he can only play as well as the green permits and in the British Isles the standard of bowling greens is depressingly poor. Consequently, my interest in seeing greens, and helping those in charge to raise them to Australian standards, grows stronger month by month. There is no reason why our greens should be poor and if one thinks back forty years or so British greens enjoyed enviable fame. But that was before the tradition of grandfather, father and son succeeding one another as greenkeepers disappeared. Also, inflation has made it impossible for clubs to employ full-time greenkeepers of professional quality.

Sadly, the information and advice issued by turf advisory bureaux is, by bowls requirements, positively harmful. In my experience, they tend to think in terms of a soft lush, healthy turf rather than a smooth, closely cut playing surface. Certainly, the grass is kept looking nice but the half a dozen or so 'musts' for producing and maintaining championship standard greens are seldom, if ever, observed.

Special, custom-made equipment is a necessity and the cost of a complete set is far beyond the available funds of all but a handful of the thousands of clubs scattered around the United Kingdom. I have been instrumental in encouraging a knowledgeable friend to purchase all the vital equipment and to set up a contracting company to deal with many clubs in my county, Somerset. Both economically and in the quality of the greens now found around the county, outside contractors appear to be the thing of the future. But it must be emphasised that they acquire profound knowledge of their profession before seeking employment from clubs.

This is another example of my overall interest in bowls and one

Bowls greens vary enormously in quality, mainly because highly skilled, dedicated greenkeepers are a disappearing race. Of the hundreds I've played on I have to rate the old championship green at Watneys, Mortlake, the best, followed closely by Worthing. Maybe significantly, both Ben Drury at Watneys and Jock Munro at Worthing played up to National Championship levels; they knew what was wanted from personal experience.

which I expect to extend in the coming years. Following the inauguration of the CIS United Kingdom Indoor Bowls Singles Championship at Preston in 1983, the danger of outdoor bowling losing out to the indoor game is undoubtedly growing.

Presentation and certainty of play have quickly become inherent in the indoor events. In order to compete the outdoor game may have to think in terms of a green modelled on the centre court at Wimbledon. I visualise one rink surrounded by permanent stands. Protection against rain could be obtained with an air balloon similar to the one installed at Leicester City Football Club's ground. And maybe natural grass will give way to one of the ever-improving artificial surfaces. Giant television screens, with knowledgeable, quiet commentators and a bowl by bowl assessment projected by a digital screen would, surely, revolutionise the game. Like that once famous advertisement 'they laughed when I sat down at the piano but when I began to play ...', my prophecy that this could all one day happen may not be too improbable. Why, even as I write, I am told that a new, major sponsor near to London is seriously considering such a bowls temple in the company's own grounds and they have 110 acres to experiment with. Could this new aspect of bowls be the future of our game?

- Good sportsmanship makes friends, and friends help you to like yourself. Liking yourself is an important factor in your total mental make-up.
- Master the facets of 'psychological warfare' and use them to prove to your opponent who is boss. Show it in your confident walk and through your 'body language' transmitting command of every situation.
- Your concentration can vary as quickly as every three or four seconds. Learn from experience your best time from 'on the mat until grassing your bowl' and then try to stick to it.
- Each time you deliver, be aware of which hand should bring you the best outcome. Do not cast out sensible analysis and stick unthinkingly to one hand shot after shot.

CHAPTER SIXTEEN

So far I have written about experience, the art of winning, accepting and coping with defeat, overcoming stress, the effect of money on the game and a host of other intangibles. 1984 turned out to be the year in which I experienced all these again, won more money than ever before, but suffered the sadness of the two main honours slipping away in circumstances which many people considered unfavourable though, in some ways, inevitable.

All competitive bowlers knew that it would be an unprecedented year. Forgetting the British Isles and National Championships, various 'Masters' and a host of other events with high-calibre entries, we knew there would be the big four. They were, in chronological order, the Embassy World Indoor Championship, the Gateway International Masters, the World Championships (outdoors) and the CIS Insurance UK Singles Championship. There were also strong rumours of other possible major events which proved correct, especially the Granada Superbowl promoted by Granada Television who injected a massive prize money pool with a £10,000 first prize, the biggest yet offered anywhere in the world.

Before Granada's entry into bowls, the biggest first prize had been £5,500 and tongues began to wag about the troubles brought to tennis by money; was bowls to suffer the same fate?

All those events were scheduled for extensive TV coverage and although the game should be greater than the media, there could be no denying that such coverage was bound to increase general interest in bowls. Thus, it was incumbent on us to produce outstanding form. Preparing for five major events and timing that campaign so that I peaked at the correct times was worse than a 1,000 piece jig-saw puzzle. Accepting that there were other major events which simply could not be ignored – e.g. the international Team Championships – also added to the strain.

My campaign began with the shedding of a considerable amount of weight; my target for the World Championship at Aberdeen was 23lbs. I achieved it with a strange diet of porridge for breakfast and supper and a light, salad meal mid-day. Porridge, I am told, helps to dispel fat and, certainly, the diet worked well for me, and without undue suffering.

During the earlier part of the year I reasoned that as I was over fifty I was possibly not quite so supple as in 1974. This led to two small changes in my driving. Prior to 1984 I sighted the target with my weight equally divided between my feet. To simplify the driving technique I now take all the weight on my right foot (the back foot) and using my left foot as a prop lean into the drive. This method during delivery requires one weight transfer as compared to two with the other.

I have always sighted with my right arm pointing at the target and then gone straight into my swing. To overcome troubles of body inertia and to develop smooth rhythm, I turned to moving my arm smoothly up and down before going into my swing. Both changes brought about good results and, mentally, I chalked up another mark for good experimentation.

Already, the growth in numbers of bowlers and, especially, skills among teenagers and those in their early twenties was exerting ever-growing interest in bowls. 1984 was going to emphasise that young bowlers would prove to be the pacemakers. The game has the appeal of octogenarians down to teenagers or even younger being able to play together on equal terms. But nowadays it is the older brigade who have to put in the hard work to keep up. Tactics they may know but youngsters learn extremely quickly. Added to their physical advantages, they are the group who apply the pressure.

My first reminder of this came at Coatbridge where I was extremely eager to win back the Embassy Indoor Bowls World Championship but I knew almost before the event began that I had some way to go before I reached the peak I had in mind for Aberdeen in July.

Nevertheless, I survived considerable resistance from Terry Sullivan and David Corkhill in my first two matches. Sullivan, with impressive calm and control, took everything in his stride and just kept on drawing, drawing, drawing. I felt I could cope with it at my best but I wasn't really happy with my form. I played too many loose ends and that was to prove my downfall later on.

Corkhill is a bit of a flamboyant character and that, in many ways, helps to make him an extremely difficult opponent. David Rhys Jones, my partner in so many EBA Championships finals, wrote later in *Bowls International* 'The Bryant–Corkhill quarter-final proved the most tactical game of singles I have ever seen, together with a magnificent finish'.

Later, I played a poor end after taking a 14–5 lead over Nigel
Smith in our semi-final. Until then I seemed in total control but
young Nigel began bowling, carpet code, at the age of three, and
with parents who never made the mistake of applying pressure
about winning. Consequently, Nigel has developed a remarkably
equable temperament and he just kept on plugging away. So,
helped by a four, he moved from 5–14 to 18–15, he then man-
oeuvered a match lie of three shots. There was no option. I had
to fire, was smack on target and the jack crashed out of bounds.
Without even the slightest qualms, he set up three shots again and
this time I missed, leaving him the finalist.

So the 19-year-old bowler, who only obtained a place in the
qualifying competition because someone else dropped out, was
within one match of becoming the Indoor World Champion. If
any greater evidence of escalating numbers of top class players
was needed, that result provided it. In an interview he said, 'David
has always been my hero in the game.' Maybe that pleased me
enough to take him under my wing via my management company
a few months later.

Defeat in such a major championship must hurt but losing in
bowls is an occupational hazard and, to a degree, it was Aberdeen
that filled most of my planned preparation. However, there was
another major international event on which I had set my sights,
the Gateway International Masters (hitherto the Kodak Masters)
at Worthing. The entry included Peter Belliss (New Zealand) and
my knowledge of him warned me of the dangers that had to be
faced and overcome.

Each year eight international champions are split into two
groups in which all play all, the top two going through to the
semi-finals. Belliss and I were put in the same group and each of
us defeated John Bell and Frank Souza, USA, though Belliss won
his two matches with greater ease than I. Bell led 17–10 but I
managed to move up to a higher level to score a two at 19–20.
Playing Souza, I reached 20–18 but he held three shots when I
delivered my fourth bowl. It was a beauty which left puzzled
Souza saying, 'I only played two bad bowls throughout the match
and he punished me for it. But, then, you have to expect that from
David. He is the best because he is always in the match.'

Both Belliss and I had made our places certain when we met
for our group match. I did not especially wish to lose but I had
survived two near misses on the previous day and I was experi-

enced enough to know that a dose of mental rest would regenerate my eagerness and inner calmness. Probably he felt the same way so that our match, which he won 21–16, was in some ways a 'nothing' contest.

Our semi-finals were uneventful, Belliss beating George Souza, Hong Kong, 21–10 and the surprisingly versatile Dan Milligan, Canada, letting me score nine points for the loss of only one in a seven ends spell in the middle of our match, so helping me to a 21–13 win.

In our group match I found my length sooner than Belliss and led 12–8 after 12 ends. Clearly, Belliss had no intention of letting me set up an immediate lead in the final and on the first four ends he scored 2,1,1,1.

Here my experience of the Worthing green came to my aid. The wind made use of the backhand unreliable so I switched to the forehand. Scoring 2,2,1, I lost a single but immediately rallied with a single and a four to lead 10–6.

Fortune smiled on me at 13–12 with Belliss holding two shots. I drew for the jack and for a while it looked as if I hadn't saved the two but my bowl finally toppled inwards for a tied end. Belliss replied with a three but, somehow, I took control of the last six ends, scoring eight shots for the loss of only one and winning 21–16.

The beautiful trophy and cheque for £5,500, then the richest prize in Open bowls, obviously pleased me enormously but not quite so much as winning the Masters again. It was just the confidence builder I needed with Aberdeen in mind. However, I pride myself on being realistic and it was all too apparent that Belliss had improved year by year at Worthing. I knew that he was remaining in the UK to prepare for Aberdeen and that he would prove a serious opponent for the holder, at the World Championship singles.

Almost simultaneously with the Gateways Masters, the format for the World Championships was made public. I was far from alone in claiming that it was wrong and I published my hopes that there would be a change before Aberdeen got under way.

I had long been a critic of the two section system they had proposed for the championships, supposedly to reduce the number of matches that would have been necessary with twenty-two competitors playing all against all. That would have entailed 231 matches. By dividing the event into two groups, each of eleven players, the total reduced to 110 plus two matches to place the positions 1, 2, 3, 4.

The unsatisfactory and unfair part was that a player could win every match in his group while in the other the winner might have lost three times, only to win the final.

If the committee considered it imperative to use a group system – and I am far from sure that it was – there is a fairer, superior system which needs very few extra matches. The twenty-two countries could have been divided into two groups. On completion of the group matches, the top three go forward into a small, final league of six countries. All six carry forward the shots and points already won. Thus 1, 2 and 3 of A group would play 1, 2, 3 of Group B. They would not play the teams from their own group again. Those matches, added to those already won or lost in the original groups, would produce the six final positions and everyone would know that all the best teams had played one another. This would add only a few extra matches to the full schedule and would be much fairer than the number ones of the two groups contesting for the gold and silver medals while the number twos have to be satisfied with battling for the bronze medal.

At Kyeemagh in 1966 and Frankston in 1980 I contested thirty-four singles matches, losing only once at each venue. In each case I went home with the gold medal. At Aberdeen I also lost only once (in my group) and yet I was not given any chance of playing for gold.

That said, one must give praise to the splendid facility and greens that were produced for the championships. Much of the time the main, show green played well but there was too much watering as well as the Aberdeen rain so that, at times, the greens were waterlogged and heavy.

Crowds fell far below expectations but that was not surprising considering the wet and cold. A major, international tournament each year in the future is anticipated and much can be expected.

Traditionally, the championships began with the pairs and triples. Tony Allcock and I met Bill Haining and David Broad of Malawi, and, despite one or two indifferent ends, finished comfortably ahead 26–14. In group play one has to think not merely of winning but also of scoring freely in case of tied points at the end of the group programme.

The favourites, Willie Wood and David Gourlay, fell to the West Samoans Falevi Petana and Loapo Iosia. This was the big-

gest upset of the entire championships and was all the more remarkable because Petana was a last-minute substitute.

Our solitary defeat in the group could have endangered our
chances of contesting for gold or silver as it was inflicted by Ron
Jones and Bill Boettger of Canada who ultimately finished third
with 14 points against our 18. Ireland finished runner up in the
section on 16 points.

Both groups remained in the balance until the last day. The
other group somewhat reddened the Scottish selectors' faces as
they had chosen Wood and Gourlay and overlooked George Adrain, one of their fellow international team-mates. So Adrain became substitute for any player of the 22 pairs who might fall ill.
Fate decreed that it would be Jim Candelet, skip of Skippy Arculli
for the USA ... and his first match was against, you've guessed it,
Wood and Gourlay. A little agonising left Adrain clear in his
mind that he had to go all out. He did so to such effect that the
USA headed the group and we opposed them in the 'gold or
silver' play off.

It was an absorbing match. On a late, crucial end Arcullis,
trying a difficult shot, knocked the jack from two USA potential
scorers into three of ours and then calmly stole singles on the next
two ends with sweet little wicks.

The 21st end was intensified dramatically by a sudden downpour that sent many onlookers scuttling for cover. Tony and I
looked to be winning but the head was dangerous and, unluckily,
one shot went wrong and we were left holding three shots. Tony
faced the alternative of a difficult draw shot to tie or a more
adventurous one that would have won the match. After a little
conference, we chose the 'all or nothing' take out shot and it
looked on target when his bowl sped down the green. Alas, it
missed by an inch or even less so it was silver for Tony and me
... and a gold medal stamped USA for George Adrain, the Scot.
Arcullis, his skip, was left with only one tinge of sadness, explaining 'George was a wonderful partner but I don't suppose we will
ever be able to play together again.'

A welcome day of rest enabled me to go fishing and, refreshed,
I began the defence of my singles title against Spencer Wilshire of
Wales which was no joy ride, especially when he had the chance
of a match lie when leading 18–17 on the 25th end. It wasn't an
easy lie but it was well within his capabilities and when his bowl
left his hand he thought he was home. Then, ruefully, he said, 'as

my bowl neared the jack I saw it going straight on instead of turning. I don't know why. I must have used too much strength.'

I was still 17–20 down and in danger but here my years of concentration and self-discipline paid a rich dividend. My mind only on each bowl I delivered, I scored a two and followed with perhaps my best shots of the match for another two and victory.

My next match was with Cecil Bransky, Israel, who was one of South Africa's finest bowlers prior to his emigration in 1980. There is no questioning his class and it was touch and go before I squeezed home 21–20.

Then came the crucial match with Willie Wood and if ever there has been an example of bowls proving it is a game which players win rather than their opponents lose, this must have been it. Throughout 27 ends plus replays Willie gave a wonderful demonstration of take-outs, promotions, micrometrically accurate shots that saved the end and all the other shots that bring about conversions. Labelling all as take-outs, Willie produced ten which converted about 14 of my potential scorers into 12 of his own. That is a conversion of 26 shots yet I believe I played really well on that day. Willie said afterwards that it was the best match ever

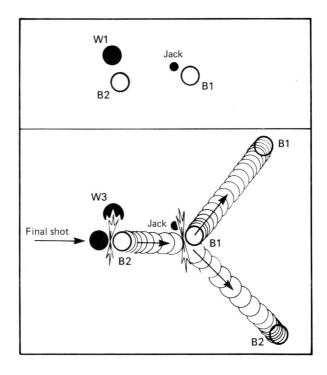

between the two of us and the bowling magazines rated it higher even than that. Perhaps the *Daily Telegraph* told it best, its later paragraphs saying 'Wood moved into top form from 11–13 down to 18–13 ahead with three of those conversions (10), the result of outstanding shots worth eight points.

'Never yielding, Bryant retaliated with some breathtaking shots of his own to reach 18–20. He looked about to level on the 27th end, only for Wood to drive the jack out of bounds for a replay.

'Unabashed, Bryant re-established a one shot position with Wood holding the final bowl. With true champion's opportunism, Wood produced his wonder shot.'

My bowl was a beauty snuggling close on the jack and beating it demanded not only perfect land but also the exact running speed to nudge his own short bowl to within an inch of the jack. Willie could not have bettered that winning shot even with guidance from the best computer in the country.

There was no chance for me to have an extra bowl. The rules had given Willie the chance to survive and he took it ... oh, how he took it. That bowl looked right on track from the moment it left his hand. Willie reckoned it was the best bowl of his career and the packed crowd of jubilant Scots clearly inferred 'we agree' through the noise they made.

So I was left with the task of winning my next six matches while hoping Willie lost one of his. Willie obliged against diminutive Ronnie Jones and it was touch and go whether or not David Corkhill scored a second win, Willie scraping home 21–20 after an indifferent last end from David.

As we were level on points, shots became vital. I scored 42 for the loss of only 15 on my last two matches but Willie dropped only 25 so he topped the group and qualified for the shot at the gold medal while I, only fractionally less successful, qualified for a bronze-or-nothing prize. My opponent turned out to be Kenny Williams, Australia. We played simultaneously with Willie Wood and Peter Belliss, who won the gold metal. We were on the adjacent green where 3,000 or so spectators virtually had their backs to us watching the other match. It was a tremendous test of concentration and I was pleased that mine stood up to the situation.

Thus I ended the 1984 World Championships with nineteen wins out of twenty-two matches and silver and bronze medals for seventeen days of pressure. Will that, I wonder, plus my extra years in 1988 mean those were the last of my appearances in outdoor World Championships? Thinking about that would be negative and I pride myself on always being positive. I believe I can maintain my current standard so I shall look at my record occasionally while directing all my attention to remaining a winner. My record runs:

Year	Singles	Triples	Pairs
1966	won 14, lost 1 (gold)	—	won 9, lost 2 (bronze)
1972	won 9, lost 6 —	won 9, lost 6	—
1976	won 11, lost 4 (bronze)	won 12, lost 3 (silver)	—
1980	won 18, lost 1 (gold)	won 18, lost 1 (gold)	—
1984	won 10, lost 1 (bronze)	—	won 9, lost 2 (silver)

Summarising, I have contested ten events in which I have won three gold medals, two silver and three bronze. Perhaps strangely, Worthing in 1972 was the only venue of which I had extensive knowledge ... and I was never anywhere near winning a medal. Truly, bowls is a strange game.

But time waits for no man and I faced a heavy programme of tasks and obligations, so after a short break it was back to full duties. Almost immediately, I turned my mind to the Granada Superbowl, with its £10,000 first prize, and my chance of restoring myself as a master contender on the green.

The entry looked like a who's who in bowls with sets scoring instead of 21 up. This was as expected because there would be extensive television coverage and TV producers demand maximum excitement. Without going into details, I can assure you that sets scoring ensures that 65 per cent of total time can be rated critical, a vast increase on the 16 per cent or so when 21 up is in play.

That increases the likelihood of upsets and there were a few: Noel Burrows, of crown green fame, beat Michael Dunlop, the British Isles Indoor Singles Champion; Karen Galvin, 20 years old, crown green, overthrew Jean Valls, British Isles Outdoor Singles Champion; Norma Shaw beat Jim Baker, the World Indoor Singles Champion; Norma Shaw beat Robert Corsie; Norma Shaw beat Willie Wood, Outdoor World Singles Championship, silver medallist. So who says women cannot compete with men?

Attitudes and concentration are imperative for success under the 21 up rule. Sets scoring makes the game even more demanding and I believe my skills in the intangibles; my general concentration and ability to focus attention so intensely that nothing else gets into my mind or hearing, are my greatest weapons. Also, I know that I can cope with crisis situations free of panic. This does not mean I never fail. Failure is an occupational hazard. I am happier when I win from such situations; from any situation. But I do not fear losing and that, paradoxically, allows me to scorn it and so play my best shots with valuable relaxation.

I needed all that to avenge my semi-final defeat in the Indoor World Singles Championship by Nigel Smith, score 7–3 6–7 7–5 and even more in the final against the 1983 EBA National Champion John Bell.

John is a tremendous competitor and he held a match lie on several occasions but the Superbowl produced a new hazard by inviting Ladbroke to set up a betting bureau. It proved itself to be a valuable ancillary and it played its part in a constant ebb and flow of spectators from their seats. As we were playing on the transportable, one rink arena specially devised for the CIS UK Indoor Singles Championship in 1983, there was an unusual nearness of players and public.

John made all the running for most of the 155 minutes we were playing but he is much more of an extrovert than me – as well as more emotional, at least in appearance. His best chance of winning came at 5-all in the third set. He drew two shots, so making me use a little force. My shot ran the jack out to the string but around ten feet from the nearest bowl which was mine. John beat it but only by a couple of feet and, given eight feet to play with in a crisis, I will expect to score 19 times out of 20. He levelled at 6-all but I obliterated all thoughts except the jack and my bowls. John's opening shots were poor and I scored the match winner: a three.

I am sure that many people believe that the £10,000 cheque was my motivation but, hand on heart, I know it wasn't. It was a new bowls record but had it been only one penny my true incentive and reward is the honour of winning and the joy of playing – especially against so formidable a rival and friend – and of proving myself the better player on the day.

If this book seems rather serious then it is because I believe that serious application to any worthy task breeds its own brand of pleasure and satisfaction. Add that to the value of exercise to one's health and you will, I hope, learn to improve your skills and attitudes and so discover new horizons in your life. I know that I have never stopped seeking them.

If you have digested the text, assessed yourself through the test and charts at the end of the book and assimilated my examples of

'Houdini-like' escapes, you are ready to practise the finer shots of competitive bowls. To help you develop some of the feelings of 'being there before', take out a lot of bowls, set them up in the patterns I saw during crises in high-level matches and which are illustrated in the diagrams on pages 220–223 and, with determination and unwavering concentration, practise and practise until they seem commonplace. Then think up similar situations. It won't be quite like the real thing but it will provide you with valuable experience.

EPILOGUE

The two diagrams on page 218 reveal the personality make-up of David Bryant and his three-pronged plan on which you should base any serious effort to achieve significant improvement as a player and competitor.

The plan lists more than thirty isolated factors on which you can work, either by following generally accepted methods or, better still, by using your imagination to expand the ideas and experiences outlined in this book.

SIX MINUTES CONCENTRATION TEST

```
A: 2 9 1 4 8 7 5  6  3 9 4 6 7 8 8  3  1 2 3 4 5 6 7  8  9 8 7 6 5 4 5 7 3
B: 9 8 7 6 5 4 3  2  1 9 8 7 6 5 4  3  1 4 2 1 5 2 1  6  2 1 7 2 8 1 9 2 3
C: 1 2 3 4 5 6 7  8  9 1 2 3 4 5 6  7  1 5 2 1 6 3 1  7  4 6 1 3 5 1 2 4 2
D: 3 3 4 6 7 3 8  2  9 1 4 6 7 5 3  4  9 1 2 9 1 2 3  1  9 8 7 6 5 1 9 3 8
E: 5 3 9 8 2 7 7  4  6 7 5 3 7 0 9  8  8 0 2 8 3 8 2  0  8 2 4 6 5 9 3 4 7
F: 2 0 5 6 3 7 7  0  8 9 5 7 4 9 7  4  5 5 0 5 5 3 3  5  5 4 4 6 5 5 0 5 6
G: 2 4 6 2 8 9 7 (0) 3 7 8 2 0 9 3  8  2 4 5 7 8 6 4  0  1 8 2 5 8 6 4 0 8
H: 7 6 5 5 4 7 4  4  4 6 6 6 8 8 8  3  1 3 4 5 1 8 7  9  1 3 1 4 1 5 6 1 3
I: 3 2 1 3 2 1 1  2  3 1 2 3 5 4 3  7  8 2 3 9 2 3 7  2  3 6 3 2 4 3 7 5 4
J: 9 8 7 9 8 7 8  7  6 8 2 6 7 5 7  0  1 9 8 6 8 4 7  4  3 2 6 8 2 6 4 1 4
K: 1 9 8 7 3 8 2  6  4 5 5 9 1 0 8  8  4 2 3 4 5 6 8  3  4 5 6 7 9 4 6 7 7
L: 2 4 6 8 2 4 6  8  3 6 9 1 1 8 1  9  4 4 5 5 5 6 6  6  6 7 7 7 7 7 3 6 7
M: 8 3 6 5 9 1 7  2  3 7 5 9 4 3 7 (0) 7 7 6 6 5 5 4  4  3 3 2 2 1 1 9 9 5
N: 9 1 8 2 7 3 6  4  5 5 8 1 8 3 7  2  9 1 0 8 2 0 7  4  5 6 7 8 9 2 3 4 8
O: 2 7 3 4 8 5 5  6  4 7 2 3 7 8 0  2  6 7 7 5 6 7 5  6  7 5 6 4 5 7 6 6 5
P: 6 3 8 6 0 9 1  8  7 6 4 3 8 2 9  2  8 7 6 5 4 6 5  4  3 5 4 3 2 3 2 1 5
Q: 9 7 5 4 3 3 5  4  6 8 2 2 5 4 6  8  5 7 6 4 6 3 5  2  9 6 6 4 5 3 4 2 5
R: 4 0 4 3 9 3 4  7  3 6 8 2 4 7 4  6  3 6 4 7 5 8 6  9  7 2 8 3 7 2 8 5 7
S: 9 0 1 6 1 9 8  4  6 3 2 8 7 6 4  2  8 4 8 7 6 5 9 (0) 7 1 1 5 1 6 8 2 6
T: 8 3 6 5 4 2 8  9  6 6 1 0 3 6 8  2  6 7 5 4 6 9 8  4  5 7 3 4 2 8 9 1 6
U: 4 6 8 5 4 8 7  6  9 8 3 4 7 3 8  9  6 4 7 4 6 7 6  4  7 6 4 7 3 4 6 8 8
V: 8 9 5 7 3 8 6  9  0 1 0 2 8 5 3  7  8 2 3 2 8 1 8  1  7 1 6 1 5 6 4 8 6
W: 6 4 2 8 6 4 9  7  6 2 8 0 1 8 3  6  5 2 8 3 6 6 7  7  8 8 9 9 1 1 2 2 6
X: 4 8 2 9 5 1 6  3  8 3 7 8 4 6 7  5  2 2 6 6 3 3 7  7  4 4 8 8 5 5 9 9 5
Y: 6 2 4 8 2 7 4  6  3 8 9 6 1 9 8  4  8 3 2 8 4 5 5  9  1 8 2 6 4 3 7 9 9
```

. . . . . 31;   . . . . . . 34;   . . . . . . 37;   . . . . 41;   . . . . 143.

If you suffer any doubts about your powers of concentration, tenacity and visual awareness, spend six minutes measuring yourself on the table of figures on page 216. During those six minutes read through the lines of figures, underlining any pairs that add up to ten. Stop on the completion of the six minutes – do not mislead yourself by adding on any seconds – and add up the number of tens you have noted; there are 143 altogether.

DO NOT READ BEYOND HERE BEFORE COMPLETING YOUR SIX MINUTES AND COUNTING THE PAIRS MAKING TEN THAT YOU HAVE FOUND.

Measurements: 133 to 143, excellent. 123 to 132 good. 100 to 122, moderate. Below 100, you must develop your powers of concentration if you wish to become a more successful competitor on the bowling green.

If you look carefully at lines G, M, S you will find this figure (0) in each of them. They, together with the 9 at the end of line Y, divide the table into quarters. Count the tens you found in the first quarter and pencil it in beside the 31 at the foot of the table.

Repeat the operation from lines G to M and record the number of tens against the 34 at the foot of the table. Continue with the third and fourth quarters.

You will probably fall short of 100% in each of those four quarters. However, if you are truly tenacious, the number you missed in the third and fourth quarters will be less than the number you missed in the first quarter.

Ideally, your perception of pairs adding up to ten should improve in each succeeding quarter but, frequently, there is a fall away on the second quarter which in this test can be condoned.

If you score badly on both measurements, read this book once or twice more ... but with a great deal more attention and determination to learn. In particular understand that the vital skill of concentration lies in applying one's mind to one's task second by second without agonising about the past or worrying about the future. The past has gone forever and you can't tell what the future holds. So make the most of each moment.

Spend as much time as you can practising drawing to the jack at all lengths and on all the types and speeds of greens you can find. Never shirk such practice as the draw shot is the bread and butter of bowls.

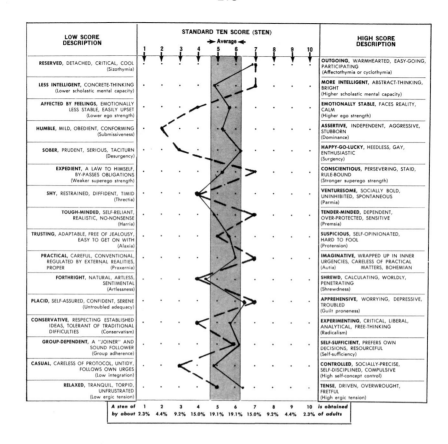

LOW SCORE DESCRIPTION	STANDARD TEN SCORE (STEN)	HIGH SCORE DESCRIPTION

RESERVED, DETACHED, CRITICAL, COOL (Sizothymia) — OUTGOING, WARMHEARTED, EASY-GOING, PARTICIPATING (Affectothymia or cyclothymia)

LESS INTELLIGENT, CONCRETE-THINKING (Lower scholastic mental capacity) — MORE INTELLIGENT, ABSTRACT-THINKING, BRIGHT (Higher scholastic mental capacity)

AFFECTED BY FEELINGS, EMOTIONALLY LESS STABLE, EASILY UPSET (Lower ego strength) — EMOTIONALLY STABLE, FACES REALITY, CALM (Higher ego strength)

HUMBLE, MILD, OBEDIENT, CONFORMING (Submissiveness) — ASSERTIVE, INDEPENDENT, AGGRESSIVE, STUBBORN (Dominance)

SOBER, PRUDENT, SERIOUS, TACITURN (Desurgency) — HAPPY-GO-LUCKY, HEEDLESS, GAY, ENTHUSIASTIC (Surgency)

EXPEDIENT, A LAW TO HIMSELF, BY-PASSES OBLIGATIONS (Weaker superego strength) — CONSCIENTIOUS, PERSEVERING, STAID, RULE-BOUND (Stronger superego strength)

SHY, RESTRAINED, DIFFIDENT, TIMID (Threctia) — VENTURESOME, SOCIALLY BOLD, UNINHIBITED, SPONTANEOUS (Parmia)

TOUGH-MINDED, SELF-RELIANT, REALISTIC, NO-NONSENSE (Harria) — TENDER-MINDED, DEPENDENT, OVER-PROTECTED, SENSITIVE (Premsia)

TRUSTING, ADAPTABLE, FREE OF JEALOUSY, EASY TO GET ON WITH (Alaxia) — SUSPICIOUS, SELF-OPINIONATED, HARD TO FOOL (Protension)

PRACTICAL, CAREFUL, CONVENTIONAL, REGULATED BY EXTERNAL REALITIES, PROPER (Praxernia) — IMAGINATIVE, WRAPPED UP IN INNER URGENCIES, CARELESS OF PRACTICAL MATTERS, BOHEMIAN (Autia)

FORTHRIGHT, NATURAL, ARTLESS, SENTIMENTAL (Artlessness) — SHREWD, CALCULATING, WORLDLY, PENETRATING (Shrewdness)

PLACID, SELF-ASSURED, CONFIDENT, SERENE (Untroubled adequacy) — APPREHENSIVE, WORRYING, DEPRESSIVE, TROUBLED (Guilt proneness)

CONSERVATIVE, RESPECTING ESTABLISHED IDEAS, TOLERANT OF TRADITIONAL DIFFICULTIES (Conservatism) — EXPERIMENTING, CRITICAL, LIBERAL, ANALYTICAL, FREE-THINKING (Radicalism)

GROUP-DEPENDENT, A "JOINER" AND SOUND FOLLOWER (Group adherence) — SELF-SUFFICIENT, PREFERS OWN DECISIONS, RESOURCEFUL (Self-sufficiency)

CASUAL, CARELESS OF PROTOCOL, UNTIDY, FOLLOWS OWN URGES (Low integration) — CONTROLLED, SOCIALLY-PRECISE, SELF-DISCIPLINED, COMPULSIVE (High self-concept control)

RELAXED, TRANQUIL, TORPID, UNFRUSTRATED (Low ergic tension) — TENSE, DRIVEN, OVERWROUGHT, FRETFUL (High ergic tension)

A sten of 1 2 3 4 5 6 7 8 9 10 is obtained by about 2.3% 4.4% 9.2% 15.0% 19.1% 19.1% 15.0% 9.2% 4.4% 2.3% of adults

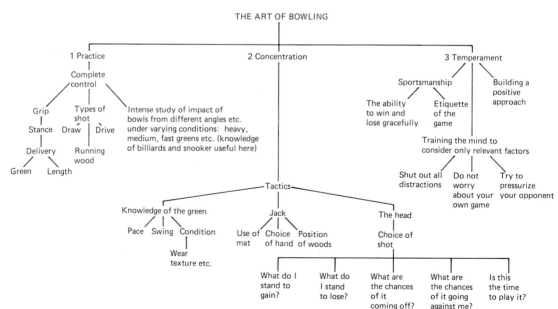

THE ART OF BOWLING

1 Practice — 2 Concentration — 3 Temperament

1 Practice: Complete control — Grip, Types of shot, Stance, Draw, Drive, Delivery, Running wood, Green, Length

Intense study of impact of bowls from different angles etc. under varying conditions: heavy, medium, fast greens etc. (knowledge of billiards and snooker useful here)

2 Concentration: Tactics

Knowledge of the green — Pace, Swing, Condition (Wear texture etc.)

Jack — Use of mat, Choice of hand, Position of woods

The head — Choice of shot — What do I stand to gain? / What do I stand to lose? / What are the chances of it coming off? / What are the chances of it going against me? / Is this the time to play it?

3 Temperament: Sportsmanship, Building a positive approach

Sportsmanship — The ability to win and lose gracefully / Etiquette of the game

Training the mind to consider only relevant factors — Shut out all distractions / Do not worry about your own game / Try to pressurize your opponent

But as you progress, realise that you need to produce many other shots to win at high levels. 'Being there' to play such shots is the ultimate form of experience but it can be sampled a great deal by 'being there' on the practice green; at least you learn how and what to do and, hopefully, gather some confidence through knowing you can cope.

To help you to practise match winning or saving matches, here are a few crisis positions I have seen, heard about or faced in play. Only the effective bowls are in the diagrams; the strays have been omitted.

Set up these heads and practise the shots used in the matches. Do not be afraid to try out your own ideas of how the situations might have been tackled; experiment; learn.

The more you think and practise, the more you will learn what to do so that whenever such heads arise, you will have 'been there' and so know how to deal with the situation.

When you have tried out my selection of situations, start compiling your own list by watching matches in such events as the National Championships, International Team Matches, Middleton and Denny Cup and so on. Concentrate on 'big' matches so that the man dealing with each one is bowling under pressure. To increase your understanding of big match tension, spend time looking at the man – his eyes, face, posture etc – to see how he reacts and think about what you might do in his place.

Now to the first practise example, maybe the finest shot of the whole inaugural World Championships; excuse my immodesty.

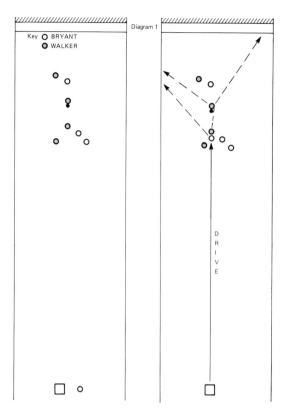

Diagram 1

Key ○ BRYANT
◉ WALKER

D
R
I
V
E

Bryant v Walker (Diagram 1)

Diagram 1 shows the position on the final end of
the match against Snowy Walker in the First
World Championships at Kyeemagh Sydney in
1966. The score was 20—18 in my favour but
Snowy was holding two which would have tied
the game at 20 all. I elected to drive endeavour-
ing to at least reduce the count to give myself a
better chance on the next end. The result was
devastating as my strike made full contact with
the second shot which, narrowly missing the
jack, removed the back toucher leaving me game.

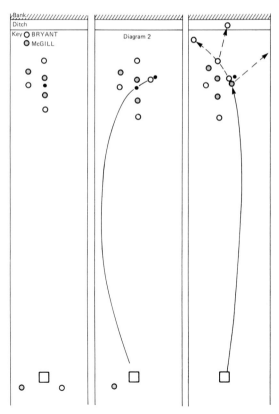

Bank
Ditch

Key ○ BRYANT
◉ McGILL

Diagram 2

Bryant v McGill (Diagram 2)

Diagram 2 illustrates the last two deliveries from
a memorable match in a semi-final clash between
David McGill and myself in the 1982 Kodak
Masters Singles at Beach House Park, Worthing.
During any tight game certain ends are vital and
this is a perfect example. Stepping on to the mat
to make my final delivery of the end David was
holding two very good shots close to the jack in
a perfect line. As the jack was obscured and the
target was a single bowl I decided to draw.
Having trailed the jack diagonally across the
head for one shot I was naturally satisfied with
my effort particularly as I also held third bowl.
David's final delivery however, destroyed my
position for a firm running shot off the forehand
cannoned my shot bowl on to my third bowl to
leave him three. A similar brilliant running shot
later in the game brought another count and he
went on to win 21—16.

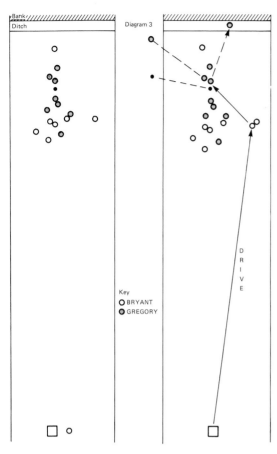

Key
O BRYANT
◉ GREGORY

Bryant v Gregory (Diagram 3)

Diagram 3 is of a Middleton Cup Trial Match early in the season on a slow unresponsive green. It shows what can be done if one has the courage to attempt the unlikely. Faced with a count of seven shots against me with two very narrow hands I had to decide what to attempt with the final bowl of the end. The back hand was nearly straight so the draw to save was completely impossible. The forehand however, although narrow did offer a better chance. After careful consideration I came to the conclusion I could only finish two feet jack high at the best cutting out one shot or possibly two.

As perfect green and perfect weight are not achieved that often I elected to drive at a solitary shot bowl some five to six feet wide of the head and probably ten feet to twelve from the jack. Although there were numerous permutations of contact (if indeed I hit at all) I knew if I caught it half bowl I would certainly cannon into the head and save something. Alternatively as it was our bowl the perfect contact on the outside could possibly send it into the cluster of shots. The result surpassed my wildest dreams as a half bowl wick saw my drive career into the head, swallow the jack and carry it safely across the string for a dead end.

Bryant v Wood (Diagram 4)

Diagram 4 shows the conclusion of the final end of a highly important match between Willie Wood and myself in the World Championships at Aberdeen in July 1984.

With the score 20–18 against me I stepped onto the mat to play what turned out to be my final bowl of the match. I was holding a good shot which if undisturbed would bring me within two shots of game but there was a chance of wresting Willie's second bowl for three shots and a game lie. The problem was, however, it was far from easy and extremely dangerous because if I was slightly overweight and the jack moved more than fifteen inches I could lose the shot and the match. After deliberating for some little time I decided to 'Take the Bull by the Horns' and have a go but still trying to play only enough weight to turn Willie's bowl over twice which would have been sufficient to have given me three shots. Unfortunately my line was not as accurate as my weight for my delivery cut away narrow just missing the object. I was far from dejected, however, as I was still holding shot and if it remained unaltered I had already planned my tactics for the next end which I believed gave me a very good chance.

It was not to be; Willie played the absolutely perfect bowl! Drawing on his forehand he nudged his second shot to within an inch of the jack for victory and eventually a place in the final against Peter Bellis.

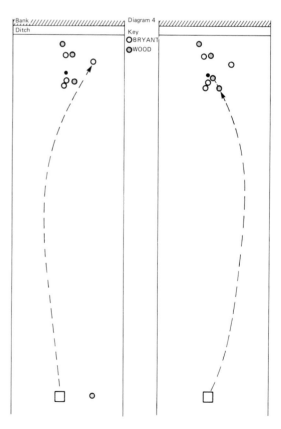

Key
O BRYANT
◉ WOOD

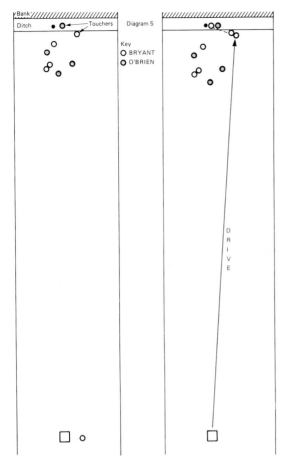

Diagram 5

Key
○ BRYANT
◯ O'BRIEN

D
R
I
V
E

Bryant v O'Brien (Diagram 5)

Diagram 5 is of another head where it pays to have a go even if the chances of success are remote. This particular situation arose in a Somerset Middleton Cup Trial at Victoria Bowling Club Weston-super-Mare. My four were holding several shots when Jimmy O'Brien drove and ditched the jack. Left with the last bowl I had the choice of drawing to the extreme edge of the ditch which had a slight slope or of ditching our toucher which would have to pass over their toucher if it was to count. As the shot bowl was less than a foot from the jack both were extremely difficult and most people I feel would have settled for the draw. However, my decision was swayed by the slope at the edge of the green as I knew I would have to draw within a couple of inches to score. I therefore settled for a very firm running bowl which I hoped would swing enough to clip the outer edge of our toucher. It was the kind of shot you play a hundred times and get it once and this was the occasion as the right contact was made and our toucher hopped over the bowl in the ditch and finished nestled against the jack. A hundred to one shot but there are situations now and again when it is the correct shot to play.

Bryant v Murray (Diagram 6)

Diagram 6 is of the final end of my match against Arthur Murray in the 1984 Granada Superbowl Tournament.

One set up and leading 4—0 in the second an opportunity presented itself which could give me a game lie. In a tighter situation I probably would not have considered it seriously as Arthur had the last bowl. However, as I was well on top and bowling with confidence I decided to play the more difficult shot. I was holding a close shot with my toucher in the ditch and there was little danger of not scoring even if I made a mess of things as Arthur's nearest bowl was some four feet from the jack and about eighteen inches from the ditch. The shot I elected to play was a running bowl off the forehand to ditch my other toucher but with weight to follow through for third shot. I felt that it was an all or nothing shot in as much that unless I made full contact with the toucher neither would finish in a scoring position as the object bowl was fully six feet from the ditch. As you can see from the second diagram the result was ideal and was made even more important as Arthur failed to save game with his final delivery.

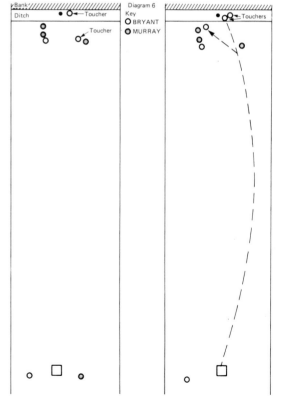

Diagram 6

Key
○ BRYANT
◯ MURRAY

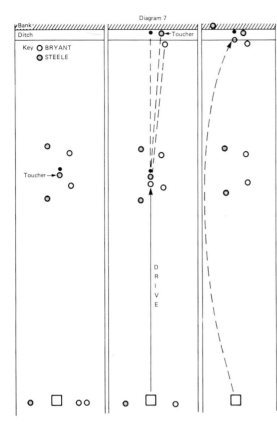

Diagram 7

Key ○ BRYANT
○ STEELE

Ditch

Bank

Toucher

Toucher

D
R
I
V
E

Bryant v Steele (Diagram 7)

Diagram 7 is of the final end of an eventful match against John Steele in the 1984 U.K. Singles at Preston. Many readers will remember the game as it was televised and we had already shaken hands several ends before, when I had apparently won the second set 7—1 only to be told a full seven minutes later that the electronic scoreboard had gone wrong and that the actual score was 6—1. Although the break did not help my game it did not noticeably appear detrimental to it. John, however, who had been really struggling suddenly hit a purple patch and could do no wrong and three ends later the set was tied at 6 all. The final end is one that I shall remember for the rest of my life as it had the spectators perched on the edge of their seats.

After the first four deliveries I was holding two shots but John would not be denied and played the perfect front toucher dead in line. I had no option but to drive and as the jack was reasonably short there was every chance that the jack and toucher would finish well apart if indeed the toucher remained within the confines of the rink. Imagine my consternation when a full bowl contact propelled the jack and toucher into the ditch within a foot of each other. In fact the contact was so full that my firing bowl followed through and had it fallen against the bias instead of with it would have been shot.

I shall never forget my last delivery as I believed it was essential that I won the second set in view of John's excellent form over the previous three ends. A third set would have been a real battle. John having kept well away with his last bowl and indeed finishing in the ditch I had only one option that of a draw. Although I could have played off the forehand and possibly turned or used my own bowl I settled for the backhand draw on the principle that if I could finish level with my second shot it would be good enough to score. Watching the bowl down the green I knew I was close but the last couple of yards I had my doubts and when the marker put his hand into the ditch to catch the bowl I feared the worst. However, it stopped two thirds on the green and one third overhanging the ditch and even as I looked at it I was expecting it to fall. It didn't and John and I shook hands for the second time which again must be some kind of record.

Black Diamonds

Lynette Rees